JEFF BUCKLEY

MYSTERY WHITE BOY BLUES

JEFF BUCKLEY

MYSTERY WHITE BOY BLUES

Anthony Reynolds

Plexus, London

For Jan and Julia Kahn

All rights reserved including the right of
reproduction in whole or in part in any form
Copyright © 2009 by Anthony Reynolds
Published by Plexus Publishing Limited
25 Mallinson Road
London SW11 1BW
First printing 2009
www.plexusbooks.com

British Library Cataloguing in Publication Data

Reynolds, Anthony
  Jeff Buckley : mystery white boy blues
  1. Buckley, Jeff, 1966-1997 2. Rock musicians - United
  States - Biography
  I. Title
  782.4'2166'092

  ISBN-10: 0-85965-406-0
  ISBN-13: 978-085965-406-7

Cover photograph by Niels Van Iperen/ Retna Ltd
Book and cover design by Coco Wake-Porter
Printed in Great Britain by Cromwell Press Group

CONTENTS

PRELUDE

The American singer-songwriter Tim Buckley, a slight man with a voice made of mountains and oceans, was born into a dysfunctional military household in the late 1940s. His abusive father was a whacked-out marine veteran with a steel plate in his cranium. The physically refined Tim was nevertheless endowed with a mighty musical spirit, in part inherited from his father's Irish ancestry.

Tim Buckley started early, finding a writing partner at school in the shape of poet Larry Beckett, who provided many – although not all – of the lyrics for Tim's progressive song structures (including the classic 'Song to the Siren'). Tim also finished too soon – his life cut short at the age of 28 – but he maintained a unique position as a musician during his decade-long journey within the industry.

At the beginning of his career, with the release of his highly acclaimed and beloved album triptych of *Tim Buckley, Goodbye and Hello* and *Happy Sad*, all released between 1966 and 1969, Tim Buckley fully embodied the classical child-poet features of a folk-era pin-up, reminding one of a less contrived Marc Bolan or a more narcotically erotic Simon and Garfunkel. Despite the regular shoals of teenage girls who could be found crouched at the foot of the stage during those early days, this was not a role that Tim was satisfied with playing, and as his work developed his looks also morphed, maturing with the decade into a hard and handsome set of Hollywood features. Yet his later work and image would never capture hearts and minds in the way those first albums did. Tim Buckley didn't come close to approaching the celebrity sex symbol status that some of his lesser-qualified contemporaries and friends (including the Monkees) achieved.

Although already dead before the end of his third decade, the nine albums recorded during his lifetime – *Tim Buckley, Goodbye and Hello, Happy Sad, Blue Afternoon, Lorca, Starsailor, Greetings from LA, Sefronia* and *Look at the Fool* – serve as a series of rich aural witnesses to a life lived as intensely and deeply as it was briefly.

There were forays into other professions – principally acting and scriptwriting (these ventures were almost always driven by a need for the

Jeff Buckley photographed in 1994, three months prior to the release of Grace.

money that his records did not provide), but in the final analysis Tim was a pure musician. He was blessed with a singing voice that was untypically impressive and technically exquisite. He also possessed (or was possessed by) an inherent musicality that sometimes allowed him to take this voice beyond its already transcendent potential. Buckley not only had a great voice – he also knew how to sing. Yet he was never particularly revered as a vocalist on any major level, not even amongst his peers. Whilst Elvis named Roy Orbison as the 'world's greatest singer' and Sinatra very publicly endowed Tony Bennett with praise, Tim Buckley remained removed from the outright adoration of both the public at large and the industry as a whole. Although critically acclaimed, he was hardly hyped. His worldwide sales remained as average as his talents were extraordinary.

Coming to light in the mid- to late sixties amongst a phalanx of other 'folkie' singer-songwriters called Tim and Tom – Rush, Paxton, Hardin and Rose – Buckley, who unlike many in the burgeoning folk movement never preached through his lyrics, would create his own personal musical vocabulary. By the end of his life he had fiercely and rapidly outgrown his folk roots and occupied a hitherto unpopulated hinterland somewhere between the music of Bob Dylan and Miles Davis and the writings of Federico García Lorca and Joseph Conrad. The journeying between these two poles encompassed the acoustic balladeering of the earlier albums, through lushly orchestrated suites and concept LPs, and even included roaring, pumped-up AOR sex-rock.

He was one of the first among his peers to use his voice as an instrument. Inspired by various jazz horn players, Tim pushed his three-and-a-half octaves to convey a sound beyond the boundaries of language, a sound that was – for the relative few who heard it – either beautifully seductive or weirdly alienating.

The effect of this on Tim's domestic and personal life was predictably detrimental. He entered into his first marriage, to aspiring actress and musician Mary Guibert, while still a teenager. They were high school sweethearts and their union was over years before their official divorce was granted in 1967. Tim was not even around in 1966 when his first and only child – a son called Jeffrey – was born.

Tim would move on, always unapologetically committed to his muse. He was initially signed to the mighty Elektra Records, where the potential of his talent was keenly recognised but never truly realised – at least not commercially. Elektra would later become home to groundbreaking acts like the Doors and the Stooges, and was the first of many labels to invest in Buckley's strangely unclassifiable but pure talent.

In the meantime Tim would occasionally tour – including well-received concerts in Europe – and marry again, becoming stepfather to Taylor, the son of his new wife Judy.

For the majority of his life, Tim was largely unconcerned with the day-to-day domesticity of civilian existence, and was married to the road, his band and his music. He lubricated the awkward space between work, his home life, and sometime financial famine with alcohol and narcotics. Although never a fully-fledged addict of anything but music, he freely indulged in and celebrated the use of everything from hard liquor to ludes, cocaine, amphetamines and heroin.

In many ways he was in his own time an unrecognised pioneer, ahead of the tide in terms of his attitude to artistic integrity and his dealings with the media. (He was the most reluctant and surly of chat show guests and these opportunities soon fizzled out after this became apparent.) Whilst posterity grants some sort of retrospective reward for such artists, the lives of these individuals are often fraught. His focus had always been on the next opportunity – the next gig, the next album, the next project. By the mid-seventies, although as a live draw he was on the up, he was out of contract and barely making a living.

Following a sell-out show in Dallas to almost 2,000 people at the end of June 1975, Tim – who had recently been on a health kick – decided to indulge himself, partying with friends and colleagues in his home neighbourhood. Cocaine and heroin were ubiquitous on the American music scene during the mid-seventies, and after some heavy drinking Tim mistook the latter for the former.

He was dead by accidental overdose at the age of 28.

His reputation in the following years, as so often happens with talents struck-down before their time, would only grow, and was furthered by a series of reissues, compilations and tribute albums.

And while it was beyond debate that he left behind nine albums of soaring, sometimes flawed ambition and majesty, his greatest legacy would arguably be the son he hardly knew – Jeffrey Scott Buckley.

1. BORN INTO THIS

'I've felt this season before
As a child playing dead near the road'

(Excerpt from 'Fullerton Road Trick', a poem by Jeff Buckley)

Jeffrey Scotty Buckley, AKA Scotty Moorhead, AKA Jeff Buckley, was born on 17 November 1966, in Anaheim ('home by the Santa Ana river'), California. His mother Mary endured 21 hours of labour during the delivery. No one knew where the baby's father – her husband – was.

Outside the hospital, it was snowing. Johnny Rivers' 'Poor Side of Town' was topping the US *Billboard* singles chart, the war in Vietnam was grinding inexorably on, and just nine days earlier, across the ocean, in another world, the Beatles had begun to fall apart.

Anaheim was an agricultural state, a once rich and thriving panorama of vineyards. Yet its life as a wine producing area had been extinct since a blight during the late 1880s. A renewed prosperity was built on oranges rather than grapes, and thus Jeff Buckley's place of entrance into the world became known as 'Orange County'.

And even in America, among a nation of exiles, within a land born of immigrants, Scotty was a rich hybrid. His father, Tim Buckley, was famously of Irish origin, descended from Cork with all the characteristics of a true Celtic ballad singer and the flighty, charismatic disposition of the fatally sensitive. Poetic, endearing, prone to introversion and extremes of mood, he was also physically beautiful, borderline androgynous with a powerful, celestial, near-operatic tenor singing voice.

'He was *absolutely* beautiful,' insisted Mary, recalling one of her initial meetings with Tim. 'This burr of curly black-brown hair and these long curly lashes that reached all the way up to his eyebrows and this... very sensitive mouth, and just... this way of looking at me. I'd be walking past him and he'd be sitting with his back to the wall. He'd stick both legs out so I'd have to step over him. He gave me a look like he knew what I

Jeff as the man he would become, circa 1995.

looked like naked. That was the way it started, this little love affair. He'd write me these erotic poems, and at sixteen that was so grown-up and so awakening, it was amazing.'

Mary Guibert was also physically beautiful, perhaps less glaringly so than Tim. Her looks were more aesthetically subtle, reflecting her richer racial heritage. She was a Panamanian of Greek, Russian and French descent who had actually lived in Panama until she was three. She was also a natural and classically trained musician who played cello and piano.

She and Tim were high school sweethearts who married much too young. Tim's sometime writing partner Larry Beckett remembered 'riding around in a car with them and him saying, "I just want you to do the laundry and clean the house," and she's saying, "You don't want a wife, you want a maid!" We were all unbelievably immature.'

She christened her son after a friend called Geoff because she thought it sounded 'cool'. The 'Scotty' came from the middle name of Mary's neighbour (and childhood 'hero'), John 'Scotty' Scott, who had died accidentally in a fall in 1965, aged seventeen.

By the time their son was born, Tim Buckley was 'completely out of the picture'. This absence was not particularly surprising to his estranged wife. 'He hadn't been faithful to me for very long,' she stated. 'And I thought that was perfectly acceptable because, after all, he was so wonderful, and I was so nobody.'

Tim, a pioneering musical man-child of just eighteen years, had left for New York City during the previous summer to perform a date at the Night Owl in New York's Greenwich Village. Mary's assessment of her relationship with her husband was, in a skewed sense, accurate. While it was harsh to define herself as a 'nobody', by default Tim certainly wanted to be a somebody. Or maybe he felt that he already was and just needed the world to acknowledge it. Little else seemed as important as his work.

'We weren't fighting or anything… just drifting apart,' recalled Mary. 'I think we were just reaching the lifespan of the average teenage relationship. Had we not gotten married we might have just ended like many other "puppy love" romances then did.'

Jeff's conception had become apparent in March of 1966. The child was not planned and both parents were naturally frightened by the prospect – though it was more likely a fear of the unknown, rather than of the actual arrival of a child, that worried the teenagers. For Tim, someone who had suffered a truly dysfunctional childhood, the prospect of impending fatherhood hit upon another deeper phobia, playing mightily upon his ingrained fear of home. In addition, 'The marriage was a disaster,' asserted

Tim's then bass player, Jim Felder. 'Mary was full of life and talent... Tim's equal. But the pregnancy made it go sour, as neither of them was ready for it. To Tim it was draining his creative force, and Mary wasn't willing to take the chance on his career, putting it to him, like, "Settle down and raise a baby or we're through." That kind of showdown.'

Whatever the travails of the lovers' young hearts, Mary wanted the baby and that was enough for her. This was the sixties and Tim was a man – a musician – who was moving on. Speaking on US radio in 1973, he was at least able to articulate his somewhat complex – and perversely sophisticated – feelings regarding relationships when he said, 'Usually men treat their women like head ornaments on Cadillacs – "Look what I got." But once it gets beyond that, it starts getting into commitment. Then you're talking about more of a universal thought, more of a personal, human thought and more of a frightening thought, because then you're cutting right to the bone of what life is.' Tim was in no minority as far as such views went. In the mid-sixties it was assumed by some people that the child was the mother's responsibility, and this was an assumption that Mary gracefully accepted and lived by.

Lee Underwood, guitarist in Tim's band, remembers the situation being a topic of discussion while he and Tim were in New York that summer. Given the choice of returning to Mary and Orange County or following what Underwood calls 'his destined natural way', Tim 'decided to be true to himself and his music, fully aware that he would be accepting a lifetime burden of guilt. Tim left, not because he didn't care about his soon-to-be-born child, but because his musical life was just beginning. He did not abandon Jeff; he abandoned Mary.'

That autumn, back in Anaheim, Tim met with Mary in an anonymous coffee shop. As far as the marriage and child were concerned, he left both decisions to her. Upon his departure, Tim returned to the road, Mary to her parents.

Whatever Underwood's take on the situation, Tim's actions spoke clearly. When Jeffrey was born there was no word from his father. 'I thought I'd hear from him, but I didn't,' said Mary flatly. Her mood possibly amplified by post-natal depression, she burned her cache of Tim's love letters shortly after the birth, and a divorce was granted during the first few months of Jeff's life.

Mary proved to be a single-minded, strong, acutely perceptive and driven seventeen-year-old single mom – an unusual phenomenon in the mid-sixties, even within the hippy sanctuary of California. Initially she worked as a bank clerk until illness forced her to quit the job and move back into the sometimes dysfunctional home of her parents.

Whatever her own personal feelings towards her ex-husband, Mary never forgot that her son needed some kind of contact with his biological father. She always made an effort to introduce the two, whenever Tim's seemingly shambolic gypsy life allowed. Later, when Tim was living out in Venice Beach, Mary visited him with an eight-month-old Jeff. Tim appeared somewhat overawed on such occasions, although he was always affectionate and engaging. Mary continued these introductions and reintroductions, which only amounted to three visits during Jeff's first year of life. Yet they made an impression. Years later, as an adult, Jeff would tell his mother about a recurring dream which bothered him. In it, Jeff was at the beach, the sound of waves crashing gently nearby. It was either dusk or dawn. Twilight. Jeff was sitting on his father's shoulders, and a few feet away Mary lay on a blanket.

She was moved by her son's description. 'I told him, "That's not a dream, that really happened." I don't ever remember telling him. It must have been one of his earliest memories. There was someone who told me later… that Tim actually walked with [Jeff] to her house down the street; she saw Jeff when he was just a little baby asleep in his arms. So I know at least [Tim] was proud, he wanted to show her his baby boy. Then he moved and left no forwarding address. I was nineteen years old. If he ripped my heart out before, this time he spat in the hole.'

To compound such brutal heartache, Mary was having a hard time living with her parents. There had often been a violent undertone to life in the family home, and the festive season of 1967 witnessed a particularly tense and aggravated Christmas within the Guibert household. Mary's father, George, continued his legacy of occasional violence towards his children, and so, reluctantly – yet with little other choice – the young mother took to the road. Sometimes, with no lack of irony, it must have seemed as though both she and Tim shared the nomadic lifestyle of the true bohemian.

Mary settled into a humble apartment in North Hollywood, taking temporary jobs to support herself and Scotty, who she now saw only on weekends. During the week her family looked after the baby. George Guibert's outbursts were neither a constant factor nor a seriously considered threat to Scotty, yet it was hardly a stable environment for the boy.

Whilst Tim had so far made only cameo appearances in the early years of his son's life, he was not unaware of what was going on. On 14 July 1968, he recorded 'The Father Song' at TTG Studios, Hollywood. Written for Hall Bartlett's film *Changes*, it remained unreleased for decades. The lyrics speak for themselves. 'I know I'll never be the man you want me to be / Oh tell me, father, is there shame in your heart for me?'

These rare meetings of father and son would be repeated over the next few years – albeit seeming more like stolen moments than quality time together. Still, it appeared that the reality of Scotty being Tim's son was slowly and deeply dawning on the young father, although in conversations with his friends and fellow musicians it sometimes seemed that he was more moved by the phenomenon of having sired a son than the actual son himself. Despite having no real commercial success as a recording artist or songwriter, Tim paid his family dues. Regular child support payments ($80 a month) made to Mary via his accountant were a more tangible sign of his awareness and commitment, however remote it may have seemed.

Baby Scotty was rarely truly conscious during these times. As with the dream-like Venice Beach episode, this period would haunt him throughout his life as a series of impressionistic fragments, time-corrupted snatches of cinéfilm woven at random into his memory.

Beyond the orbit of his father, Scotty began to bloom and flower in a myriad of ways. His vivid musicality, in particular, manifested itself at an early age. 'As a baby he was vocalising,' said Mary. 'I have little snap shots of him raised on the hearth of the fireplace: that was his little stage where he would sing songs for his grandma.'

Little Scotty began school at the tender age of two-and-a-half, albeit at the 'progressive' Montessori school in the Anaheim hills. The institution, conceived by its founder, Maria Montessori, was admirably forward-thinking even for the sixties.

'He was always playing toy instruments, even as a little boy – singing, reciting poetry,' recounted Mary, obviously still proud decades on. 'I believed very strongly in the Montessori method... and he just loved it [the school]. He used to imitate his Ceylonese Montessori teacher when he was three... had us all in stitches.'

In 1969, tired of being separated from her child, Mary abandoned the tiny rented apartment in North Hollywood and returned to Orange County to be with Scotty.

It was here and now, back in the place of her son's birth, that twenty-year-old Mary would meet Tim's romantic successor, mechanic Ron Moorhead. Ron was built along more 'regular' lines than Tim – tall, macho, blue-eyed and blue-collar. But he was also a 100-mile-per-hour music lover, addicted to a bountiful and frequently replenished supply of vinyl albums. Ron, Mary and Scotty hit it off immediately. So well, in fact, that Ron and Mary were married in December of that year, with three-year-old Scotty appointed as best man. The family moved into a new home the following year; a compact but cosy house in Orange County's Fullerton that was notoriously sandwiched between the noise, grind and fumes of an aluminium factory and an airport. 'I loved this atmosphere,' remembered Jeff fondly. 'The noise was like music for me: the trains on the track which adjoined the house, the aircrafts passing overhead at low altitude…'

It was in this cinematic setting that Scotty would experience having a father for the first time. The tall and athletic Ron worked at his own business as a Volkswagen repairman during the day, and indulged his love of contemporary rock and pop in the evenings and on weekends.

This era was a rich time for popular music in America, and between the constant AM radio and his stepdad's various stereos (both in house and in car: 'I can remember being obsessed with my stepfather's stereo,' Jeff would recall), little Scotty's infant ears were exposed to the finest (and then freshly minted) works of the Doors, Crosby, Stills & Nash, Pink Floyd, the Who, and the group that would exert a profound and lasting influence on the young boy: no one could predict it then, but Jeff would, in effect, one day become a hybrid of both Robert Plant and Jimmy Page. Hearing the soaring stomp and blur of Led Zeppelin amongst the industrial roar of Fullerton Airport and the steelworks signalled a kind of homecoming for the young boy. Meanwhile, Mary used this newfound domestic stability to indulge her own musical passions. She returned to studying piano and cello, and her listening tastes filtered down to her son in tandem and contrast with those of her husband. As well as developing a taste for the bombastic, guitar-driven rock sounds that Ron loved so much, through his mother Jeff was equally well-versed in the works of Joni Mitchell, Barbara Streisand and Fleetwood Mac, as well as absorbing a classical supplement of Chopin, Bach and Stravinsky.

This was a fecund environment for any child, especially one imbued with Jeff's nascent talents. Yet, along with the richness of noise and the novelty of cosy domesticity, nagging financial troubles were causing problems between Mary and Ron. Exacerbating this sometimes tense relationship were the periodic arrivals – via Tim Buckley's management – of Tim's latest albums. Ron was an averagely macho young guy living and working in early seventies America. He was not particularly comfortable with his wife's forays into amateur dramatics and general artiness, nor by the occasional manifestation of Mary and Scotty's seemingly exotic past in the shape of albums recorded by the man who had helped conceive and then abandoned the child. Mary would obviously play the records to her son, and this understandably made Ron feel uncomfortable, even threatened. Not that Jeff reacted to the music in any particular way. Indeed, in comparison with the ecstatic reactions he afforded when listening to Led Zeppelin, he seemed almost indifferent to Tim Buckley's two masterworks to date, *Lorca* and *Starsailor*. Besides, as Jeff would later admit, he was deep into *Sesame Street* at this point.

Despite the undertow of marital strife, another son – Corey – followed in March of 1972. Meanwhile, the firstborn continued to come into being musically, even if the opportunities for doing so were less than glamorous. 'My stepfather got drunk and fell asleep in front of everyone and my grandmother got really embarrassed,' Jeff would remember. 'So to direct attention away from him I sang every Elton John song I knew.'

Such scenes were typical amongst any family, particularly a work-oriented, blue-collar one like the Moorheads. Yet, outside of this, Mary was not happy in herself, and was certainly not happy in the role her hard-working husband expected her to play. 'My mother would have dreamed of playing Mendelssohn instead of doing housework,' reckoned Jeff years later. 'When her husband unexpectedly returned from work, it made him crazy to find her sitting at the piano…'

By early 1973, all of the various stresses and strains had finally ruptured the marriage, and the couple sadly but inexorably separated. Mary retained the house, the car, and the children. She was still only 24 years old.

The next few years witnessed a pattern familiar enough for any estranged family unit. Mary moved from job to job, made do despite the odds, and kept the family together. All the while she was conscious of the fact that her first son was growing up fast, and without any real relationship with his biological father. 'After the break-up of my second marriage,' said Mary, 'I began to think it really sad that there's this boy who had no contact with his father. There were no birthday cards, no Christmas cards…'

Scotty, at least, now had a permanent chum – as they grew, he and his half-brother Corey came to share an impish sense of fun and mischief, and often played together in each new location they called 'home'. Life went on.

By 1975 Mary had become enamoured enough of another self-employed man by the name of George Vandergrift to buy a house with him in Riverside, 50 miles east of Scotty's birthplace. Luckily such a transient life seemed to suit Scotty's nature. 'I hated comfort,' he would tell a French journalist years later. 'I refused stability, lethargy, a comfortable environment. In a place like California, everything was "right" – Americana in all its horror. Life in suburbia… cooking, cookies, the horror! However, there was the desert, mountains, sea, and of course, incredible artists. Fortunately, my mother spent her time on the move; it put a little spice in my life. It was exciting and frightening not to have roots. Yet, I was sometimes ashamed. To my school friends, I represented a failure, someone lacking something…'

The year of this move – 1975 – was to be the year of the first and last of Jeff's substantial meetings with his blood father. It occurred in April, when he was eight.

Mary Guibert noticed a listing in a local newspaper for an upcoming Tim Buckley show. Tim's career had by now, in many minds, peaked – at least commercially – and he was certainly struggling financially, which forced him to diversify (unsuccessfully) into film projects and take to the road full-time. Yet those close to him say that he had found a second-wind artistically and that this was beginning to be reflected in a somewhat commercial return to form in terms of his live performances, as he was currently without a recording contract for the first time since the sixties.

Mary and Scotty undertook the hour-long drive to Huntington Beach, an oceanside town ten miles southwest of Orange County, and arrived at the Golden Bear club just before Tim walked onstage. They took a seat on a bench in the second row. Scotty's reactions to his father's actual recordings had been muted. But now, breathing the same air, his eyes fixed on the stage, he encountered his dad's quixotic pop music in a way that would prove to be far more satisfying for all concerned.

'I think the band came on and started cookin' first,' Mary remembered decades later. 'Yeah, and here's little Scotty, he's got blonde hair down to here, he's bouncing in his seat, he's chair-dancing to his dad's music, and Tim's wailing, and I saw – or I imagine I saw, I don't know which – his eyes were closed, and he'd open them a little bit to see Scotty in the second row, and Scotty was grooving. I was watching the two of them and I thought, "This is really going to be amazing." '

Scotty continued to bop throughout the gig, not seeming to tire even when the initial novelty of such a loud, kinetic experience had passed. 'Scotty was in love,' Mary said. 'He was immediately entranced. His little eyes were just dancing in his head.'

From where Mary was sitting, it was obvious that still Tim still had 'it'. He still appeared to be tuned into something otherworldly. His countenance had changed though. Although still youthful and even more handsome than she remembered, the cherubic face once featured on the *Happy Sad* album cover had been erased by the countless road miles that

Jeff's father Tim Buckley, who died from an overdose in 1975, aged 28.

a lack of commercial success had forced him to travel. At the end of the set, Mary asked her son if he wanted to meet his father. The answer was instant and physical. The kid shot out of the stalls and scampered backstage. As they entered the cramped dressing room, Jeff clutched his mother's long skirt. It seemed a foreign and frightening world to him, until he heard someone shout out, 'Jeff!' Although no one had called him that before in his life – he was still 'Scotty' to everyone – Jeff instinctively recognised the voice of his dad and ran across the room to a table where Tim was resting after the show.

'He leapt at the sound of his father's voice,' said Mary, 'across the room into his arms, and he was sitting on his lap and chattering a mile a minute. He said things like, "My dog's name is King, he's white," and he was telling [Tim] everything he could think about himself to tell his father. He was sitting on his dad's lap facing [Tim] and I could see Tim's face over Jeff's shoulder and tears were just running down his face. So I thought, "I'll just let this be," and I went back to the audience.'

'I sat on his knees for fifteen minutes,' Jeff wrote later. 'He was hot and sweaty. I kept on feeling his legs. "Wow, you need an iceberg to cool you off!" I was very embarrassing – doing my George Carlin impression for him for no reason. Very embarrassing. He smiled the whole time. Me too.'

Tim's drummer, Buddy Helm, remembered: 'It was a very personal moment. The kid seemed very genuine, totally in love with his dad. It was like wanting to connect. He didn't know anything personally about Tim but was there ready to do it.' It seemed that finally, after years of absence, Tim too was ready to reciprocate this feeling. Between sets (Tim was due to go on again that night) Judy, Tim's new partner, asked Mary if it would be cool for Scotty to spend a few days with her and Tim. After that night, Tim had a couple of days off and wanted to use them to catch up with his son. It was the start of the Easter holidays for Scotty, so Mary acquiesced. The next morning, she packed his clothes into a brown paper bag and drove him to Santa Monica to spend a handful of happy days with Tim and his wife. He returned to Mary the following Thursday evening, among his new possessions was a matchbox with his daddy's phone number written on the back.

Two months later, Tim Buckley was dead.

Although at the time there were various contradictory accounts and accusations as to why and how the young singer had died, decades later, the truth has settled upon the following sequence of events.

While winding down at the home of Richard Keeling (a friend from his time at UCLA) after another tour, Tim had snorted a line of heroin. With a few scotches already inside him, he apparently thought the dope was cocaine and sucked it straight up, no chaser. He almost immediately started losing control and began to stagger around Keeling's apartment.

Keeling and Jackie McGuire, a female acquaintance, escorted Tim back to Judy, his wife, at their nearby apartment. With their help, she got Tim to bed. Mumbling, 'bye bye baby' – a reference to 'Drifting Blues', a Ray Charles song he loved – Tim slipped into an unconsciousness from which he would never wake.

Various murder and the inevitable suicide conspiracies abounded in the immediate wake of his passing. Police would even charge Richard Keeling – the immediate source of the lethal dose – with murder and distribution of heroin. Ultimately the evidence (and one would assume the motive) proved insufficient and, at a hearing on 14 August, in the Municipal Court, Keeling pleaded guilty to involuntary manslaughter. Tim's friend was given the chance to avoid time in jail by doing community work, but failed to keep his side of the bargain. He was sentenced to 120 days in jail and four years probation.

None of these judicial processes would bring Tim back. The toxicology report placed the cause of death as 'acute morphine/heroin intoxication' and in time no one was ultimately blamed for this seemingly senseless death, not even Tim himself.

Mary was devastated, both for Tim, herself, and their son. 'It was cruel. Scotty was ripped away from the possibility of ever having known him.' What she might not have realised was the extent to which this permanent departure would shape Scotty's own life. Tim Buckley's passing bruised his son in countless subtle shades. Among these was the heavy shadow that his legacy would cast over the child's development. Within this shadow grew the primary source of Jeff's reticence where embracing his own particular musical destiny was concerned. 'I knew there would be [comparisons] from the time I was a small child,' Jeff admitted years down the line. 'From the time that his manager started calling my house when I was six or seven. I found my grandmother's guitar and [his manager] started calling the house: "Has he written songs yet?" So I've been waiting and doing the maths in my head about the inevitable comparisons all my life. But I don't care.'

Another slight but profound change following his father's death manifested itself when it was time for Scotty to enrol for a new term at school. Jeff chose to do so using his father's name. He stopped using 'Moorhead', and for the first time took on 'Buckley'.

'The reasons behind this decision are too entirely personal and private to share,' admitted Mary. 'But I supported his choice.'

Neither Mary nor Scotty was invited to Tim's funeral. Many of the deceased's friends and acquaintances were unaware that he even had a son. A time would come when that very son would somehow seem to blame Tim himself for not inviting him to the funeral. Bad seeds were sown.

Tim's music and reputation would not only survive his death, but actually prosper and thrive in the coming decade. This again would have unforeseen consequences for the newly fatherless Scotty. As Lee Underwood succinctly observes, 'Jeff suffered because his tormented father was physically present as a critical adversary but absent as a loving mentor.'

Despite the constant coming and going of various father figures within Scotty's life, two things remained a source of constant love and security for the boy: his mother and music. 'As a child,' Jeff would remark, 'there were my mother's breasts and then there was music. I was basically raised by my mother. Me, my little brother and she. I was raised by my mother's side of the family and there was music all the time. My grandmother, she had this acoustic guitar. This gut-string in the closet. I claimed it for my own. And that's how I started playing...

'It was the only constant. Anything from, like, Aerosmith down to the soundtrack of *Close Encounters of the Third Kind*. Anything that I liked was mine and I could appreciate the whole world through it...' Scott Buckley, as he was now known, had a ravenous appetite for music – as a listener and, increasingly, as a performer. 'I felt the pull from an early age,' Jeff would reminisce. 'I must have been about twelve when I started to think about its bright lights.' In addition, his mother would acknowledge the 'slight preservation of European tradition in my family', and inferred that this had touched her son as he was growing up, lending him a slightly more cosmopolitan edge than your average (as Jeff would describe himself) 'trailer trash' figure.

Obviously, Scotty did not think of his life in terms of tragic rock folklore. The father he barely knew had disappeared again, this time forever. As heartbreaking as this was, in real material terms it made little difference in Scotty's day-to-day life. By now a toothsome blonde, he continued his studies at Riverside High School, made friends, began to notice girls, became enamoured of glam heavy metal music (Kiss and Styx were early favourites), and generally got on with growing up. At the same time, the grown-ups that he and Corey shared a life and house with were beginning to come undone. By the end of the decade, Mary and her long-term partner George Vandergrift had parted. She, the thirteen-year-old Jeff, and the seven-year-old Corey were alone together and on the road again. In 1979 they had resettled in Sunnymead, just ten miles on from Riverside. They moved into a pink cottage, and once again the single mother struggled to make ends meet, this time by starting up her own business, Emerald Enterprises, through which she grew and sold vegetables. Mary also faced the fresh problem of having to deal with the two wayward boys in her midst. While Scotty had long ago acclimatised to the absence of an enduring father figure – he knew no different – Corey in particular now seemed resentful of being estranged from his very much alive father, Ron Moorhead. Mary, Corey and Scotty were forced to take advantage of their extended families as financial pressures meant that both boys would occasionally spend time with various fathers, grandparents and great grandparents. Despite such enforced wanderlust, Scotty would never seem to hold it against his mother. 'She was quite a gypsy,' was about as far as his judgement went. Yet, whatever their domestic situation, the boys' school studies continued for the most part unabated, and fundamentally they had an emotionally supportive upbringing.

For Christmas 1979, through the combined effort of his mother and her parents, Scotty received his first electric guitar – a copy of a black Les Paul. He instantly learned the immortal pop hit 'My Sharona' by the Knack, and played it to the point of distraction. Simultaneously, he fell in love with his tape recorder, obsessively recording favourite TV and radio shows on it and playing along with the tapes in his bedroom.

In the cheap Les Paul copy, Jeff had acquired a lifelong friend. 'I didn't really start playing, really getting proficient until I was about thirteen. An electric guitar comes into a kid's life, it'll just... the potential is, like, to take him away forever. And that's what happened.'

Jeff was the first to admit that he 'hated' high school: 'My family would always be moving, so I was always the new guy in town. Any school I went to, I would always be introduced to the class. I would be judged in hand immediately. I would always be singled out... Kids are cold and disgusting because they learn it all from their parents.'

Despite his social difficulties, Jeff's academic life continued, and this of course included music studies. He received the bare amount of formal musical training that the curriculum endowed, within which he dabbled in cello for a year and, as instructed by his tutor, 'plinked on the piano' at home. However, it soon became apparent that it was the guitar that would be his first instrument of choice. Mary remembers her son playing along religiously with favoured albums, until 'one couldn't tell whether it was Jeff or the stereo playing'.

All the while he continued to grow, get into fights, join school bands, foster crushes and watch TV, Jeff was evolving into a slightly gawky-looking teenager, a self-confessed 'geek and outsider'. His mother would concur, reasoning that the extra responsibilities foisted on her son in looking after his family had prematurely aged him. (As well as being preoccupied with the traumas of puberty and schoolwork, for some time Jeff had also been helping out his mother, both around the home and in her business.) In turn this led him to seek a kind of escape – a refuge –

within the music he loved. As he progressed through high school he found it hard to break out of such absorption, as if what he found in music was much more profound and meaningful than the somewhat transient and relatively shallow social whirl of the teen. 'He was a very sensitive and introverted guy – especially for a teenager,' remembered Mary. Jeff was – no doubt about it – a music nerd. At one point his most favoured possessions were all four Kiss albums and a Rush picture disc.

The American seventies – with their growing economy and madness for technology, the future, and plain old consumerist crap – were in many ways the perfect decade for someone as sponge-like as Jeff. 'There was an overspill of rock life,' he mused years later, 'which becomes coffee-table material with books on Kiss and rock stars on TV. I knew it was possible for some people to do it for a living. I spent hours listening to *Magical Mystery Tour...*'

Tellingly, he did not cite his father's works as part of this inspiration (although in later life, Jeff would put this down to a mere matter of taste), and neither did he initially find many others of a similar disposition at school. 'I had friends, just nobody to talk music with,' he remembered in 1994. 'I did not want to share it with anyone, it was my secret. I spent whole days learning albums by heart.' He rarely exhibited his talents outside of the family home (whichever house or apartment that happened to be at any given time), giving his first public performance at the age of thirteen when he sang at a dance for a Northern Californian Methodist church. He practiced mostly in the solitude of his poster-plastered bedroom, and his visible musical focus was as a fan. As such he continued to be utterly enamoured of music on television, including the house bands of regular chat shows and the occasional mega-concert, in particular the huge glam-fests staged by such evergreen favourites as Elton John.

By the early 1980s, Jeff outwardly seemed like any other fourteen-year-old music fan. Usually dressed in jeans and a T-shirt, his tastes were all-American in so far as he loved the FM radio-friendly sounds of Kiss, Rush, Led Zeppelin, Foreigner and their ilk. At this point his listening habits ran no further afield than avant-garde prog-rock. Amongst the modest tape, eight-track and vinyl collection kept stacked beside his bed was the occasional triple-album opus produced by such ornately-packaged groups as Yes, Genesis, Asia and ELP. (He would outgrow these groups to the point where he found comparisons with them distasteful.) But for all his passion, Jeff was still discerning. As such he was certainly not enamoured of the new-wave sounds of English ska groups, or by the likes of Ian Dury and Elvis Costello, who were causing a moderate US media stir at the dawn of the new decade. Nor, a few years hence, would he be queuing up to see the bastions of the 'second English invasion' such as Duran Duran and Flock of Seagulls. (Although he would thrill at the reggae-pop fusion of the Police.) Yet compared to what they would eventually become, Jeff's tastes as an adolescent were unextraordinary. A minor epiphany came in the form of a 1981 Def Leppard arena gig that he attended with his friend Willie Osborn. In the pyrotechnics and elaborate light display of the spandexed rockers' pantomime show, Jeff saw a possible future for himself. At this point his aspirations couldn't have seemed more distant from the esoteric folk-funk fusion that Tim Buckley had pioneered at far more intimate venues less then a decade earlier.

During the first summer of 1980, Jeff and his half-brother wearily made yet another 'home' when he and Corey moved in with Ron Moorhead and his new family, south of San Francisco. Yet this proved to be another temporary refuge. By the following fall, the nucleus of Jeff and Mary were once again in transit, this time leaving Corey to spend more time with his father Ron, while mother and son rented house after house in Orange County. As a rising star years later, constantly going over his childhood in press interviews, Jeff would often mythologise this roaming aspect of his youth. 'I'm being thrust into my old ways, ways I've grown up with, and I have to hang on: moving from place to place, grabbing onto people, making fast friends, letting them go.' He was equally fond of declaring: 'I was rootless trailer trash.'

To his mother, this was merely funny. 'Jeff would sometimes make things up,' Mary countered. 'I would see the "poor white trailer trash" reference in interviews and I'd be like, "Oh my God Scotty! We never lived in a trailer! Where is this coming from? What kind of picture are you trying to paint?"'

Jeff seemed, on the surface at least, able to accept his situation whilst having some awareness that it was merely provisional. He was, in effect, marking time. He saw his environment as essentially harmless and 'really middle of the road, conservative, white neighbourhoods, very segregated. I was just in dreamland about... everything. I just didn't appreciate it. It didn't include me. There's a huge world outside. If you don't know that then, it's too late for you already.'

His school life continued when and where it could, but unlike many others who suffered similar periods of rootlessness, the constant ritual of having to make new friends and forge fresh teacher-pupil relationships never seemed to damage him. Jeff appeared to travel in a self-contained bubble that consisted primarily of himself, his imagination, his music and his mom. Although as a student he got passable grades, he was not noted for particularly good or bad behaviour at any school he attended. Academia and the environment it fostered were not for him, but rather than rebel against it, he merely sat it out. 'High school was just a joke. Not the information but the people,' Jeff would reckon years on. 'I sometimes felt like an outsider, already too old for my age.'

The next school he attended had deeper connotations for Jeff than any joke could have. How must he have felt to now be attending Loara High School, the place where both his parents schooled and courted? If the young man did feel haunted, there is no record of it, and while he was no social pariah, Jeff was certainly no jock either. He made little effort to be anything other than himself and did not court popularity or peer approval. But neither did he make much of a disruption. Jeff was simply Jeff; slightly weird, likeable, somewhat goofy, and a little too cool for school. When he did relate to his fellow students it was usually through music, and he wasn't self conscious about his talent, or at least one particular strain of it.

'I was in band at Loara High School with Jeff. I remember him well,' recalled one ex-Loara muso. 'Jeff was the class clown in the school stage band but he got away with quite a bit because he was truly a child prodigy. I remember thinking it was like he was born with a guitar in his hands. I feel honoured even now to think that I performed with Jeff...'

Jeff's main musical chops centred on his guitar. He spent countless sun-bleached California mornings jamming in garages and shacks with fellow music-fixated buddies throughout the early 1980s, and hardly any of them heard evidence of the one thing the young rocker would eventually become best known for – his singing voice.

Whether it was a reaction – conscious or otherwise – against the legacy of his father that he found seeded within him, Jeff seemed utterly focused on being a guitarist. During rehearsals he would amiably if only occasionally sing backing vocals or launch into an impression of a then popular pop singer, but for the fifteen-year-old Jeff Buckley, singing seemed to be one of the few musical endeavors that he *wasn't* interested in.

By 1982 Jeff had begun gigging properly with his first serious band, Mahre Bukham. Alongside Robin Horry and Jason Hamel, Jeff mostly played lead guitar throughout a set of spirited and highly proficient covers of artists such as Hendrix and the Police, wherein he also indulged his spandex tendencies. No one who witnessed Jeff during this group's four-gig history would have thought for a second that he was keeping anything back. The preening, joyous, long-haired teen rocking out onstage could not have seemed less like a frustrated devotee of jazz, folk-rock, and chanson singer Edith Piaf. To all who saw him play during this era, Jeff appeared to be a consummate guitar god in the making.

Finally, as the decade moved into its midpoint, Jeff's tastes began to mature. In 1984 he became 'obsessed' with Miles Davis for a while (as his father had been, particularly with the trumpeter's seminal *In a Silent Way*). In turn his own music began to reflect this new passion – Jeff now performed at school functions in low-key jazz-fusion outfits, often playing his original, fret-heavy instrumental compositions to mostly indifferent and overly made-up examples of early eighties youth.

Throughout his teens, Jeff was a 'cool nerd', untypical, a minor enigma. He was a true maverick – too subtly weird even to be portrayed in any of the John Hughes films that epitomised that era, existing beyond the labels and clichés of the schoolyard. Jeff rarely indulged in alcohol, did not smoke and was, to a degree, anti-drugs. (He shared a joint now and then.) While not popular as such, he thrived in a small group of select and sincere friends and his social life, revolving as it did around music, was rich, expansive and busy. By contrast he loved his own company and spent hours in his bedroom, practicing guitar and listening hungrily to music which now included the pantheon of jazz – an obsessive's delight. While undoubtedly attractive, if still mawkish-looking, Jeff didn't seem to have one major girlfriend throughout these formative years, although he had the occasional crush on girls who would invariably become friends. But, as ever, music remained the constant factor, and was, in many ways, the first love of Jeff Buckley's life.

His relationship with his immediate family – Mary and Corey – remained stable and affectionately civil. Years later, without expounding on the fact, Jeff would admit: 'Everybody's childhood places a devil inside of them.' Yet for someone with such a potentially traumatic background, as a teenager Jeff seemed to have come through his own particular storm of childhood pretty much unscathed.

By late 1984, Jeff was ready to move on again – this time on his own. With what was perhaps no small touch of irony, he would one day look back on his eighteen-year-old self and say that the reason he left home at this particular point was because, 'I was tired of moving around.'

But Jeff wasn't about to take off into the vastness of America by jumping a train or hitting the road thumbing. (Although such fantasies no doubt appealed to the Kerouac fan in him.) Despite his natural disdain for academia, Jeff planned to move away solo under the cloak of further education – albeit this time a purely musical one.

Located near Sunset Boulevard, the Los Angeles Music Institute, and in particular its own Department of Guitar Technology, seemed like a natural destination for a fretwork freak like Jeff. A year's tuition cost $4,000, and he would obviously need help with living expenses on top of that. Once again the spectre of his father loomed. With Mary's full approval, they used a trust fund that had been set up for Jeff in the wake of Tim's passing to finance the venture.

The course lasted a year. Jeff arrived for the term beginning in the autumn of 1984. During his time at the institute he bonded with like-minded jazz-fusion enthusiasts, was a respected and well-liked student, and to this day is listed on the institute's 'Roll of Honour'. Yet the appreciation was hardly reciprocated. Speaking of his time there, Jeff was brutally dismissive of the school: 'I went to this really crappy guitar school for a year. This is the kind of school where you give them a shitload of money in order to spend a year learning the curriculum, and pretty soon you have all this shit inside you and then they give you this paper that says you have what it takes to be a professional musician. In the end, I think, the only true product of that kind of learning is to get you gigs… on the session guy circuit.' It was, he concluded, 'the biggest waste of time I have ever seen'. Tellingly, none of his peers ever recall hearing Jeff sing a word.

By 1985 Jeff had graduated and moved into central Hollywood. Despite his fresh certificate from the institute, he remained essentially a freelance musician, living gig-to-gig.

It was now that he began a pattern of odd jobs and Pyrrhic musical activities that would discolour the next few years of his life. He hooked up with bands of varying styles and genres, always as a guitarist, and always on what seemed to be a temporary basis. Jeff gravitated towards reggae and ska bands in particular, one of his most rewarding gigs being with the AKB Band, led by saxophonist Al Kirk and the heavily dreadlocked vocalist Pablove Black. Jeff would reflect on this group with a fondness he was unable to afford his memories of the Los Angeles Music Institute. A handful of years on, he reminisced that, 'Pablove, the Rasta… everything he said about playing makes sense now.'

Beyond reggae, Jeff drifted back onto the spandex highway for his musical detours – but would be utterly dismissive of such groups in the future. 'Forget the next band,' he opined in an interview in 1992, referring curtly to his time as pocket-sized guitar god with the soft-metal, Fleetwood Mac-lite outfit Group Therapy.

Jeff was constantly active. Some of his earliest recordings occurred on a demo with one of the ex-teachers from the institute. By September 1987,

Jeff had ended up sharing an apartment with bass tutor John Humphrey. In late 1988 John recorded some amateur demos on the four-track reel-to-reel of a friend. Jeff provided guitar and some reluctant backing vocals. 'I had to talk him into singing,' recalls Humphrey. Despite his vocal reticence, Jeff gigged with John for a while until they parted company in the summer of 1989. Jeff had nothing concrete to concentrate on. He was listless. A malaise of the soul was setting in.

Following this last pleasant but futile musical misdemeanour, Jeff decided 'not to spread myself that thin. I didn't like California, South LA especially. Hollywood isn't a real town, but that's the reality of it.' He had perhaps always been aware on some level that his recent musical ventures had been just that: sonic excursions, ultimately diversions. Jeff wasn't particularly passionate about anything he was involved in – neither the groups he played with, nor the music he was writing, and certainly not his day job at a mediocre hotel. Five years away from home had flown by, and all he had to show for it was a long list of seemingly random gigs with a cornucopia of middling groups, and a few bashed-up demo tapes of his own generic-sounding fusion compositions.

Meanwhile, his long-dead father, Tim, was making something of a comeback. Slowly but surely, and particularly in Europe and the UK, the music of Tim Buckley – in almost direct parallel with Nick Drake – was becoming cool again. As such, labels were beginning to re-release and repackage his works, particularly as part of the CD boom. Jeff would even visit the offices of one of these labels – Enigma Records – to listen to a playback of a recently discovered Tim Buckley concert from London, circa 1968. Eventually released as *Dream Letter*, the album was almost instantly hailed as a classic of its genre, and the Tim Buckley revival seemed to be in full swing. Yet in almost every retrospective piece published on the dead singer – and there were plenty in the latter years of the eighties and early nineties – hardly anyone mentioned the fact that Tim had a son.

One would have to scour some of the more obscure Tim Buckley fanzines to stumble upon even the vaguest of references to young Jeff.

In 1989, writing to the editor of *Tim Buckley Fanzine 2*, Lee Underwood wrote: 'Meanwhile, Jeffrey Scott Buckley, Tim's son by his first marriage, has grown up. I am not in touch with him, nor have I ever seen or met him. However, other people tell me he looks exactly like Tim; he plays jazz and rock guitar, he has a band of his own, is about 25 or 26 now, and goes by the name of Jeff Scott. You and I should both keep our ears and eyes open. If Jeff's any good, we'll probably be hearing about him soon.'

2. MUSIC IS MY RADAR

'I guess I felt blocked. I felt like I was dying… I was still. I was stagnant. I felt like I was rotting away in Los Angeles.'

Jeff Buckley

By the first winter of 1990 it seemed as though the 23-year-old Jeff had reached some sort of impasse within himself. He was unarguably at a stalemate of sorts. In his own words: 'I was staring at the wall. Just blankly putting tapes in the player and pulling them out, putting them back in again. Just doing nothing, really. Just depressed. Depressed beyond belief. So I decided not to die anymore.' So much for Hollywood.

Jeff seemed to have gotten as far as he could within the centrally-heated pond of the Californian music scene. Ultimately what he needed to change was himself. In this regard he seemed to have hit a road block in LA. It was time for a change of scenery. If he couldn't change himself he would shift his geography. Jeff went to New York.

The boy Buckley was no movie freak – the fair share of his nebbish nerd energy went into his fanatical love of music, but he enjoyed a classic movie as much as the next art-throb muso geek. *On the Waterfront, Duck Soup, Street of Crocodiles,* and *Notorious* were confirmed favourites, but Jeff was also surely familiar with John Schlesinger's *Midnight Cowboy,* and the films of Scorsese, Warhol and Woody Allen. All these names often embodied New York City itself as the star of their movies. As such, like millions of others before and after him, New York already existed in a very real sense within Jeff's own fertile imagination. 'I'd never been there before,' he admitted. 'But when you're a kid in America New York kind of permeates every bit of the media. Everybody seems to have made it big in Paris, England or New York, y'know? Bugs Bunny had a Brooklyn accent…'

The move wasn't only about the lure of the Big Apple. Jeff also ended up there by default, as he felt that there was no conceivable way

Jeff Buckley in 1992: still rocking the Californian funkster look as Gods and Monsters' vocalist.

he could remain on the West Coast. 'The future just kept on pointing to the east,' he would later say. 'At the time I was feeling cancerous and I just had to get out.'

He arrived at JFK Airport in the freezing February of 1990.

Buzzing with wonder and utterly energised – just being out of LA was a shot in the arm – Jeff first found digs in the magic desolation and jive of Harlem. The apartment was small and he shared amenities with a drummer, but he was living in New York City. He was hip, talented, cool, young and beautiful. If he could make it here he could make it anywhere. His bedroom was tiny, but so what? He didn't feel much like sleeping anyway.

If LA had been stunting him, then the Big Apple would provide the changeling Jeff with a rich soil in which to grow. 'This is where I blossomed,' he grinned, still a gypsy at heart. 'This place turned out to be everything I knew it to be. It stinks like hell – a fucking majestic cesspool.'

Yet even those existing in a cesspool had to sustain themselves, and thus Jeff took on the wearisome work of looking for a job. He auditioned for the occasional acting part – failing to get onboard TV show of the moment *Murphy's Law* – and skirted the outer twilight zone of celebrity further by working for Denzel Washington's answering service. He soon realised, as the other millions had and would, that starting from the bottom was as hard as ever, even when you lived – perhaps *especially* when you lived – within mooching distance of the legendary Apollo Theatre.

'New York was just so overtly romantic that I thought that it had to be the place,' he would counter just two years on, speaking with all the grim authority of a true ex-refugee. 'It's the wrong place to run out of money and not have food – it's the wrong place, baby. 'Cause you'd be walking down the street and doors are open and there's food everywhere – there's food on the street. And you think about stealing it, some huge, beautiful pretzel that I wouldn't even buy now, but at the time it was like, "Ooh, Thanksgiving dinner, right there." '

Luckily for him, even while he subsisted on popcorn and air, Jeff made friends and kept them easily. By spring he had moved in with another companion, the actress Brooke Smith. (But not before his drumming flatmate had exposed Jeff to some of the most important music of his life – the devotional music of the Pakistani-born singer Nusrat Fateh Ali Khan.)

Jeff had met Smith during her filming stint on *The Silence of the Lambs* in California. She was of rare pedigree – an actual successful movie actress – and as such she had a lease on her own two-bedroom apartment in the swanky area of West Eighty-Ninth Street on Manhattan's Upper West Side. Jeff had barely been in the city a season and was already working his way up and in.

Aside from busking on corners and in subways, usually accompanied by a borrowed acoustic guitar, Jeff continued to look for 'proper' employment. His rent was $500 a month, and he wasn't making that singing Bob Dylan and Paul Simon songs all day. Eventually he landed a job folding shirts in the trendy populist boutique Banana Republic. While it was a step above waiting tables and many mountains beneath playing Carnegie Hall, he sensed that he would end up doing one or the other someday.

Once the boutique had closed up for the night, New York's latest immigrant joyfully let himself be swallowed up by the teeming masses of what Henry Miller so aptly called 'The Air-Conditioned Nightmare'. At this point, New York was far from being a bad dream for the young musician, who found ecstasy in mere observation during those early Manhattan nights. Walking the carnival of the city's streets, Jeff let the faces and the sounds and the steam and the smells and the accents and the voices and the lights and the smoke and the people soak into him. As he did so it was as if he were feeding and nurturing himself in some way, sucking up all the mess and beauty for some future purpose. Compared to the stagnant pond of LA, New York provided constant grist for the mill. He wrote letters, composed poetry, and kept scrappy notes in journals. In addition, music seemed to be everywhere, drifting from cafés and diners, screaming from cars, ebbing and pounding out of the boom-boxes on the street and, of course, forever percolating and ricocheting inside of him.

So he wandered, letting the sidewalk guide his feet, those 'stupid shoes' he had once written about in an early fusion composition soon coming to recognise the area he would shortly make his home.

'The Lower East Side is a region of Manhattan that's just intoxicated with its own eccentricity,' raved Jeff. 'I appreciate that. It's easier to be me there. Southern California is kinda dead. There was always a lot of life there but there's a certain electricity missing that New York will always have above everywhere else. That's just my opinion, though. New York has this caffeinated frenzy. Anything that's excellent that comes out of Los Angeles, like the Doors or Jane's Addiction, you just can't figure it out. [But NYC] It's freaky. It's great.'

Jeff's newly adopted city, the very city which had claimed his father so shortly after his conception back in 1966, had now more or less forgotten Tim Buckley. Some very well-received reissues had come out recently (namely *Dream Letter: Live in London*), but the currency of Tim Buckley's genius was still too rarefied and subtle for the masses as a whole. He remained a cool and cultish concern poised somewhere – if at all – between Nick Drake and Tim Hardin in the public's consciousness. Occasionally a wandering Jeff would stumble across the odd vinyl LP in a second-hand store. Other times he would actively seek him out in rock'n'roll reference books or in the old back copies of *Creem* and *ZigZag* that were piled high in the Gotham Book Mart.

But, as an orphan of sorts, Jeff would have felt at home in such a city of exiles. More than this, he told some friends that he actually felt 'reborn'.

Like a clipped minor chord sent shivering through one of his favoured digital FX pedals, a single riff from Jeff's past kept recurring. This was his unreadiness to become Jeff Buckley – singer-songwriter and frontman.

He still auditioned for groups, but seemingly always as a sideman, offering his services as a highly proficient guitarist. It was as if he had learnt little from the session guitarist ping-pong he played in LA. As in Hollywood, the groups he went for in New York seemed to share little stylistically. The one thing they held in common was how little they had in common. He went from playing for ska groups on a Thursday to trying out for hardcore moshpit skinheads on a Friday. On some level he arguably didn't *want* to be exclusively accepted as a guitarist, and so by setting himself up against such inappropriate groups perhaps he was subconsciously willing himself to fail. Perhaps some unconscious system of elimination was at work. Tim Buckley's ex-sideman, Lee Underwood, would follow Jeff's life and career from an informed distance. His perception was that Jeff's lack of confidence in the most profound part of himself – his musical ability – was something that the boy would never come to terms with.

'Jeff felt uncertain of his musical direction… all the way to the end. He did not know himself,' is Underwood's diagnosis. '[He did not know] which musical direction he might want to commit himself to, because taking a stand, making a commitment to a direction, or even to composing and then successfully completing the recording of a single song, was extremely difficult for him. On the one hand, creativity was his calling. On the other hand, any creative gesture that offered the possibility of success terrified him. Hence, his creative inertia, his inability to write very much or very often, his inability to make a commitment.'

Despite this being a seemingly harsh call, Jeff did acknowledge such evaluations of himself at various times throughout his life. His later solo tours would attempt to address this very stigma.

Although in those early months of 1990 he was creatively scattergunning all over the place and missing every target, Jeff's social life was as fluent and healthy as ever. One of the first friends he made was the handsome actor Michael Tighe, who would play a major role in Jeff's musical future.

For now, though, they were merely friends who shared a massive passion for music that stretched seasons and decades beyond what was 'current' or 'hot' within the *Billboard* chart. 'At the time I was listening to mainly soul and blues,' remembered Tighe. 'That was the first language we shared. Then he opened me up to countless other bands.' Jeff's talent for absorbing, processing, appreciating and assimilating music as well as making and performing it staggered and impressed Tighe, who saw Jeff's appetite as verging on 'superhuman'. Jeff seemed intent on eating the world before it ate him, despite the odds. New York could indeed be an electric jungle, particularly for the fragile and poor, but Jeff loved it so.

'I was more interested in being in a place that was more cosmopolitan and more artistic in every way, shape or form,' he said. 'But wherever the human race is involved, unspeakable horrors lurk just around the corner. Whether it's religious, political or just plain insanity. And because of Reagan, there are a lot of mentally ill people out on the streets. They're in a dream anyway. They're not really dangerous or bad, they're just very eccentric. They just need a lot of love and care from people who understand them. It's a hard life, man. It's fucking hard.'

Yet for all the sensual fiesta of sight and sound that the city offered, and in spite of the pivotal and profound friends he was making, Jeff soon found himself face-to-face with yet another impasse. After a trumped-up dispute at the clothes store where he worked, when he was accused of stealing and threatened with police action, he was once again backed against a wall – he had been sacked. Jeff had never felt wholly at ease working at a schmuck job like the one he had at Banana Republic, but still, he couldn't seem to move beyond it. Now that he'd been fired from that position, by default an important decision had been made for him, although at the time such an event would have seemed much more like a crisis than an opportunity. While Jeff reeled – his $500 a month rent was a constant drain; what the hell was he going to do now? – fate stepped in from his father's past.

As if he had been waiting for just this very moment, Tim's old manager from the sixties and seventies – Herb Cohen – materialised.

Cohen had been in constant touch with Jeff and his mother throughout Jeff's childhood, regularly checking in on his progress. Had he inherited more than his father's looks? How musical was he? Could he play anything? Had he written any songs?

However, over the years, Jeff had remained aloof to such come-ons, rebuffing the businessman's enquiries as to how and when Tim's apparent heir was going to carry on the gloriously unfulfilled Buckley legacy.

But now, going nowhere musically, fired from a crappy job and seemingly at yet another dead end, Cohen's offer of some solid dollar for Jeff to record a demo seemed inexorably logical and appealing. As a bonus, Cohen wanted to hear the boy's own tunes. Jeff was adrift artistically, unemployed, broke, and at best seemingly in freefall towards another thankless, drudging job like the one he had just been sacked from. Faced with Cohen's proposition he could only ask himself, 'Why not?' His mistrust of his dad's old business associate was a childhood prejudice that would have to be set aside for the time being. Gathering himself, Jeff decided that it made the most sense for him to record the demos on familiar sonic territory. This much was obvious. He'd head back to California.

Although during his initial seven-month tenure in New York he had successfully located a new chamber of his heart, Jeff hadn't convincingly set down any musical roots, either in the business or even at street-level. So that September he decided to take his old man's ex-manager's money, and returned to LA to record demo versions of his own songs.

In Hollywood once more, Jeff stayed with friends – his musician buddies and ex-Group Therapy members Kathryn Grimm and Mark Frere – crashing at their apartment and turning a bashed-up living room couch into both a home and place of work, where he completed the songs that would eventually become 'Eternal Life' and 'Last Goodbye'.

He recorded at the generically named Eurosound Studio in San Fernando Valley, alone with only the resident engineer for company. Jeff played or programmed all of the instrumentation (bass, guitars, drum machine) himself, and within a couple of days he had completed a four-song, seven-track demo, mastered to cassette tape, featuring 'Eternal Life', 'Unforgiven', 'Radio' and 'Strawberry Street' (the title of which, if not the music, was very redolent of his father's era).

The Babylon Dungeon Sessions, as Jeff named the cassette, surprised all those friends who heard it, as if it had come out of nowhere. Although most people who knew Jeff realised he was extremely musical – albeit primarily as a great lead guitarist – very few knew he could sing lead and fewer still that he did so with such range and authority. His mother was one of the first to receive a copy. 'There was one song called "Unforgiven",' she recalled, 'which became "Last Goodbye". But it was a diamond among a lot of dark and scary stuff.'

'Unforgiven'/'Last Goodbye' particularly was an odd sonic rose to bloom from a low-budget demo studio in the San Fernando Valley. It is much more redolent of early nineties UK indie pop – the Cocteau Twins, the Sundays, Morrissey – than the liquid white-boy proto-funk which was then so rife in California.

The other songs included the hysterical punked-up sonic rant of 'Radio'. 'Radio, why are you so lame?' screamed Jeff, sounding as if he were having more fun than a barrelful of monkeys. An instrumental mix was also included.

'Eternal Life' was guitar FX-heavy and instrumental. In addition there was another, clearer-voiced mix of 'Unforgiven' and two versions of the Bolan-esque glam stomp of 'Strawberry Street' – again also featured as an instrumental mix. The vocal version sounded eerily like a lost track from androgynous Britpop provocateurs Suede.

Jeff passed the tape onto Herb Cohen and let the businessman do his thing.

After so briefly flaming into being, he returned to his friends' brown couch and the existence of a poverty-stricken artist, finding himself again ensconced in the Hollywood mire. Still, his life in all other respects was rich. He now had an impressive demo in the hands of a potential manager, and musically he continued to be besotted with UK pop particularly. Socially he kept on making notable friends. He also finally began to explore the roots and branches of the Buckley family tree.

As outwardly aloof as Jeff was, for the most part, towards his dad's musical legacy, he was not immune to his own genetic curiosity. Without any particular fanfare, perhaps piqued by his recent dealing with Herb Cohen – a prominent figure in his father's life – Jeff began to stealthily investigate those survivors from Tim's past, including friends and family alike. Judy, Tim's widow, had actually got in touch with Jeff as early as 1987 in order to assign him his share of his father's royalties. (Most likely publishing royalties, as it's unlikely that Tim had recouped all of his recording advances for his albums.) Oddly, Jeff managed to track down his father's mother via her chiropractor. The meeting was amiable, but Jeff remained reserved and sceptical. 'She always knew I'd show up,' he reckoned. 'I talked with all the cast of characters and then I was done with it. I revealed a lot of ugliness I can't talk about.'

Tim's old gunslinger, lead guitarist Lee Underwood, was among that cast of characters. Jeff's attitude toward his father and his work upset him.

'What about the beauty and creativity he heard about?' asks Underwood. 'The humour and intelligence and high integrity? Clearly, everything positive said about Tim was wasted. Jeff visited me and several others and selected those negatives that fit with his negative preconceptions about Tim. A shame, and very sad.' Lee is one of the few to write at any length of meeting with Jeff (which had actually occurred late in the previous year, 1989). His account is worth reproducing here in full.

When I answered the knock and opened the door Jeff Buckley stood leaning against the porch wall, jacket draped over one shoulder, hand in pocket, knee slightly bent, intentionally striking precisely the same pose as Tim had on the first album cover. He looked almost exactly like Tim too, astonishingly so – a full head of hair, high cheekbones, full lips, bushy eyebrows, dark brown eyes, the same charming smile. He said he was soon leaving LA for New York, and was talking to Tim's friends about his father, before his departure. He had already spoken with Dan Gordon, Judy, and Daniella. Could he talk with me too? We sat in the living room. 'You ask, I'll answer,' I said.

He leaned forward, his voice a hiss. 'How did he die?'

'Ha! You go right for the jugular, don't you?'

We started with the death, moved into the albums, travelled through the various creative stages. For two hours, I painted the most honest portrait of Tim that I could – his love of music, his dedication to it, his honesty, wit, intelligence, and creative evolution. When I mentioned that Tim loved him, Jeff spat out, 'He did not!'

'Have you listened to the song, "Dream Letter"?'

'Yes. Other than that, what did he say?'

'Well, "Dream Letter" says a lot. To me personally, he expressed his love for you, and the guilt he felt at not being able to take you into his life. He told me he fully intended to talk with you when you got older. He hoped to make things up. His departure before your birth had nothing to do with you. He said he didn't know Mary was pregnant when he left. That's no small thing, man. When he split for New York, he did not know Mary was pregnant. Even if he did, he did not leave you – he left your mother. Besides, given the choice – her and you, or fulfilling his calling as a musician – would you have had him give up music and keep working at the Taco Bell? Is that what you would have done in the same circumstances?'

Jeff returned two days later. This time, he had slashed half his hair off, leaving one side bald, the other side with a Mohawk on top, long hair on the sides. It was as if he had intentionally decimated his beauty and was defiantly and belligerently presenting himself as an ugly stupid two-bit sleazy grunge-rock street-rat. I ignored his appearance, and we talked another two hours. Except for that 'He did not!' in our first visit, Jeff did not indicate the profound and deep-seated antipathy he felt toward Tim. In this way, he was dishonest. From my side, I regret the fact that we talked only of Tim, not of Jeff. Looking back, I can see how Jeff gave subtle indications of his rage. But at the time, I missed them. I had no idea Jeff felt so hostile toward Tim, no idea of the extent of his inwardly searing love/hate conflicts. I thought he would welcome hearing the truth about his father. Otherwise, why did he contact me? If I had asked questions, opened Jeff up, become aware of his anger, I might have framed some of my answers differently, perhaps helping him come to terms with his own animosity and with Tim. From Tim he got his voice, his looks, his intelligence, his exceptional musical talent. Mary obviously contributed talent too, for she was also a musician. But the distinctive and characteristic cast of Jeff's handsome features, the particular tone and range of his voice, the oblique slant of his sparkling intellect, and the idiosyncratic Buckley viewpoint – its brilliant insight and verbally poetic expressiveness – seemed to descend from his warrior grandfather, down through Tim, directly to him. Physically, intellectually and musically, Jeff was a Buckley to the core. If you looked, you saw it. If you listened, you heard it. The resemblance was uncanny, unequivocal, and indubitable.

Among all of those old comrades, lovers, buddies and business cronies that Jeff had met up with, each one would comment on how obviously Jeff was Tim's son. It was not just in his appearance but in his aura, his voice, and most of all, his movements, which shared the musicality of his late father's body language.

Jeff came away from most of those meetings unimpressed and unconvinced. He had a natural contempt for the sentimentality of his father's friends, especially those who only knew Tim as the flighty, charismatic, romantic minstrel and not the errant father and wayward husband. He did, however, connect mightily with one of Tim's old Venice Beach friends, Daniella Sapriel, who was now living in North California with her little daughter. Honing in on Jeff's little-boy-lost vibe, she invited him to move into her spare room. Jeff gratefully agreed, no doubt relieved that he was finally able to abandon the brown couch at Frere and Grimm's Hollywood apartment.

Sapriel had no outstanding issues with Tim and by extension felt only warmth and protectiveness towards Jeff and his curiosity. This extended as far as her innocently organising him a twenty-fourth birthday party to which both sides of Jeff's ancestry were invited. Guests from the Guibert and Buckley families seemed intrigued and weirdly fascinated by Jeff. For all those who missed their long-absent friend, it was as if in Jeff – high cheekbones, bushy monobrow, cat-like grace, deep-set olive-black eyes – Tim had actually been reincarnated. Understandably, Jeff was never comfortable with this kind of attention. Yet as he suffered the cheek-pinching, power handshakes and bear hugs from the assembled population of his father's past, he was, in effect, partaking in a weird dress rehearsal for a much more public demonstration of the same variety, which would occur within months at Brooklyn's St Ann's Church, New York.

Since 1985 Janine Nichols had been a member of the programme staff of St Ann's. As programme director she had most famously reunited the estranged John Cale and Lou Reed in Andy Warhol's memory for the classic *Songs for Drella* project in 1989. The live performance of that album at St Ann's would help define the church as what *Rolling Stone* magazine described as 'the guiding light of New York's avant-rock scene'. Nichols ensured that the venue lived up to this title, organising 'Art at St Ann's' nights which included the work of Brecht, Weill, Marianne Faithfull and Nick Drake. Her project for the spring of 1991 was to celebrate the work of one Tim Buckley.

The event itself had its seed in record producer and A&R man Hal Willner, best-known for his artfully conceived and executed tribute albums to artists such as Thelonius Monk. 'For some reason,' he stated, 'I thought Buckley's music would work better live – and in this type of multi-artist situation – than on LP.'

Nichols herself outlined the brief in what would become the show's programme: 'Artists were approached by our thinking they could do something interesting with the music. In some cases, the artist was already a fan of Buckley's. This was the case with Shelley Hirsch, the Horse Flies (who had to drop out because of their touring schedule), G. E. Smith, Loren Mazzacane and Suzanne Langille, known then as Guitar Robert, got wind of the project and got in touch with us. Other times, the music was new to the artist but the affinity was instant – Mary Margaret O'Hara (who also had to withdraw in order to finish a film soundtrack) and Richard Hell fell into this category. Herb Cohen, Buckley's manager, revealed that Buckley had a son, now a young man

Jeff onstage during the 'Greetings from Tim Buckley'
tribute concert at St Ann's Church, New York, in April 1991.
He would perform his father's material on only two public occasions. This was the first.
(© Jack Vartoogian/FrontRowPhotos)

and a remarkable musician in his own right...'

Thus Nichols tracked down Jeff, then living with Sapriel, and phoned him out of the blue. (Others report that it was Jeff who got in touch with Nichols via Cohen, but given Jeff's personality, this seems unlikely.)

Whatever the dynamic of the introduction, by the fall of 1990 Nichols and Jeff had spoken and the question that she had asked him was heavy in its plainness. Would Buckley Junior consider singing at a tribute concert for his father?

Putting down the phone after such a question must have set off quiet storms within the 24-year-old Jeff. His life in Hollywood, although temporarily and cosmetically comfortable (he felt more at home with Sapriel and her dog and daughter than he ever previously had in LA) had nevertheless once again reached a familiar impasse. Besides which, Jeff had never felt entirely comfortable with comfort.

The Babylon Dungeon Sessions tape had elicited barely any response outside of Jeff's immediate circle of friends and family, and there is some doubt as to whether Herb Cohen had even circulated it within the music industry. For a man who had been troubling Jeff and Mary for some kind of evidence of his father's continuing musical legacy since the former's childhood, this would seem perverse in the extreme. It surely only served to deepen Jeff's already cool disposition towards his father's old manager.

Meanwhile, Jeff wrote snippets and fragments, practiced his guitar scales, and worked out the chords to his favourite songs, which he sang mostly to himself or Sapriel's dog. But, as ever, such moments of inspiration were thin on the ground. There was little cohesion or focus to his musical activity and, depressingly, for a buck he was working on other people's songs at a demo studio with an old associate named Jeff Clouse, arranging and adding instrumentation to the tracks of any would-be musicians who could stump up the cash. He also engaged in a brief, Pyrrhic writing relationship with the legendary songwriter Carole King. (The meeting may have come via Jeff's old roommate and fellow band member John Humphrey, who was now playing bass for King). Nothing concrete came from the collaboration insofar as no recordings now exist, and it seemed as if in going to New York and then returning to record his demo in LA, Jeff had taken one step forward and three steps back. Snakes and ladders.

After consulting his mother, reviewing the dire LA options, and surely realising that he would always have unfinished business with his father – ignoring it would not make it disappear – Jeff concluded the argument with himself, and on 20 April, with a ticket paid for by St Ann's (and in a way by Tim), Jeff once again flew to New York.

He arrived at the church's rehearsals straight from the airport wearing the actual Navy-issued pea jacket his father had once worn. (A gift from Sapriel, who had kept it all those years.) Gary Lucas, a 38-year-old local guitar hero and ex-Captain Beefheart guitarist and manager, was rehearsing when the skinny kid in the navy-coloured coat arrived. He was instantly smitten. Oddly, Lucas also remembers that it was Jeff who made the move to become involved in the project.

'Hal Willner told me, "You know we've been contacted by this young person who is the son of Tim, a kid named Jeff." "I never knew Tim had a son!" I said. "You'd be good to work with him," Hal said. Anyway, I agreed to meet with him and I just saw this young kid come up to me who was so electric and alive and vibing…'

Jeff, who was as charming as ever, was also aware of Lucas's cult reputation and made sure he knew it. 'I know you, I read about you in *Guitar Player*!' he gushed. 'I love your work with Beefheart.'

Lucas was smitten. 'I invited him back to my house,' he says, 'set up some guitar parts on the computer, and Jeff started to wail. I thought, "My God, this kid is amazing." ' Lucas let him know it, too. 'After he stopped singing my jaw dropped and I said, "Jeff! You're a star, man!" And he was just… very self-effacing. Like, "You really think so?" Yet he was one of the most brilliant musicians I've ever known.'

Jeff Buckley was a New York citizen again, swimming with the tide, among his own kind within a city he loved. It felt good. Despite the ambiguity of his feelings about the actual reason that had brought him there – the father he never knew – it felt as if he had a real focus at last. As a consequence his perspectives were sharpening. He was finally closing in on something real.

As his new foil, Gary Lucas was both sympathetic and receptive. 'I found out that he had come out of this very negative, self-destructive scene in LA,' recalls the eccentrically-quiffed guitarist. 'He was hanging out with people hoping to get their approval and they used to really berate him. They told him he sucked… and he half believed it.'

Jeff missed little of his old stomping ground. 'In LA and in Hollywood, especially, it's an industry town. It's like a steel town except it's the fame industry. Irish people would hate it in Los Angeles. They always do. They fucking hate it, man. It's all who-you-know. It's like you have to sweep up the names dripping down everybody in restaurants. It's just boring. Even the architecture is set up for maximum schmooze capacity. It's a game, the rules of which I've never understood.'

In the days of dress rehearsal that followed, all involved in the show became enamoured of Jeff, although beyond the besotted Lucas, there seemed to be no particular recognition of his talent.

Pale, underfed and eminently motherable, Jeff continued to make friends of both sexes, also meeting a new girlfriend – a pretty, dark-haired girl with a china-doll complexion called Rebecca, daughter of the Fluxus art movement founder Peter Moore.

Come showtime, St Ann's was packed but not sold-out. To the uninitiated, Tim Buckley remained an unknown quantity. In many ways he had been a musician's musician, and two dozen of this breed, ranging from cellists, pianists, and experimental singers to guitarists, turned up to channel Tim's more esoteric, progressive music – mostly culled from his *Starsailor* opus. Even so, the line-up was low-key, with punk and new-wave legends Richard Hell and Bob Quine being the most famous names on the bill.

About halfway through the gig, Jeff and Gary ambled onstage with no introduction other than Lucas's pedal steel guitar loops. It was surely not by chance that they opened with 'I Never Asked to Be Your Mountain', the song Tim had written about Mary and Jeff after they parted ways. Lucas's sonic architecture was all zig-zags and clean angles, setting up a weirdly skeletal, edgy energy. Into this came Jeff – strumming solidly on an acoustic. It sounded strange, yet oddly authentic; of a new age but obviously indebted to Tim's folk café roots. Few in the audience had any idea of who this was or where it was going. And then, after some ecclesial humming, Jeff began to sing.

'Shock waves went through the audience,' remembers Lucas, who was so blown away by his partner's performance and presence that he experienced a transcendence of sorts. 'This skinny kid with this unearthly voice just wailing. I was next to him playing the guitar but I was really just watching…' The evening had perceptibly tilted for the better, and it was utterly unexpected for most of the people in the pews. The fact that Tim had sired a son was never widely advertised, but the resemblance, visually, aesthetically and – most of all – sonically, was arresting, enthralling and inarguable. Those familiar with Jeff and Lucas's opening song would even have noticed a new verse at its end. Jeff had added lyrics, finished backstage just minutes beforehand. In hindsight they were grotesquely prophetic.

'I want to feel the tide pull through me / Let the water take my skin.'

The song occasionally threatened to amble and stray, but never truly veered into overindulgence. Just as James Dean was said to symbolise 'fuck you' and 'love me' both simultaneously and equally, so Jeff sounded at once pissed-off and full of yearning, hope and heartbreak. After a wonderfully controlled and crazed jam, the piece slid to a standstill.

The audience's response, having grown somewhat worn-down and muted by the earlier acts, now resonated with a rich and enthusiastic timbre. It sounded like someone or something had arrived. One could have joked – who would have anticipated Tim Buckley to be at his own tribute concert? But to many, that's how it seemed.

'Thank you,' said Jeff meekly as the applause faded. His voice carried shock and he was clearly in awe himself, sounding much more like Scotty Moorhead than Tim Buckley Junior. 'Sefronia' followed, again introduced by an infinitely spiralling guitar loop, which only heightened the starkness of Jeff's strumming. This oscillating ended the song, too, before its descent into complete pin-drop silence. 'Phantasmagoria in Two' came next, and with the addition of some Yoko Ono-style vocals provided by Julia Haywood, the trick was starting to sound a little thin. Then the son did what many had been secretly wishing for. He came back on solo. In a genial, sing-song voice a million light years away from the cosmic shaman songs of the previous minutes, Jeff introduced 'Once I Was'.

'A long time ago, when I was a little kid, my mom sat on a bed and put this record on...' This was surely the apex of the ritual. 'Once I Was' sounded like the song which seemed to encapsulate everything that the ghost of a dead father symbolised.

The song was lent an eerily haunting coda when Jeff accidentally snapped a guitar string in the last verse and was forced to finish the piece *a capella* in the midst of the church's yawning acoustics – effectively turning the song into a hymn.

No one followed Jeff. He closed the show.

His performance was 'spooky but impressive', according to local DJ Nicholas Hill. 'It was the first time I became aware of Jeff. And it was pretty mind-blowing, y'know? Here's this guy who basically looks like Tim and has Tim's voice...'

For others, the performance had been an even more moving affair. When Willner gave his professional and educated opinion, he spoke simply for many in attendance. 'He just absolutely had it. It's definitely a voice from heaven.'

Jeff also stood out because the tone and timbre of the evening had veered between the near-unlistenable avant-garde of Shelley Hirsch and the twee finger-in-the-ear folk of the Shams, and was populated by a host of other obscure and marginally better-known performers. (Richard Hell – dubbed 'the low point' of the evening by the *New York*

Times – decided to do a Ramones cover dedicated to his recently deceased friend Johnny Thunders.)

Jeff being Jeff, the event could never have been a purely victorious affair.

'See, I sacrificed something for my father's memory,' he sighed a few years hence. 'Technically the tribute will be seen as my debut in New York…'

Although he was not present, Lee Underwood had a most emphatic perspective of Jeff's performance that night in April. 'Jeff fiercely turned his back on Tim. "Genetics be damned," he told writer Robert Hilburn. Even as he denied the biological influence, so he denied the artistic influence. He said in print numerous times that he had not listened to Tim's music, and yet at the St Ann's Church commemoration he sang four of Tim's songs…' Underwood's argument is disingenuous. Jeff could have hardly shown up to perform at a Tim Buckley tribute without knowing the work of the man in question.

The son himself justified his 'sacrifice' as some kind of ritual compensation for having not been able to attend his own father's funeral. It was a way of acknowledging his dad, both privately and publicly. 'I probably wouldn't ever have had another chance to pay my respects. No matter what kind of twisted feelings I have about Tim, no matter what kind of pain or anger I have against him, whatever I haven't come to terms with, the fact that I never got to go to his funeral always bothered me.'

This wished-for process of closure would not serve to be so tidy. The meaning of his father as a man and particularly as a musician would continue to haunt Jeff during his few remaining years, and despite Gary Lucas's enthusiasm, his performance at the tribute show did not lead to an instantaneous musical career.

Despite featuring a picture of him crooning into the microphone, the *New York Times* review gave Jeff only one line.

Jeff Buckley was slowly burning into being, but on that night, no star was born.

Gary Lucas's musical project, Gods and Monsters, had been limping, bouncing and hopping along in fits and starts since the late 1980s, suffering almost terminally from a lack of singer commitment. For whatever reason, Gary could not get a vocalist to stick around for any length of time. (Many would argue that this was because he saw himself as the non-singing frontman of the band. Jared Nickerson, then a highly regarded bassist on the amateur session circuit, who was often employed by Lucas, puts it more plainly: 'Being with Gary in different musical configurations I can easily say that he was, and most likely still is, a control freak.')

Like many others in attendance at the tribute show, the guitarist had been utterly beguiled by the 'skinny kid with the unearthly voice'. But now he was certain that he'd found his perfect foil. 'We really hit it off, from the word go,' reckons Lucas. To this extent, he went as far as introducing Jeff to a Columbia Records A&R man as his new singer. Jeff, who was already co-writing with Lucas at the guitarist's apartment, offered no statement to the contrary, but his lack of verbal reciprocation was telling. At this point, it may have saved both some hassle if they had taken the time to differentiate between definitions of 'frontman' and 'singer'.

Another early warning sign that should have registered for Lucas was that Jeff wasn't merely a unique and accomplished singer – he was also an extremely gifted and competent guitarist. A guitarist with occasional MOR-rock tastes that Lucas found baffling. 'He was an excellent guitarist,' says Lucas. 'I could tell he was a good player instantly upon hearing him… but later on he revealed a passion for Rush, a group I never really got.'

While Lucas set about making plans for the newly rejuvenated Gods and Monsters, Jeff continued to soak up the invites, good vibes and general jewellery box of opportunities that New York was now offering him. He was drawn to the rich underground scene as much as he was to the glamorous lunches at the Russian Tea Room that Hal Willner occasionally treated him to. He was also utterly moon-eyed over Rebecca Moore and the leftfield Fluxus art attitude she had inherited and was now introducing him to.

Despite such apparent progress, in mid-May of '91 he returned to LA, where, perversely, he once again began dabbling in sub-Red Hot Chili Peppers pseudo-funk with his old buddies Carla Azar and Chris Dowd, within which Jeff limited himself to pyrotechnic guitar riffs and the occasional vocal. After the celebratory nature of the tribute gig, and in particular stumbling across the blueprint for his future via the near-*a capella* 'Once I Was', Jeff was yet again playing with inappropriate musicians in an unsympathetic environment. Writer David Fricke reported seeing Jeff in this 'heavy punk funk band'. His verdict: 'Not very graceful.'

Why Jeff was in California at all remains something of a mystery. In New York he had a cool, connected girlfriend who he was head over heels in love with, and in turn had met a driven, brilliant guitarist.

During his absence from NYC, Lucas courted Jeff; mailing him instrumentals, desperate for the two of them to make beautiful music together. (Another warning sign of the pair's ultimate incompatibility was evident at this stage. Lucas would send guitar instrumentals with titles. Fully-loaded, lyrical titles like 'Rise Up to Be' and 'Fool's Cap'. This suggests that the guitarist was at heart more of a frustrated singer-songwriter, rather than an equal musical foil in the tradition of Johnny Marr or Keith Richards. While Jeff loved to gorge himself on other musicians' compositions as a listener and interpreter, as lyricist, singer and composer of his own melodies, he would never work to another's title or let such titles dictate the words.)

Yet all this positivity didn't seem to be enough. Perhaps the Harlem slumming and bogus job experiences of his initial New York sojourn had left a scar deeper than the combined balm of St Ann's, a new girlfriend and the enthusiastic Lucas could soothe. So rather than simply turn up at JFK airport again – albeit into the arms of Rebecca Moore and the eager guitarist – Jeff sought to secure a concrete gig in New York prior to what would be his final departure from LA. His muse was in full flight, though, which was surely more than some consolation. At this point he was already working on the lyrics for what became the title song of his first and final album. '[When I wrote the words to "Grace"] I was anticipating leaving LA for New York, so I was waiting to go. I'm not afraid to die... and I'm not afraid to leave this place or any place. I had somebody who loved me in New York... a lot... and it was amazing.'

Surreally, Jeff's ticket to New York came via an Alan Parker film about a rough, working-class soul group from Dublin. *The Commitments* was a huge hit upon its cinema release in 1991, and part of the promotional work for the movie was a string of actual live gigs by Andrew Strong, the singer in the film, backed by a full band. After a chance encounter with the band members in question at an LA rehearsal space he'd been hanging out at with old friend Chris Dowd, Jeff was hired as a behind-the-scenes member of the touring entourage.

One has to remember that at this point few 'knew' that Jeff Buckley was 'Jeff Buckley', as Strong's lack of recall makes plain. 'I remember those shows at the time. We would perform after each premiere... Wow. It seems he [Jeff] did work with us, so I guess I must have met Jeff... still, I can't place him at that moment in time which is a real shame. It's bizarre to think he was actually involved with the Commitments in this capacity...'

Jeff was, however, remembered by other members of the Commitments gang. He landed the gig as guitar technician for one of the band members, Glen Hansard, who struck up an instant and intense rapport with Jeff. 'Me and him just got on so well because he was a Bob Dylan freak and a Van Morrison fan and so was I,' Glen recalled. 'And every night we would just rattle on about Van, we were traveling through America, and when we got to Chicago I remember sitting at the sound check with Jeff and I started playing "Once I Was" by Tim Buckley, 'cause I'd just gotten into him at the time. And Jeff was like, "He was my da, y'know." And I looked at him and I was like, "No way. Wow. That makes a lot of sense. That's mental!" And he says, "Well I didn't really know him that well to be honest, but he was my da... anyway, what was that song you were playing?" So we sort of left it at that.'

Thus, although ever-haunted, Jeff was back in NYC in style. The mini-tour came with hotel accommodation and a $2,000-a-week salary, and on the night of the last gig an Irishman called Shane Doyle was in attendance. Doyle ran a tiny venue in the East Village called Sin-é. Impressed by his fellow countrymen's soulful set, he invited the band down. The café was tiny and intimate, but it would play a huge, expansive and profound part in Jeff Buckley's future.

Jeff was elated to be back home. Upon returning to New York, he found that his love affair with the city that never slept was unabated. 'It's full of strange beautiful people,' he cooed. 'Ginsberg, Quentin Crisp... not even really famous people.'

Perhaps this provided an unintended insight as to what Jeff saw himself becoming. Strange and beautiful, but cool and chic. Well-known, but too modish to be truly megastar famous.

All the while, Lucas and Jeff continued to write together, although it was mainly at the former's instigation. The writing process was informal. Usually the two of them would hang out at Lucas's record-filled apartment. This was a favoured environment for the control-conscious Lucas, as Jared Nickerson remembers: 'Man, I sat in Gary's living room for countless hours learning his basslines. He's an accomplished finger-picker and I play primarily with my thumb, so the thumb parts of his finger-picking were right up my alley.'

As Jeff lay back on the couch or rifled through the guitarist's extensive collection of alphabetised vinyl, Lucas played chord progressions on one of his many guitars. Occasionally something triggered inside the singer and Jeff would improvise melody and words over the top, sometimes using entries from his journals and poetry as the raw material for his lyrics. As with 'Grace', (originally titled 'Rise Up to Be' and/or 'Fool's Cap') Jeff had already worked to the tape Lucas had posted to him in

A 25-year-old Jeff poses with Gods and Monsters
guitarist Gary Lucas, co-writer of both 'Grace' and 'Mojo Pin'.
(© Jack Vartoogian/FrontRowPhotos)

LA. From Lucas's side of the court, their bouts of co-writing seemed like exquisite games of tennis.

'It was profoundly easy, in a way,' he reminisced. 'Much easier than a line by line thrash-out with another collaborator. I would first come up with fully-realised instrumental compositions... motifs, chord structures, rhythms intact, all there... mail them or play them directly to Jeff... he'd go away, sometimes for months, usually just weeks... and damned if he didn't always come back with *perfect* lyrics and a *perfect* melody line that sinuously entwined itself *inside* the matrix of my instrumental, for all time... Only once or twice did he offer any modification at all to the basic underlying music, such as asking me to repeat one section of "Mojo Pin" to stretch it out to double verse length because he had more lyrics that he wanted to fit in that section... and he added a vocal section over the bridge of "Grace" when he came to ultimately record it...'

Whatever the minutiae of the process, the two had soon birthed two modern pop-rock classics: 'Mojo Pin' and the aforementioned 'Grace'.

The combination of both men's talents made for a sound that was quixotic and intoxicating and, furthermore, unique to both. Each cancelled out many of the other's weaknesses – for example, Lucas's tendency to overplay while placing proficiency and dazzle before poetry and emotion. For his own part, Lucas forced Jeff into a role he had so far successfully evaded – that of sole lyricist and singer. Both were eager – Lucas perhaps just a bit more so – to catch the newfound alchemy on tape. Lucas booked a cheap studio downtown and assembled a rhythm section. Jared Nickerson was on bass and Tony 'Thunder' Smith on drums. Jared remembers: 'We cut the tunes without Jeff. The music was completely Lucas-written with our interpretations of what Gary wanted from bass and drums. There was no Jeff-input on the musical side of those recordings. The studio was like a living room with an isolation booth where the drum kit was set up. I tracked directly into the board. Nice low-lighting atmosphere like a Keith-Richards-with-scarves-over-the-lamps type thing... I knew the material was "hot" right away, even before Jeff did his thing.'

Jeff 'did his thing' as an overdub. 'The fact that Jeff was a once-in-a-lifetime vocalist just put it over the top,' states the bassist, who nevertheless found that Jeff 'did not mingle much. He was slightly aloof and distant, but not in an unpleasant way... more in a don't-know-you way, which is usually true with everybody, in that position.'

In this hit-and-run fashion they would record an album's worth of material, piecemeal to be released a lifetime later.

One of the standout tracks, 'Grace' was obviously something special, yet lyrically, Jeff saw it as pretty straightforward. 'It's about not fearing death, or any of those slings and arrows that you constantly suffer... because somebody loves you. You're not afraid to go, you're not afraid to withstand what you have to withstand because there's a tremendous energy inside that is constantly refuelled because of somebody's love for you. That's what "Grace" is about.' He paused. 'And it's about life sometimes being too long.'

It seemed like full-steam ahead for the strange-looking duo. There was an obvious chemistry between them as musicians, and for Lucas in particular, the affable kid with the mysterious heritage definitely filled a hitherto vacant shape in the guitarist's operation. Jeff in turn seemed eager to please, often asking Lucas's approval of his contributions, while also seeming queerly absent from the proceedings in some indefinable sense. Still, the guitarist was only too used to singers and their strange emotional weather (Gods and Monsters had ploughed through a choir's worth in the preceding years), and so he plugged away regardless, arranging a fistful of local shows and submitting their latest demos to NYC-based record labels and music publishers. With a buzz building via word-of-mouth and their local radio appearances, the focus settled upon a forthcoming show at the venue that had first brought Gary and Jeff together – St Ann's, scheduled for that March.

At this juncture, Imago Records – a successful independent record label – were closest to signing the band. Tellingly, Jeff brought in his own lawyer to dissect their proffered contract rather than approach it as a united front with Lucas and his manager. Thus Jeff met George Stein – a relatively hip and perceptive attorney who would from this point on become Jeff's 'man in the field' and ultimately his exclusive legal representative. Whilst reviewing the contract Stein seemed to pick up on Jeff's underlying doubts. In the most explicit terms, not only did Jeff not want to sign the deal, neither did he want to work with Lucas.

But for now, Jeff kept these feelings hidden both from himself and Gary. In a spirit of awkward comradeship, the two attempted to play the game as much as their limited budget would allow, financing not only most of their musical activities but also the occasional photo shoot. One such activity took them on a day trip to Coney Island, where photographer Chris Buck remembered Jeff as 'just a regular struggling musician'. Remarkably, Buck also appears to have introduced Jeff to the Velvet Underground. 'Jeff said he'd never heard them... I played him some... he seemed to get off on it'.

Such happy excursions were rare.

The Gods and Monsters rhythm section of Tony Smith and Jared

Nickerson was broken up when Smith was sacked at Jeff's request a mere fortnight prior to the gig. 'Jeff wanted to use his own drummer for the show,' remembers Jared. 'Gary agreed as it would provide Jeff with a certain amount of comfort in not being in a band of complete strangers. As the days before the show were ticking away we were finally able to jam with this drummer and the cat was terrible – could hardly play due to the fact that he hadn't "seriously" played in a few years. He was so humble and nice that we couldn't really get mad at him, but it did put up a red flag in our minds. Then in comes Tony Lewis, who I knew from his playing with the Michael Hills Bluesland at various Black Rock Coalitions multi-band functions around NYC.'

Tony Lewis also noticed the unevenness in Gary and Jeff's dynamic. 'There were probably more details behind the scenes Jared or I never saw, that forced Gary to have a "vibe" with Jeff,' he observes. 'It seemed to me that Jeff and Gary had different concepts about how they wanted their own music to be performed. There were moments of anarchy between the two, yet they would concede to each other after a while.'

As a consequence of this weird energy, the material went up a gear, as Jared affirms. 'The music became even crazier – in a good way in my estimation – due to Tony Lewis's Keith Moon-style of drumming, making a three-piece sound like a five. Rehearsals were at Vinny's and were what they were – who am I to say how they sounded? Jeff was fine with it at first, but then seemed to get a bit more uncomfortable as the days passed...'

Lucas was undoubtedly a man with a vision and could come across as stifling in his need to dictate, but, as Jared counters, such behaviour was not unusual in bands, and Gary's need to control his music was 'no more than any other band leader who knows how he wants his material to sound. Gary respected Jeff's musical ability immensely, gave him free reign, and tried to accommodate Jeff's requests.'

However convincing and creatively-stoked the music was sounding, as a band the members were hardly a healthy social unit.

The drummer in particular did not hit it off with Buckley. 'Jeff was young and had different yet interesting ideas as a musician, but as a human, he was an asshole,' says Lewis. 'I say this because at that time I was involved in a car accident and when I explained to the band what had happened he seemed to have a very dark view about it, like it was some sort of funny thing. I wanted to take him out back and have him drawn and quartered, but that's how I felt at the time. He really had the attitude of a jerk and needed to be put in his place. I'd seen him and Gary go at it and he treated Gary like he had no idea what he was saying or doing.

Almost like a father telling his young son to do something he says because he is the experienced one and the young one doesn't know any better. The time I was in the band was very limited, and I had to move on.'

'I've been raised to know that if you can't say anything good, then don't say anything at all,' states Jared more tactfully. 'So I won't mention the relationship Jeff had with Tony and myself, or how we felt about him, but suffice it to say, we didn't hang out.'

There was little love to be lost among the misfit gang, and Jared was next for the chop. 'The next day at rehearsal Jeff insisted that a particular song needed to be played with a pick on bass. I didn't agree. Feeling a bit leery I insisted that Gary take me to the bank machine and pay me my rehearsal pay right after rehearsal. That night I received a call from Jeff saying that they [Jeff and Gary] wanted to use another bass player who would use a pick. I said fine. Tony was let go soon after...'

Gary Lucas, no doubt bug-eyed and chomping at his knuckles in dread of his latest singer doing a runner, agreed to Jeff's unreasonable, prissy demand. This presented the nervy guitarist with a dodo-sized egg to suck. The St Ann's show was a mere fortnight away, and the Gods and Monsters repertoire hardly consisted of your basic G-A-D chord trick. Bassist Tony Maimone (who, for the record, played all his parts with a pick) and drummer Anton Frier were hastily brought in. The sound they would have to integrate with was, in part, highly dependent on tricky time signatures and colourful guitar effects.

'FX was just something we used,' says Lucas. 'There was no particular philosophy. We both just liked experimenting with different sounds, and set-up wise, I used the same rig I have now – a Roland JC-120, sometimes with a Gallien-Krueger 250ml split.'

The demos that Gods and Monsters had submitted to Imago and other interested parties were assured and solid, but also multi-layered and mellifluous. There was a trace of Jeff's rock-fusion past in the occasional twisting time signature or florid guitar trill, but this was mostly down to Lucas's excesses as a guitarist, one who at times seemed to be competing with the vocalist rather than accompanying him.

Jeff's role in these exercises was almost exclusively as singer – what this group didn't need was another guitarist – but he did occasionally let rip on an unconvincing-sounding mouth organ (as on the early draft of 'Grace'), wherein his frustration at being 'merely' the singer is arguably apparent. Yet for all their assuredness and imagination, the recordings sound strangely pedestrian, as if Lucas and Buckley – never mind the other session musicians brought in on a budget – are never truly connecting. At its best it is as though Jeff is singing along to an exquisite, if averagely recorded, backing track. But then these demos were just that – demonstrations of a potential that would never be realised. Musically, Jeff was just passing through, and in doing so learning how to become a singer in a band – and he knew it. Lucas dared not admit it to himself, but perhaps he knew it too.

As a Gods and Monsters showcase the St Ann's show that mid-March was an anticlimax. Purposes were crossed and it showed, with Gary and Jeff rarely gelling – when they did it was more like a lucky collision. Jared didn't hold enough of a grudge not to attend the show and duly turned up as a punter. 'I went to the show and it was very interesting,' he remembers. 'Tony and Anton are fab musicians, but either they didn't have the time, or they were not interested in learning the intricacies of Gary's tunes. The tunes in no way resembled the way Tony and myself performed them. I think to this day Gary rues that decision. I know that I remember looking at the pew with the label folks whose expressions were like, "We flew in for this?" It was kind of funny.'

Musical car crashes aside, even aesthetically, and especially visually, the duo were not convincing. As unquestionably talented and adept as Lucas was as a guitarist and composer, he lacked the final mysterious quality of cool that would have sealed him and Jeff as a true proposition. Had Gods and Monsters been an instrumental, jazz-folk fusion group from the 1970s, perhaps the occasional and endearing innocent goofiness of the guitarist's demeanour would not have mattered so much. But the visual chasm between Jeff's obvious MTV, movie-star looks and the rest of the band's plain, down-home gawkiness – in particular Lucas's 'haystack in a high wind' receding hair-do and the fourteen years he had on the boyish-looking Jeff – only accentuated a deeper flaw. Too often, the quartet came across as merely a deeply proficient group of musos at a high-level amateur band night. There were no doubts as to their musical chops (Lucas's choices were never in question, as his taste in superbly efficient rhythm sections would confirm), but this in itself was not enough. It very rarely is. Anyone coming in off the street to view a Gods and Monsters performance would have soon been guessing as to what the musicians' day jobs were, with the exception of the singer. The boys in the band just didn't have 'it', while Jeff brought 'it' in spades. Yet he was no perfect musical deity either. In fact, he seemed a bit bored on stage, as if restless to move on already, and as a result he often ploughed parody in his performance, indulging in cod-blues patois and riffing on his lamest Robert Plant affectations. Such an uneven marriage could never last long, and it didn't.

Jeff sang the penultimate song of the set alone – a version of the standard 'Satisfied Mind' – which seemed to make more sense than the rest of the show put together. There was no celebration after the gig. Jeff and Gary left independently of one another, albeit with Gary still in denial. Jeff, however, had his mind made up.

'It was after that night,' Jeff said of quitting Gods and Monsters, 'that I knew I needed to invoke the real essence of my voice. I didn't know what it tasted like at all. I knew I had to get down to work and that anything else would be a distraction. In that band there were conflicts. It was really crazy, a desperate situation. I just didn't need things to be desperate. I needed them to be natural.'

Jared, who had perhaps one of the most objective seats in the house on the matter, puts it in more metaphorical terms. 'This was sad to me in the fact that Jeff simply had to sit in the passenger seat of the musical car Gary had constructed and do his thing. So Jeff disassembled the car.'

Jeff phoned in his resignation the very next day.

While Lucas was sent reeling by this news and its repercussions (the Imago deal was off, for starters), spinning into a hell of feverish insomnia by night and nail-gnawing marathons by day, to Jeff, the reason for the split was plainly obvious: Lucas, although gifted, was ultimately unnecessary. There was no real role for him to fulfil within Jeff's current musical life. The singer would never need a Jimmy Page, or even a Johnny Marr for that matter. 'I am the constant factor,' he admitted in 1994, finally freed of all false modesty. 'Morrissey needs a partner because he can't play the guitar himself, but I can sing and play guitar.'

By the time he left Gods and Monsters in early 1992, Jeff Buckley had some notion of where he wanted to go, but still had no idea of how to get there. He had no band, and, general good will aside, he had no real concrete prospects. Rather than start his own group immediately, he was determined to learn how to be a performer the hard way, by playing solo around Greenwich Village. (Weirdly, these activities also included a few shows as a duo with Gary Lucas.) Jeff also wanted to understand how the best songwriters did what they did, so he began a self-imposed course of study. One night he came into an East Village restaurant carrying a new CD of Van Morrison's *Astral Weeks*. He had heard the song 'Sweet Thing' on the *Best of Van Morrison* album and wanted to follow that trail back to its source. Within a couple of weeks he was adding *Astral Weeks* material to his solo sets, along with Edith Piaf, Mutabaruka and Bob Dylan songs. An initially gutted Lucas eventually regained his pragmatism and returned to the wingless albatross of Gods and Monsters. He and Jeff remained on civil if distant terms. While Lucas would always speak affectionately of his fleeting writing partner, Jeff could be cruelly comic in his honesty. 'I thought playing with Gary would be interesting but it turned out to be a disaster,' he stated in his first ever *Mojo* magazine interview less than a year later. 'We had two completely different paths... the cart was before the horse.'

Jeff's personal and creative reconstruction continued, as always fed by a voracious diet of music. Looking back on that period of individuation, he stated: 'Before I left for New York for the last time all I was obsessing about in my notebooks was that there's this... this place I want to get to. And I was remarking to myself that there are no teachers. There was nobody to show me. Well, actually there was, but they weren't alive or else they weren't... I'm not going to be able to walk up to Ray Charles and be his protégé...

'I went into those cafés [to perform] because I also really felt I had to go to an impossibly intimate setting where there's no escape, where there's no hiding yourself. And it wasn't easy at first. I mean, when I first walked into Sin-é or the Cornelia Street Café, people talked their asses off. They didn't want to hear it. And that was a problem and it made me frustrated. Until I made the audience a part of the music. Until I made those sounds part of the music like they were samples on a record. They were actually an interactive part of what I was playing and was going to sing. And then all of a sudden I just fell into a rhythm and I learned about what it means when the audience is responsible partly for the experience. I'm determined to start from that space again with a band. I want to get the band ready to go into these intimate places and learn how to make big magic in little areas. Things that you just can't forget.'

3. THE PRINCE OF NEW YORK

'I'm sick of the world. I'm trying to stay alive.'

Jeff Buckley, 1993

Both were petit, ungroomed and yet effortlessly hip. Louche, cool and possessed of a certain off-world charm, Jeff Buckley and Sin-é were a perfect match made in a blue Manhattan heaven.

The name 'Sin-é' is Gaelic. Pronounced *'Shin-ay'* it means literally 'That's it', 'Over', *'C'est fini'*, 'Done'. Yet for the 25-year-old Jeff, his association with this club would mean everything but.

At this point Sin-é was more of a down-home café than the rough-hewn bar it would later become. Located only a few busy streets off the beaten track of New York's East Village, this vibey cramped space would, in effect, become a literal gateway for the fledgling performer. By way of its austere décor and crappy PA system, bare walls and bedsit-kitchen, the small, bony Jeff – with his demonically angelic voice, Irish blood and American heart – would somehow be stumbling into the gateway to his future. When Buckley finally got a low-key gig at this spare, soulful club he was, in effect, hooking up with the speeding bullet train of his own destiny.

In the New York of 1990, Shane Doyle was a mellow Irishman in his forties. Originally a native of Dublin, he had settled in the States during the early eighties while following his own particular musical dream. (The details of his then band remain lovelessly anonymous.) But even before Doyle's group and their rock-star dreams petered out, he had already set about looking for a more blue-collar method of bringing in the Yankee dollar. This casual change of career plan would be an unmitigated success. By the end of the decade's first year he had opened an unpretentious coffeehouse that would become legendary within a few years – both in itself and by association with a budding artist who, if known at all in the club's early years, was known mostly as his father's son.

The Adonis turns diva: Jeff's intimate one-man performances at Sin-é in
New York's East Village made him the most sought-after unsigned artist in the city.

122 St Mark's Place was part of an area regarded by many as a hip public thoroughfare through the bustling East Village. A former art gallery that covered just under 1,000 square yards of floor space, it still conveyed an air of industry. Bare floors, steel doors and brick walls lent a gritty, soulful authenticity that would come to reflect the vibe of both its customers and the musicians who provided its very heart and blood. With that much raw atmosphere, you didn't need drapes or fancy lighting.

Nicholas Hill was a local DJ and remembers the Sin-é in its first years. 'I knew Jeff before he played at the Sin-é, so maybe that's how I discovered it – through Jeff,' he recalls. 'It was a really interesting place because of its proximity to the street. It was basically kinda *on* the street itself, like a sidewalk café. Even for New York, it was... different.'

Back in late 1990, during its first fledgling weeks of life, as if by prior arrangement, Sin-é's clientele drifted in like well-appointed actors from central casting. Floating through its heavy doors there came a slow, trickling parade of writers, musicians, poets, painters, hustlers and players – dreamers all. Fidgeting with crumpled packs of Marlboro and freshly-replenished coffee cups, they sat and mused and talked and smoked at well-worn second-hand tables illuminated by candlelight. Outside all of this, beyond the floor-to-ceiling windows and beneath the music played over the crude in-house stereo, the New York day hustled past.

Tom Clark, a guitarist, singer-songwriter, and affable borderline eccentric, took his place there too. A local musician by way of Illinois, Clark was one of the first at Sin-é to saunter from table to stage. By 'stage', one actually meant the bare, scrubbed space poked in to the left of the entrance. Nicholas Hill recounts that, 'There *was* no stage. There was a wall against which people performed, just off to the left as you came in. You were always within earshot of the kitchen. It was... well... intimate is an understatement.'

'I must've walked past this place a hundred (or a thousand) times and hadn't taken much notice of it. Another café on St Mark's Place. Big deal,' remembers Clark. 'When I finally got around to going in I figured it was gonna be a bunch of poseurs... and the first thing I noticed was my old friend Kirk Kelly up there with his acoustic guitar, singing. No mic, no PA... just up there old school. There were about ten people in the place. I sat there and Kirk asked me to do a couple of songs, so I did – why not? When I finished, the guy behind the counter, Shane, asked if I'd like to do a weekly thing there. I said, "What's it pay?" and he kind of chuckled, sinister, like. (I was playing gigs to survive then.) He said, "Nothing, but you can tell your friends to bring their own booze." Well, I don't think he realised what a can of worms he was opening there! He had no liquor licence, no beer and wine licence. I had lots of friends. All of whom liked to drink. A lot. I started playing there on Monday nights, mostly, and filling in a *lot* on other nights when he didn't have anything booked. I have old calendars of mine where I'm playing three times some weeks.'

For all its musey vibe, there was never any question that Shane Doyle was running a coffeehouse and not a mini-Carnegie Hall. The 1980s tape player that was located in the kitchen and hooked up to a basic amp and handful of speakers was about as much as the Irishman was willing to invest in musical technology. Basically, there *was* no house PA, so the eager Clark brought his own, a basic yet adequate and tinny-sounding set-up formerly used for street busking. 'It was battery-powered,' laughs Clark. 'So if you were playing that evening, you'd have to go in and charge it up during the day.'

Taking requests from his peers in such a homely, informal gathering, the buoyant and goofy Clark soon became a Monday night regular at the club, a performing 'Human Jukebox' who, in true busker style, passed around a plastic bucket at the end of each set.

Although Shane Doyle rarely ever gave the impression of being desperate in any way, shape or form ('He was... laconic,' says Nicholas Hill), it was a business necessity that he and his weird juice joint build up a regular clientele. Thus, even with characters like Clark putting on quite the floor-show, Doyle kept an open-door policy and wasn't about to start charging people to come in just yet.

'Shane would hustle his connections and get people to play,' Hill says. 'Performers wanted to play there because there was no pressure, it was casual and noncommittal. You could literally just turn up there and sing a song.'

Sin-é was starting to happen. The atmosphere was loose and Boho-funky, with a growing reputation among the plentiful hipsters of early nineties New York.

In the wake of performers like Tom Clark, actual real-life MTV celebrities eventually began to show up. Among them were restless Celts like Sinéad O'Connor, Shane McGowan and Mike Scott. Such individuals would often drop by unannounced and perform a tune or two – or maybe just sit cradling a hot chocolate and cigarette before walking out unhassled into the East Village air.

By 1992, the club had bloomed into a cool and cosy being, well-established, but still maturing. Jeff was outside, traversing the New York streets, quite literally looking for a gig.

The concert at St Ann's had given Jeff a powerful taste of what was to come and now, with the train-wreck of his old band, Gods and Monsters, burning behind him, he was by his own admission 'desperate' to move to the next level.

Thus, through the autumn of late 1991 and early '92, drawing on all the humility he could muster, Jeff dropped in at clubs and venues personally – 'cold calling', as it were – in the hope of some future chance at a show. Jeff Buckley was a man between stations, but nonetheless, deploying such humility must have been tough. Moving through the New York crowds, picking up fresh bagels at the deli or the latest copy of *Rolling Stone* at the newsstand, he was just another handsome face in scraggy duds, a citizen of a city made up of the richest, most beautiful, and ugliest people on the planet.

Whatever his true feelings for his father, the name 'Buckley' still held a sublime and discreet currency in terms of musical kudos – particularly following the minor (mainly critical) early nineties revival of Tim's back catalogue – and Jeff had inherited much more than a mere surname. Wherever he was during that season in New York, he was full of music, songs and words waiting to be born. They ached and shimmered within him – promising weird beauty and splendour against the starless, bible-black void of his future.

Daniel Harnett was yet another local aspiring singer-songwriter and artist who had gravitated inexorably towards the unique Sin-é. He felt immediately at home within its low-pressure atmosphere. 'I knew Shane to be fairly soft-spoken,' he remembers. 'I thought he was cool... and we loved playing Sin-é 'cause *he* loved it and that showed through. It wasn't all about how many beers were sold. I saw him a lot drinking red wine at a table with rolled cigarettes... he was a tall, lanky fellow.'

Within weeks Harnett and Jeff's paths would cross, with significant consequences for at least one of the young singers. 'I heard about Jeff when I was doing a play at La Mama Theatre with Rebecca Moore,' recounts Harnett. 'She told me that Jeff was looking for gigs to play. I was playing Sin-é regularly with my band Glim, so I introduced Jeff to Shane.'

Back at St Mark's Place, on Harnett's recommendation Jeff was soon submitting a copy of his demo tape and a few Xeroxed reviews from the St Ann's concert. He was in and out of the Sin-é in a matter of minutes. As far as Shane Doyle was concerned, this skinny kid was just another pretty face with a scuffed TDK C90 in his fist. Doyle had an itty bitty office overflowing with stacked and split demo tapes that he would never get around to listening to. The name 'Buckley' meant nothing to him, and the word didn't even make it into one ear, never mind out the other. Sensing this, Jeff left less inspired than when he had entered. And that was saying something.

Months would pass before Jeff actually got to play the club, and while Jeff may have known who he was, he had no way of knowing what was in store for him. So he played wherever and whenever he could under various guises, in addition to his solo self. 'Jeff and Glim did a handful of shows together at Fez and Postcrypt,' says Harnett. 'Sometimes Jeff would join us for a song or two and sometimes roll around the floor to our punkier stuff. He was very spontaneous and improvised a lot and cracked jokes… we had a good time.'

Meanwhile, the humble café was on the rise. Its reputation was built upon that rarest of combinations: the Sin-é was known as both a hip *and* classy joint. It had also acquired a modest booze licence. (Beer and wine – there was no hard liquor.) While this addition to the menu didn't hurt business, neither did it attract the hardcore lushes that more typical New York gin joints did. Although it drew in plenty of eccentrics, as Tom Clark fondly recalls.

'There were lots of regulars and colourful characters. There was Hot Dog – a four-foot-tall, foul-mouthed insane black girl who was *very* unpredictable, and drunk… all the time. She was known to just walk in and smack people, but usually just asked for money for beer. She had a loud, frog-like voice, and could curse like a sailor. Most beloved was Tree Man, whom Jeff mentions on the *Live at Sin-é* EP. He wore a sheet, and branches from various trees tied to his head. These were not twigs, they were *branches*. He was at least 60, and he would shuffle along asking for spare change. A good few times he would get up and sing a song for us. He probably made more dough than any of us! He was a pretty good guy, too. If you caught him when he wasn't "on". I wish I knew what happened to him… though it's probably better that we don't know. His legend lives on.'

True to its essential nature, and in the tradition of the 1960s counter-culture that seemed so alive within its bare walls, the Sin-é remained at heart a coffeehouse.

Jeff meanwhile, always desperate to make the rent on his and Rebecca Moore's tiny East Village apartment – never mind the bills – played where he could. 'There are a thousand places to play in New York,' he mused. He was a restless soul in search of a host, gigging at other small 'indie' venues around the city in an almost hit-and-run, guerrilla fashion. First Street Café, Cornelia Street Café, Bang On, Tramps, the Knitting Factory,

Fez – no one stumbling into any of these venues could know then that they were accidentally witnessing the forging of a future legend. In such modest places Jeff was roughly raising his mojo out of bare, parched earth. He was, by his own admission, playing 'Anywhere I could find, basically. Over and over and over again. The only way to make it – anywhere – is to put every part of your being into the thing that only you can provide.'

If the clubs where he was playing were as low-key as it was possible to get outside of one's bedroom, Jeff's growing self-confidence produced a very real alchemy. Speaking of one particularly well-known dive, the singer reflected, 'You can make a very sacred place out of the Speakeasy if you put enough heart into it.'

He was intent on transforming something internal, too. 'I wanted to put myself through a new childhood,' he reflected. 'I was disintegrating my identity to let the real one emerge. I became a one-man jukebox... discovering the basis of what I do.'

Six months after Jeff's first futile visit to the Sin-é, Daniel Harnett pressed the club's manager into giving the kid a break. Doyle acquiesced, but he was hardly fired up. 'Yeah, whatever,' he told Harnett. Jeff was, however, ecstatic – as if he sensed that he and the Sin-é had some mutual date with destiny. He first played on a mild Friday evening in April of 1992. Plugging his borrowed white Telecaster into a Vox AC30 guitar amp, there was a slight reverb-laden crackle as the lead connected.

He tentatively strummed a few exploratory chords, keeping a bony left arm and hand clamped on the neck while his right worked the AC30, stooping as he did so, adjusting the EQ on the amp until he had a guitar sound that was full yet brittle enough to cut through the sound of rattling coffee cups and chatter. ('The cappuccino machine was so loud,' says NYC-based songwriter Tom Shaner, 'that whenever anyone ordered espresso or cappuccino it would almost always drown out the artist.')

As Jeff eased himself into the set – which would almost completely be made up of covers – he did so gently and calmly. The spartan audience sat at tables so close to the microphone stand that the space between performer and spectator was easily bridged by the drifting smoke of a cigarette. When Jeff eventually got around to finishing his first song the audience's reaction was mute. Sparse clapping cut across the Marlboro air as a polite afterthought. There was no sudden, awed silence in the club, no shocking moment of shared epiphany.

Rather than 'attacking' the audience, Jeff seemed to want to shrink the club down to a communal globule within which he could snarl or sigh as the song dictated. This was a passive-aggressive attempt at seduction

*Street Life: Jeff – pictured with the ever-present boom box –
on a photo shoot for* Rolling Stone *in 1994.*

and the singer was prepared to take as long as was necessary. As he crooned through his interpretation of the Smiths' 'I Know It's Over', it seemed to some as if Jeff were singing into an invisible mirror. It was a slow, stealth-like exercise made up of the songs of Judy Garland, Edith Piaf and Nina Simone.

'People weren't into it at first,' Jeff recalled to journalist Ray Rodgers just two years later. 'I had to fight to be heard. Then I had to stop fighting. Whole months went by where people would not stop talking. I even got a headache from a performance one time.'

Shane Doyle, however, was happy enough to give the kid a regular Monday night slot. This strikingly handsome skinny boy in baggy pants and a V-neck T-shirt, hanging onto a swan-coloured guitar that appeared at times to threaten to topple his frail frame, just seemed to fit right into the place. Singing cabaret, show tunes and standards, the quiet, self-possessed musician matched the quirky soul of the club itself.

From this point on, Jeff practically moved into the Sin-é, becoming a quixotic hybrid of customer, employee and tenant.

'He basically turned the place into his living room,' says Nicholas Hill. 'He was receiving mail there; he would help out in the kitchen, and basically just hung out there even when he wasn't playing. He was friends, pretty much, with everyone who worked there.'

'I love this place,' Jeff gushed. 'Anything can happen here and it usually does.'

The gigs didn't pay much. The performers relied instead on the passing around of the faithful battered bucket at the end of each performance. But the experience was paying off in a far more substantial manner. Jeff had found a base, a space where he was safe enough to crash – musically – and get up again and crash once more if he needed to. In effect, he had found the perfect audience in the actual air, wood and brick of the Sin-é itself.

'I wanted to get to a place that was impossibly intimate,' explained Jeff of his choice of a new musical home. 'Where the people are really up close… and some people come to talk to each other and don't come to listen and sometimes there's a lot of noise… but if you can't move people close up then there wasn't much point in going any further.'

Jeff had soon taken over Tom Clark's Monday night slot with complete authority. Clark remembers that 'Jeff would sometimes just sit there and sit there… then come up and whisper, "Great show, I gotta go." So we'd say, "Ladies and gentleman, Jeff Buckley's gonna come up and do a couple with us." Then a half-hour later, you'd still be saying, "Ladies and gentleman, Jeff Buckley is *still* gonna come up and join us... aren't you Jeff? *Jeff?*" He liked to play around... he loved to entertain.'

Jeff continued gigging throughout the week when and where he could; his faith in both himself and his social circle was ever-growing.

Tom Shaner was a new friend. 'When I first met Jeff, we did hit it off. I immediately knew he was really rooted in some of the same older stuff I loved – and wasn't just superficially aping any current trend or music style like you often see in the various parades of poseurs in the music scene.

'I knew right away when we were jamming one day that he was dipping his cup in the great well of 20th-century songs. We would talk about Leonard Cohen, Dylan, and Hank Williams, Belafonte, Miles Davis, Louis Armstrong, Billie Holiday, and many others... on and on...'

It seems that, having finally accepted the singer in himself, and by default perhaps the thorn of Tim's legacy, Jeff was now on fire. He couldn't stop. Shaner bore witness to the fact that he could not stray within a few feet of Sin-é without needing to sing. 'We [Jeff and I] often hung out at the bar next door,' he laughs. 'The Anseo – which was also owned by Shane. We could play acoustic guitars in the corner. It had an Irish pub-style vibe... I remember one night us singing "Amoreena", an old Elton John song.'

With no manager, roadie, soundman or even band, Jeff was honing his chops down to a powerful minimalist armoury of guitar, voice, and presence. But although he used the rest of the week to explore New York's busy underworld of tiny clubs, it was Sin-é that remained his home port, his centre of gravity.

'He was doing this at a time when he could pretty much guarantee the smallest audience possible,' adds Nicholas Hill. 'Some nights I saw him play to five people. He was using that place as an environment where he could perform under very non-intimidating circumstances.'

Jeff concurred: 'I went into those cafés because I also really felt that I had to go to an impossibly intimate setting where there's no escape, where there's no hiding yourself. If you suck you need work, and if you don't then you have to work on making magic, and if you make magic then everybody has this great transformative experience.'

Jeff had found his niche and was making a slow but profound progress – within himself and in front of his steadily growing audience. Much of that audience was, for obvious reasons, female.

Jeff's voice could often be heard from the street. Siren-like, it drew some people to the source. They would be rewarded by the sight of a petit, handsome vocalist crooning unearthly versions of Dylan's 'If You See Her, Say Hello' or Billie Holiday's 'Strange Fruit', as well as his (and

Lucas's) own 'Grace'. Jeff's visage did not betray the beauty of his voice, and many left infatuated on multiple levels.

Years down the line, London journalist Cressida Johnson actually went so far as to exchange a passionate kiss with the exquisitely diminutive torch singer. 'He was stunningly gorgeous. He could have been used as an antidote for women who don't like short men. He was breathtaking. He was odd in that he actually looked as good as his press photos.'

Jeff was less impressed by this focus on the exterior. What say did he have in the way he looked? Much of that was down to his father, after all. 'I don't pay much attention to it,' he modestly told a journalist one year later. 'I think I look kinda goofy.'

Many different worlds occupied the same geography within New York. While Jeff did his stuff for sparse but increasingly appreciative handfuls of punters, a few blocks away major music industry did its own business. Hal Willner was something of a minor American industry legend. A self-confessed 'jazz snob' who had come up through the ranks as a producer's assistant, working alongside such classic artists as Roberta Flack and Mose Allison. From 1980 onwards, Willner had truly found his niche. By the start of the nineties he was both the musical director of TV's immortal *Saturday Night Live* and had a growing reputation as a producer of quality tribute albums. He had also been deeply touched by Tim Buckley's output during the seventies and had, of course, met Jeff briefly in April '91 at the tribute concert.

Now, over a year after the St Ann's tribute show, and quite by chance, Willner found himself and his buddy, Steve Berkowitz, approaching the Sin-é.

Actually they were meaning to pass by it. Berkowitz was a big shot at Columbia Records – an A&R and production management executive at one of the biggest and most legendary labels in the world. Strolling down St Mark's Place, Willner was taking Berkowitz back to his apartment to play him rough mixes of his latest project – a tribute album to jazz legend Charles Mingus.

But a name in the café's enormous window caught his eye. It was a handwritten sign announcing that Monday evening's gig: 'Jeff Buckley'.

Willner suggested they pop in. He had been impressed by the St Ann's performance and Berkowitz had been a fan of the original Buckley, way back when. Jeff's name had also been mentioned to Berkowitz years previously by the former's LA friend Chris Dowd. The place was full but not packed, and they easily located a table amongst the other Monday-night regulars.

A nondescript young man who had just been seen making coffee in the kitchen ambled up and out of the crowd, placed a beer on a stool, turned, plugged in, and began crooning and strumming to himself.

As soon as Tim's scruffy-looking son started singing, Berkowitz was blown away.

The kid was *weird*. He had heartthrob looks and yet the air and voice of a Delta Mississippi chanson. There was something of his father in him – an almost ethereal intensity – but something new, too. Something sellable. In his mind's eye, the A&R man in Berkowitz was already seeing this guy's face on heavy rotation MTV.

Jeff wasn't particularly aware of the attention. He was utterly *in* and *of* the music by now. Had he been any more relaxed, an adrenalin injection would have been advisable. As a consequence his shows had sometimes morphed into partial stand-up comedy, with jokes and funny voices often introducing the gig before the humour disappeared in a moment, replaced by that quicksilver singing voice and spookily evocative covers of Nina Simone's 'Be My Husband' and 'Wild Is the Wind'. Tonight was just another Monday night for the jobbing singer and he was having fun; playing in tune with the kitchen's coffee machine (in the key of B-flat), improvising new verses to old standards, talking with friends a few feet away in the audience, taking the occasional swig of beer from a nearby table.

As the set wound up, dissolving into quiet café ambience, the buzzing Berkowitz was introduced to Jeff by the ever-affable Willner.

Nothing even close to an offer was made that night, but pleasingly, the A&R man and singer found much common ground in their shared love of blues and jazz and chatted enthusiastically as the occasional audience member came up to compliment Jeff on his performance, offering him a cigarette (Jeff didn't yet smoke), or a drink (usually beer).

Jeff was cool though. In no small part this was due to the tales his mother had told him about his father and the music business of the seventies – the various hassles and double dealings that had caused so much strife back then. Jeff was rushing into nothing. 'The whole reason I was so wary of… things,' he would reason just a few years later, 'was because I suspected my lineage had everything to do with it. I didn't get the feeling that anybody had really heard of me.'

People *were* beginning to hear about Jeff Buckley, however, and increasingly those people – particularly the cult of young females who were now practically squabbling over tables at Sin-é – had never even heard of an esoteric 1970s troubadour called Tim Buckley.

4. IN BLOOM

'No, I haven't really thought about an audience. This music isn't just for me... I can offer stories people can relate to. I'm just like anyone else, with a brain, heart, loves, coffee stains, whatever. Anybody who is into music I hope will want to hear me.'

Jeff Buckley, 1994

Whatever the intensity and sincerity of the nascent hype haloing him, Jeff was far too outwardly laidback to appear excited by any attention. He hadn't even recruited a manager to deal with it. But he did allow the lawyer who had sorted out the Gods and Monsters mess the previous year to represent him, albeit unofficially.

George Stein had a naturally good rapport with Jeff and was eager to escape the dull (as he found it) world of common legal practice. Beyond this, he was eager to get into rock'n'roll management and, more specifically, keen to manage one Jeff Buckley. Jeff, still wary of almost anyone who was associated with the music business in any way other than on a purely musical level, was politely reticent. Though he eventually consented to a verbal agreement between himself and Stein, for now, nothing would be signed. His wariness was no pose – it was weaved into his genes. The attitude was ingrained, as Jeff explained: 'I can't really trust anybody in the music business. It's the way I've been brought up.'

It was perhaps some kind of reward for Stein's patience that he had to do little in the way of being proactive on his (informal) client's behalf. Good vibes and the opportunities they rode in on seemed to gravitate towards Jeff. 'He was one of those guys that everybody just fell in love with, the moment they met him,' recounted Hal Willner, speaking for the majority. Such likeability also transposed itself into Jeff's performances. It was a rare gift, but his personal charm was tangible within his stage presence. He was no gentlemen crooner onstage and paranoid, screaming monster backstage. This was yet another weirdly attractive aspect of his strange, changeling character.

A November 1994 portrait taken at New York's
Wetlands Club hints at the geek within.

As spring tilted towards summer, the buzz surrounding Jeff Buckley thickened, swelling the tiny Sin-é to bursting point. By that ripe, sweltering June of 1992, leading A&R men of major labels were in attendance whenever Jeff played or whenever there was a rumour of him playing. The sleazy, narrow backstreet that the café opened up onto was soon jammed both with limousines and the quizzical indignation on the faces of those who couldn't get in on the guest list. (There was no guest list.)

'He gets nervous when the record company limos pull up outside,' Shane Doyle told journalist David Browne that year. 'Those are never his best gigs.'

Yet even when plagued by nerves, Jeff could take the place by storm. Photographer Merri Cyr, who would eventually become a friend and colleague of Jeff's, saw him now for the first time. Her verdict was to the point: 'He was phenomenal.'

The poet Wanda Phipps was a friend of Jeff's girlfriend, Rebecca Moore, who had introduced Jeff to Wanda. 'I didn't notice him at all,' said Phipps, 'but then I saw him perform at Sin-é… When he sang he was gorgeous. It was like some channelling of the divine. I was running Monday night readings at the Poetry Project and I went to Sin-é after the readings every week. My friends thought I was crazy because I kept going back, but it was never the same. He didn't want to perfect a song in a certain form; he kept improvising – finding what else was there. Often people didn't pay much attention to the performers at Sin-é, because it was free, but once Jeff would start to sing a huge hush would descend and everybody would be totally rapt.'

Another female in the audience with a somewhat more rarefied history than the average Sin-é customer was equally succinct in delivering her professional opinion. 'Of course,' said Marianne Faithfull, there on the personal recommendation of friend Hal Willner, 'like everybody else I just fell completely in love with him.'

Even so, the club did not belong exclusively to Jeff.

Sin-é continued to host handfuls of other singer-songwriters and bands. Nicholas Hill points out that, 'You could never be sure who was playing. You might walk by and sure, Jeff would be playing, or Katell might be singing, or Marianne Faithfull. But then there were others, even lesser-known, who were still inspiring and so inspired by the place itself; Susan McKuen, Dorothy Scott, Jack McKeever, Timothy Hill. These people made Sin-é their home too. It was just such a special place.'

Jeff often jammed with whomever happened to be playing at the Sin-é when he himself wasn't. Bassist Andrew Goodsight recalls that 'I was playing with many bands at the time and one was the Adam Roth Band. We played at Sin-é on Saturdays and Jeff was there and asked Adam if he could sit in with the band, which I'm sure Adam wasn't too thrilled about, because singers don't like being blown away at their own gig by another singer. Jeff asked if I knew "What Is and What Should Never Be" by Zeppelin, which I did, so we played that. He *killed* it. The place went nuts. After he asked if I wanted to get together and jam sometime. I said, "Sure!" and gave him my number.' Jeff and Goodsight would meet again, albeit under somewhat more professional circumstances.

Outside of the cosy confines of the Sin-é the well-oiled wheels of the record industry continued to turn. As well as Columbia's Steve Berkowitz, various other record company honchos – including representatives from Ensign, Arista and the indie label Imago – were all badgering Jeff's lawyer for a demo tape. They needed something tangible to play their colleagues, something to fiddle with and mull over back at the office. Such was the nature of the business and the ritual of signing a new artist. Stein could only shrug and offer a limp smile. What could he say? Jeff was a true maverick. *The Babylon Dungeon Sessions* were unequivocally old hat, consigned by Jeff to the dustbin of posterity. The hours and hours of Gods and Monsters recordings would not surface for over a decade. They were not representative of what was now drawing audience and industry alike to the Sin-é in droves. Thus there was no demo tape. Anyone who wanted to hear Jeff Buckley literally had to fight for a table, regardless of their motivations, connections, or intentions.

The Buckley set was now fluid and assured, although still as loose on any given night as Jeff's vibe dictated. He had built a musical foundation within himself, a base from which he could take off in any number of directions. The bulk of the gig consisted of cover versions, drawn from an increasingly disparate and seductive palate. As well as Van Morrison, Bob Dylan, the Smiths and Nina Simone, Jeff was also occasionally covering hardcore metal songs and throwing in the intermittent musical nod to current chart-toppers such as the Red Hot Chili Peppers and Nirvana, often preceded by some witty dialogue or a surreal monologue that showed 'Scotty Moorhead' still existed somewhere.

Although Jeff could easily claim a handful of self-written originals that would stand up beside any of the standards he was performing, that was not quite the point. He would reflect on his choice of material, saying, 'I consciously took on my idols as teachers. One, to get into the skin of the songs that they did that I loved, and also just to learn about what they did. Not only to make it my own, but to have it call up something from me. Just like any learning at all.'

Yet even with the regular inclusion of original material – including both 'Mojo Pin' and what would one day become the title track of his debut album – Jeff's obvious strength still seemed to be his abilities as an interpretative singer. Exactly how a record company would present him was a mystery.

As Berkowitz pointed out, Jeff as an act was a prism with many viable angles. 'It could have been Jeff with the New York Symphony Orchestra, or the Jeff Buckley Big Band. Who knew?'

Nicholas Hill did not place such emphasis on who had actually written the songs Jeff was singing. 'His performances were pretty spectacular in that he so inhabited other people's songs. He rarely performed his own material at the beginning, as I recall. He was using the Sin-é as a place to woodshed. He *created* the environment that he played in.'

Perversely, despite his ongoing financial struggle and the mass industry attention coming his way, Jeff remained truer than ever to his *raison d'être*. In 1993 he would sigh, 'I'm used to the standard by which bands are measured – by how ambitious they are about getting a deal.' Reflecting on this heady time less than a year later, he continued, '[Hype] is like a huge chain reaction, a domino effect, and all those clichés. They either come to dispel the rumour that what their friends are seeing is good, or to totally get on it, so they can be a part of it. That's not real though. Those aren't real people. Because that industry thing, that buzz, can always be taken away. But what real people feel, that's there.'

Despite such acute awareness, Jeff was practical. He realised that any future he had in music – and as far as he was concerned, his future could *only* be in music – would be in making records. But Jeff was living in the dogged present, not the future, and as it was he was barely getting by on the two most basic levels – rent and food. In part, even this reflected badly on the late Buckley Senior. 'Because of my father people assumed things about me that weren't true,' Jeff claimed. 'That I was taken care of, that I lived in Beverly Hills, that I was a brat.' In reality, he was barely a few rickety steps from being a vagabond, a few heartbeats away from the bums of the bowery. He admitted that it was 'very hard' to turn down the financial offers coming his way, but he retained a wariness that was almost spiritual in its intensity. His lawyer was much less reticent and, as Stein pointed out, Jeff's time was now due. Such moments happen rarely in a singer's career – if Jeff didn't mind him referring to his client's *raison d'être* in such gross terms as a *career*. If they were ever going to act, they had to act now. But, perhaps remembering what his father had suffered at the hands of commerce, Jeff clung to his ideals. Audaciously, he told Stein that he wanted three things from a record company: 'Integrity, patience and hands off.' Knowing his client as he did, Stein could hardly be surprised at such a robust attitude. However, fully convinced of Jeff's star potential and eager to seal his trust (still nothing had been signed between the two), Stein went ahead as directed, and that summer arranged various meetings between himself, Jeff and record company presidents. Rather than acting dumb or playing smart, Jeff was, if anything, even more of himself at these meetings. At one encounter, high on the hype, legendary music mogul Clive Davis – then head of Arista – was laying his shtick on Jeff and Stein, raving about potential markets and inevitable platinum discs. Speaking deliberately quietly, Jeff asked, 'Have you heard me?' Although his demeanour was polite and ice-cream-wouldn't-melt innocent, the singer was well aware that Davis in fact hadn't heard him. It was a slyly rhetorical question. There was still no demo, and Jeff had no inclination to record one. Davis, rather taken aback, candidly admitted that, no, he hadn't actually heard Jeff, but he *had* heard that he was great. A silent beat passed. And then, to Stein's embarrassment, Buckley suggested that Davis, one of the biggest names in the music industry, come down to the Sin-é, one of the tiniest clubs in the music industry, and check him out.

No doubt beguiled by the kid's chutzpah, Davis duly took a limo down to the tiny venue, was impressed and made an offer. However, no agreement was reached at that time, either with Arista or any other label. Jeff knew what he wanted and was prepared to wait for it, although there were doubts. He was acutely aware of the pros and cons of labels and marketing. He was also media-savvy, but this was an instinctive, street-level knowledge. Jeff knew what was and wasn't cool because he was – put simply – a huge fan of pop music and, to a lesser extent, of pop culture. During his roaming seventies childhood Scotty Moorhead had gobbled up what he could in this respect, taking sustenance from all that pop offered. As well as consuming innumerable albums and singles, Jeff had bought the coffee table books, the T-shirts, hoarded the magazines, and even worn the spandex. Now, years later, by visiting Clive Davis et al in their impressive thirtieth-floor offices, Jeff was walking into the belly of the beast. And this troubled him. 'Jeff felt from an early age that he had to vindicate his father,' said his friend, performance artist Penny Arcade. 'And that's why he could never be an indie artist.'

Stein confirmed the doubts at play in Jeff's mind. 'Jeff was worried about signing to a major label and losing his soul,' he stated. To compound such procrastination, many in the industry saw the matter in grosser terms, and the general consensus was that Stein was asking for too much money.

The other recurring problem was – as Berkowitz had so astutely pointed out – how do we market Jeff Buckley?

His given name held little currency in the grunge- and dance-dominated music scene of the early nineties. On the other hand, Jeff was supremely photogenic and charismatic, with an indisputably great voice that, while not only technically stunning, was also genuinely unique. But then there was the problem of material. Was he a singer-songwriter or merely an interpretive singer? Could he be both?

Certainly, he was no Tom Jones or Frank Sinatra in the latter respect, but he obviously had a profound talent for making almost any song his own. The record labels were dealing with an unknown quantity that, while undeniably singular and precious, had little precedent.

Beyond this, the buzz and the label interest were undeniable, and this phenomenon would ultimately feed itself, with moguls like Clive Davis and Seymour Stein determined to trump one another as a matter of pride. Yet, in the midst of this potentially derailing pandemonium, and despite being stony broke, Jeff continued to take his time and consider the growing options. George Stein was patient, even fatherly with his still-unofficial client. 'He had conflicts his whole career about commercialisation,' the lawyer would later reflect. 'He was worried about selling a lot of records.'

Stein and the labels carried on playing the waiting game while Jeff went back to what he knew. He continued to gig alone at various tiny New York venues such as Skep and Tilt, as well as appearing regularly at the circus that Shane Doyle's baby had become.

By now, the Sin-é was a star in itself.

'One of the most memorable times I ever spent there was when one night I walked in and the place was just jam-packed,' says Nicholas Hill. 'And Alan Ginsberg was there, Marianne Faithfull was there, Jeff was there... all of 'em had been doing a song or two, and then out of the kitchen comes Sinéad O'Connor and Katell Keineg together.

'They did a duet of Dylan's "Mama, You Been on My Mind" and they were both barefoot and beautiful and you know, stunning. And then Katell came out solo and did this tour de force called "Gulf of Araby", the final song from her first album – it was a masterpiece. On another night I saw Vic Chestnut with Jeff... Mike Scott came down and sang a song – "Send Him Down to Waco", it was called. Pretty topical, back then. It was the kind of night that you'd only get at Sin-é.'

Despite the massive focus on Jeff, there was very little in the way of jealousy or animosity from his success-hungry peers. 'There were never any bad vibes amongst the artists that I saw,' attests Hill. 'The vibe of the place got weird much later. Shane had drug problems, which drained the cash out of the place, but this was long after Jeff had exploded.'

Jeff appeared to retain his sense of self. When Wanda Phipps went to see her friend, she found that 'there was a huge swarm of people crowding around him. I was about to leave but he grabbed my arm and held onto it really tightly so I couldn't move. Just to make sure that after all the rabid fans disappeared I could say whatever it was I'd wanted to say to him. He was really considerate and thoughtful that way. He had a nurturing way that made you feel full and joyous long after you'd parted.'

Throughout the muggy New York summer of 1992, Jeff and Stein pondered the various publishing and recording deals on the table. Another recurring question kept surfacing – did Jeff even want to go with a major record label? Imago was the most realistic indie label in the running, but compared to Sony it had meagre financial resources. Would it be able to serve Jeff's potential? After all, Jeff and Stein weren't asking for a lot – they were asking for pretty much everything. The lawyer repeated his mantra to Arista's Clive Davis, telling him face to face that he wanted just those three magical things: 'Integrity, patience and hands off.' Eventually Clive (who was used to dealing with 'difficult' artists, having worked with one of Jeff's heroes, Miles Davis, throughout the seventies and eighties) felt that he could not be forthcoming and retreated. Undaunted, Jeff told Stein to report these conditions to any label who came calling. Thus the system of elimination continued.

Eventually, after much consideration, a deal was struck. Jeff Buckley decided to go with goateed A&R man Steve Berkowitz and, under the direction of Stein (who was still acting for Jeff in a semi-official capacity as lawyer only – even now he had no manager), signed what was essentially a million-dollar recording and publishing deal with Columbia and Sony in October of 1992. Jeff had searched his indie-kid soul and come up with the following diagnosis: 'It wouldn't have happened with an independent label because I'm not alternative… I got this opportunity for the umpteenth time and I thought I should take this and parlay what I can.'

It helped that he got on with Berkowitz on a personal level. The A&R representative, with his bohemian facial hair and old school jazz demeanour, hoped that 'Jeff would make 25 albums. Columbia and Sony thought that it went Dylan... Springsteen... Buckley.' Posing for a photograph to commemorate the signing, Jeff looks like a ghostly waif beside the suits who now owned his songs. '[That picture] is almost amusing,' reckoned Stein. 'Jeff looks absolutely tortured. Everyone else had big smiles. It symbolised visually what he felt... he had real reservations.'

But despite the image Jeff projected of being a vague, somewhat aloof hipster in terms of the industry and business side of his art, he was in fact flatly pragmatic and aware of what he was allowing himself to become part of. Speaking of massive companies like the one he had just signed his future to, Jeff pointed out the pluses and minuses of such a deal when he accurately stated that it was an industry that: 'Steals, chews up, spits out and forgets... [While] it allows you to make your living by being who you are. And that's a very beautiful and lucky thing.'

While, in their corporate mind, Sony had already made plans for him as a platinum-selling 'prestige' artist in the mould of Bruce Springsteen or Van Morrison, Jeff's own vision was untainted. The actual physical result of this union between man and corporation would be, he hoped, 'To make things I've never heard before... to go as deep as I can.'

Jeff was now a potential major player and he knew it. Companies like Columbia rarely signed up individuals frivolously or recklessly, even though their judgment could sometimes invariably be wrong.

But while Jeff was obviously no Billy Ray Cyrus or Michael Bolton, nor was he a tidily marketable alternative MTV poster boy. His aesthetic, musical and otherwise, included a particular and peculiar perversity most apparent in his goofy humour and slightly skewed attitude toward authority figures. 'I've always been wilfully out of step,' Jeff would concur. 'I've always been on the outside.'

After signing a million-dollar deal with a major record company and publisher (Jeff personally netted a percentage of this, said to be $100,000, as a cash advance), he almost immediately went into the studio, for one day (8 November 1992). This seemingly futile few hours in a budget recording studio off Times Square appeared to be nothing but a token gesture – as if Jeff's new 'bosses' wanted some physical proof that their new investment could actually sing. Following that brief sojourn, Jeff returned to civilian life for a few weeks before he once again took to the stage. It was 21 November 1992, the venue was the Anthology Film Archives Theatre, situated in the East Village, and the event was sponsored by Fluxus. The audience consisted mostly of John Cage and Stockhausen aficionados. Jeff walked onstage with a plastic hair comb. Dressed in a natty seventies-style suit he stepped up to the microphone, tapped it gently, and then proceeded to blow through the comb, running his fingers along its plastic spikes. He followed this by blowing into an amplified ceramic vase.

Jeff's friend, the performance artist and former Warhol cohort Penny Arcade, reckoned that within such leftfield performances and art movements, 'Jeff found his true artistic home and an antidote to the commercial world of the entertainment industry, whose focus was on process and long-term artistic development which largely rejects "product" mentality.' Whether Jeff himself would define the joy he found in such activities in such political terms was beside the point. What was true was that by stepping out of the expected role of guitarist and singer-songwriter so immediately after signing up as just that, he was publicly alluding to the many natures at work within himself. Even so, for now, such gestures would alarm no one. In fact, blowing into vases and disposable hair combs only served to endear Jeff further to the staff at the label. The more himself he was, the more he was accepted. He concluded that night's performance by improvising with some text from a newspaper article in the style of a 1968 Yoko Ono piece. (This 'song', 'Untitled', can be found on the soundtrack of the *Fall in Light* documentary.)

Jeff's commitment to the Fluxus ethos continued when a few days later he performed at another of their sponsored happenings at the Judson Memorial Church. Fans of his more traditional songwriting talents and in particular his singing voice would have no doubt been perturbed. Wandering among the space, Jeff gleefully ironed shirts on an ironing board improvised from an electric guitar and screamed pseudo-abuse at potted plants until they wilted.

Such forays into the avant-garde were not merely empty gestures on Jeff's part; neither were they arty poses or subtle *fuck you*'s to his new parent label. At heart Jeff was a pure artist. His hunger for culture and sensation and experience was ravenous, and New York City was only too able to feed such appetites. Outside of the Fluxus events Jeff also experimented in live theatre – ultimately concluding that 'acting wasn't for me' – all the while continuing to perform musically and solo at such intimate venues as the Fez, the Knitting Factory and the reliable Sin-é. These activities were grounded by a temporarily secure domestic life with girlfriend Rebecca Moore. He was, to quote another famous NYC citizen, Al Pacino, 'getting to know the neighbourhood'.

For all this apparent extra-curricular activity, as a brand-new signing to a global multi-national company, Jeff seemed to be taking matters extremely casually; proof that both parties were standing by the oft-cited

'Integrity, patience and hands off' stipulation. Sony's mellowness seemed to draw Jeff in, and consequently he would sometimes wander through the warren of the label's offices, helping himself to coffee, chatting with the staff, and picking up carrier-bagfuls of promo CDs and tapes. Yet, although low-level, there was definitely the presence of pressure, as Andrew Goodsight observes: 'When you sign the kind of deal Jeff had, it isn't long after the cheque clears that the suits want to hear something. I think Jeff was just trying to keep the president of Sony off his back. I remember he wouldn't talk to any of those guys... only Berkowitz.'

As such, although far from feeling ready, Jeff continued to make token trips to local studios. A slightly more fundamental studio experience came in the February of the New Year when, by direct arrangement with Berkowitz, Jeff attended Steve Addabbo's recording studio on West Twenty-Seventh Street. For sixteen hours, Jeff played solo, with guitar and harmonium, running through almost every song he knew, while Addabbo recorded the whole time.

As impressive as this exercise was, it was not much more than that – an exercise that Jeff was going through with much more *élan* when live onstage.

Outside of these Columbia-instigated guerrilla attacks on minor recording studios, Jeff's civilian life continued apace that spring when he moved out of Rebecca Moore's apartment and into a swish, eccentric duplex of his own, located a five-minute walk from the Village and Sin-é. His relationship with Moore, while not officially over, had been deteriorating since he'd signed his record deal, and his promiscuity during this period was common knowledge in certain circles. ('Who wasn't one of Jeff's lovers?' asked Glen Hansard rhetorically.) With the new neighbourhood came new friends. Jeff befriended local 'underground' (although she was in fact also signed to Columbia at this time) musician Brenda Kahn. This was a contented time in the lives of both artists and the two hit it off immediately.

'I met Jeff at Columbia records when I was a signed artist and he was being courted by several labels,' recalls the pixie-faced Kahn. '[Columbia executive] David Kahne introduced us in his office. That night I had a dream about Jeff – that he was cooking Shitake mushrooms for me. I took that as a sign that I should call him, and got his number from David. We became friends after that. We played music together and hung out together. I knew Jeff when both of our lives pretty much revolved around music. I remember his apartment then... there was mostly music equipment downstairs and just a regular apartment upstairs. I remember he painted the exposed brick some strange colour. Lime. He painted it lime. We liked to walk around the East Village and go in and out of thrift stores and eat ethnic food and talk about life, but mostly we would end up with guitars, making up ridiculous songs, and sometimes quite *serious* songs.' Jeff and Kahn would go on to work together, both on record and live onstage, but for now his focus was on his own material.

While the songs were indeed coming to Jeff, they were coming slowly. No longer a scream in search of a mouth, his muse was burning with a steady equilibrium constantly stoked by his live solo shows. But still no one – the singer himself included – knew quite how to take this force into the studio. Although he had handfuls of musician friends, he still had no regular group.

That May, Jeff felt the need to experiment in the studio once again. He was feeling his way, unsure as how to progress but determined to find a direction.

Having found his recent solo studio experiences ultimately futile, Jeff decided to set up his own recording space in the kind of place he felt most comfortable with – a tiny, intimate downtown club. He chose one of his regular live venues, the Knitting Factory.

This recording session would be profoundly different to the recent solo skirmishes. Jeff wanted to play with a band. Flicking through his address book, he came up with the number of the bassist he had rocked out with at Sin-é a few months previously. Andrew Goodsight remembered Jeff fondly but had no idea that he'd just signed a megabucks contract. Nor did Jeff make this known; he simply asked Goodsight if he could recommend a drummer and if he would be able to come down to Context Rehearsal Studios. Goodsight hoofed it over and on arrival was stunned to discover that Jeff had booked the place for a week. The Knitting Factory wasn't available yet, but Jeff wanted to get going on something *now*.

Goodsight was a typical struggling musician living in NYC in the early nineties, with a raw passion for the music that moved him, including Led Zeppelin. Suffice to say, he and Jeff got on well.

'Jeff and I had the same taste in music. We could both play every Zeppelin song note for note. He could play and sing those songs as good as the original recording, so a lot of time was spent jamming. We would play Rush songs, Grateful Dead songs, Yes songs, Beatles... the list goes on and on.'

Goodsight and John McNally, the drummer he had recommended, were a bit confused as to the nature of the project, but more than happy to go along with whatever was required. Jeff certainly didn't brag about his contract, and it was only when other people mentioned the mammoth

Columbia deal to the easygoing bassist that he understood the state of play. Still, Goodsight didn't feel the need to bring it up with Jeff, and all three worked intensely according to Jeff's methods.

'We rehearsed at Context Studios for a week. Every day from 10:00am till around 5:00 or 6:00pm,' recalls Goodsight. 'Jeff recorded everything on cassette during those rehearsals and the next day he would bring in a copy of highlights from the day before. We then moved to the Knitting Factory, and I remember Jeff recording every note and conversation on cassette and DAT, and for actual takes we recorded on sixteen-track half-inch tape as well as DAT and cassette.'

The recordings, save for 'Strawberry Street', would never be officially released, but the experience was more than a mere exercise for all concerned. By the end of the three weeks, Goodsight had been blown away, both by Jeff's musicality and by the man himself. 'The guy should have been a dick. Would have been with his talent... had a right to be, even. His star quality alone would have warranted it, but he was real cool and easy to talk to. When I started playing with Jeff I did not know that he had just signed a huge deal with Sony and was getting cover stories in the *New York Times* and having sex with every girl in the East Village and packing every club. I was out of the loop. But after about 30 minutes in a rehearsal room it occurred to me that I was playing with someone special in a way that really appealed to me as a musician. His personality, his vibe; neither did anything to convey the idea that he believed or that he thought – in a pretentious way – that he was anyone special or famous or going places. He loved to laugh and had a great sense of humour... he didn't take himself too seriously at all. I've played with many people and been in signed bands. I've played with people when they were nobodies and cool, only to see them make a splash in the business and become, how I shall put it... *dickheads*. Jeff was not one of those people. At least he was not to me.'

The sessions ended with little ceremony. 'Jeff was always real secretive about his plans, and I never knew if we were going to play again till the end of the day,' concludes Goodsight. 'At the end of the day he would say, "Are you free to play tomorrow?" No talk of money. No talk of the future. There was no schedule or plan. Just fast and loose. If you're a full-time musician, that can be nerve-wracking.'

The results of this three-week recording session were ultimately inconclusive, but the next step suddenly seemed obvious. Jeff had been signed more or less on the strength of his Sin-é shows, so Berkowitz decided to go back to the source. His decision was not unanimously popular – few of Columbia's staff believed the world was ready for a solo acoustic debut. But as summer came around once again, it was decided that Jeff should be recorded solo and live at Sin-é for an EP release.

This was an audacious decision for a monolithic company like Sony to make. It was an organisation used to dealing in primary colours, as it were, and this choice proved beyond doubt that they were taking Jeff seriously, and on his own terms. Full-blown EPs, as opposed to slightly expanded CD singles, were by the early nineties a curiosity at best and offered little possibility of financial reward. Such a debut release was a weird and mysterious gesture – particularly in that it was a live recording, something that usually came midway through or at the end of an artist's career.

In other respects it could make perfect sense, commercially capturing Jeff's essence at the start of his professional career as a recording artist. As was plain by now to anyone aware of Jeff's nature and art, for him playing live was much more than the mere replication of songs. 'What I wanted to do,' he would tell Nicholas Hill, explaining the philosophy behind his Sin-é performances, 'was get to a place... somewhere that's really up close. And Sin-é was like that, y'know? Where you're right in front of the people. It's just a strength I really wanted to get into, as a natural force in my playing. If I couldn't move people really close up then there wasn't any point in going much further.'

This was the ethos inspiring what Berkowitz (who would be credited as producer) and engineer Michael Sauvage hoped to capture.

On the morning of Monday 19 July 1993, Berkowitz had his engineer and assistants set up a makeshift mobile recording studio in the Anseo bar a few doors down from Sin-é. This scenario had more in common with the blues and jazz field recordings of America's twenties and thirties than it did with any contemporary recording session. The first set was planned to commence at 3:00pm. Hardly rock'n'roll, but nonetheless appropriate for Jeff.

Attempting to appear as casual as the clothes in which he sauntered into the club (Jeff had not dressed up for the occasion of his first major label recording. He came clad, as on any other day, in baggy pants and a T-shirt), he was nevertheless edgy. Played to a near-empty room, Jeff's performance erred more on the side of nervy gags, bits and chatter than consummate musicality. Disappointed, he retired to the nearby Anseo with Merri Cyr, where under her watch he willed himself into a siesta.

Refreshed after his sleep, Jeff returned to the Sin-é for the evening performance. Sounding charged and happy, he skipped through a three-hour set that saw almost every song in his recent repertoire pour out of him. Despite the obvious improvement upon the daylight show, the evening set was still ultimately deemed mediocre by Berkowitz, his accomplices, and Jeff's friends.

'To me it was… unfortunate,' says Nicholas Hill, 'because it was only an attempt to capture his woodshedding days, but the result was not natural. There were all these hot-shot executives and Sony brought in all this gear… it was odd. Jeff went through every song he knew over a few nights but it was obvious he felt uncomfortable. The setting was contrived. The nature of his performance was that every performance was different, every night.'

Hill's opinion was pretty much the consensus, and a month later another recording session was set up – same times, same place, same songs, but with a much more relaxed Jeff channelling much more satisfactory results, the cherry-picked highlights of which would appear on the *Live at Sin-é* EP.

The formality of the event had effectively been punctured by what now proved to be the 'dummy run' of the July sessions. As a consequence Jeff was far more relaxed and powerful, stomping and swooning through a set that included pages torn from the classic American songbook – Gershwin, Dylan, and Simone – played beside his own material and that of his beloved Nusrat Fateh Ali Khan.

As these café performances demonstrated, Berkowitz and Sony had shown great patience and grace in the way they handled their sensitive artist's debut recording session. It was now beyond obvious that their faith in Jeff Buckley and his uncompromising aesthetic was for real.

Jeff did not take such belief for granted. 'I'm aware that it's hard,' he confessed. 'I know about Columbia and Sony and other big places. I'm not talking about Sire or SST. I'm talking fucking Michael Jackson money. I was wary at first that they didn't know how to do anything small, but I'm really determined to think it will work out for the best.'

The November 1993 US release of the four-song *Live at Sin-é* EP generally drew favourable notices. Yet, to some listeners, the cosmetic sheen of Jeff's voice sounded no different to other wannabe blue-eyed soul singers, albeit with souls of a much lesser indie credibility.

One New York writer compared Jeff's debut to his label-mate Michael Bolton. 'Oh my God!' Jeff spat in disgust to journalist Ray Rodgers. 'Oh shit, that's really disgusting…' This odious comparison seemed based on the assumption that both Jeff and Bolton simply wished that they were black, like their heroes. 'Really?' Jeff huffed derisively. 'But the thing is, I'm not taking from that tradition.' This reaction seemed somewhat affected, given his public love of artists such as Miles Davis, Nina

Simone, Harry Belafonte, Billie Holiday and James Brown. 'I don't want to be black,' he pouted. '*Michael Bolton* wants to be black, black, black. He also sucks.'

Bolton was a kind of *bête noire* for Jeff throughout his brief life. He perhaps sensed on some level that if he did not dig in and challenge himself, his gifts, and those around him, then he too could be drawn down the same slick cod-soul road to damnation that Bolton swaggered along so well. Bolton's poodle-haired vapidity was in some queer way almost as much of an influence on Jeff as the sacred Nusrat Fateh Ali Khan. Jeff had the skills, the looks and the backing to successfully emulate such a spiritually shallow yet fiscally deep career as Bolton's. But in the final creative audit, Jeff would choose art (i.e. life) over money (i.e. death). 'There are thousands of great artists who wouldn't be doing the same kind of work if there was no music business machine,' stated Jeff. 'The ones who are popular would be doing much different work, too. Michael Bolton would be pumping gas.'

The prospect of working a minimum-wage job now seemed a million light years away from the reality Jeff Buckley was facing. Summer was in full swing, and finally, with the gleaming machinery of a star-crossed destiny and a massive record company behind him, Jeff was poised to record his first – and final – album.

5 GRACE

'Music is the only thing I've got. It's the only thing that's been really great to me all the time.'

Jeff Buckley, 1994

As the summer of 1993 slowly ebbed away, so Jeff turned towards the realisation of his first album. Steve Berkowitz, aware of Jeff's liquid, mercurial nature, announced a definite recording date – September. He knew all too well that Jeff was apt at circling a project to the point of avoidance. The boy was so perceptive and sensitive that he could see six sides to a square.

Both Berkowitz and George Stein wanted to make the most of the momentum they now had in terms of Columbia and the sympathetic staff there, the general good vibe, and the world market. Grunge was peaking, the zeitgeist mutating, and such a new season was perfect for a new musical phase, exquisitely typified by the changeling Jeff. Focusing on a September start date would give them the whole summer to find the right producer. And the 'right' producer was essential. Columbia's new signing was obviously not a four-piece group who'd been gigging hard since leaving college, nor was he a folkie merely awaiting sympathetic backing from hired session musicians. His talent, although fierce at this juncture, was still prism-like in its nature, reflecting and refracting his catholic tastes through a variety of styles and material. Such was the scope of his singing voice that it was in some ways potentially prohibitive. If someone can sing anything, then they obviously have a harder time deciding just what it is they *want* to sing. A producer who would bring focus to Jeff's multiple elements was vital, but this same producer would also have to appreciate and respect his core talent, whilst nurturing that ability and providing it with the necessary space in which to evolve. Suffice to say, Phil Spector would not be summoned from retirement.

Various names were proffered by Columbia, Stein and friends, some obviously more predictable than others. Tom Werman, (Ted Nugent, Blue

Jeff performs at the Roseland Ballroom in New York,
clad in a dazzling jacket of glittery gold sequins. Bought second-hand,
this shabby item of women's clothing would be immortalised on the cover of Grace.

JEFF BUCKLEY: MYSTERY WHITE BOY BLUES

Öyster Cult), Mitchell Froom, (Richard Thompson, American Music Club, Suzanne Vega), Steve Lillywhite (the Pogues and Jeff's beloved Morrissey)... The list was as predictable as Jeff was unpredictable. No real 'wild cards' were brought up. Though Jeff himself aptly provided that element. (Steve Albini or Eric Jacobsen, producer of Tim Hardin and Chris Isaak, or the ubiquitous Brian Eno would have been intriguing candidates.) Jeff finally decided on the experienced, middle-aged, in vogue and highly successful Andy Wallace.

Wallace had a broad, rich CV that included the Beastie Boys through Aerosmith, right up to the then current cultural explosion of Nirvana.

Meeting with Wallace in an anonymous Columbia office that June, Sony's new signing told the sage-like producer exactly what he needed. Jeff wanted to *capture* something, not design it. He imagined an old-style recording, the sound of a band playing live in a well-miked room. Ultimately, it wouldn't happen quite that way, but Wallace got the gist. The young, softly-spoken man sat opposite Wallace was obviously more interested in style than fashion. He was no chancer, someone merely lucky to be there. This much was obvious. Jeff had not just stumbled upon a random wave in the breaking zeitgeist and surfed it into a million dollar record deal. Neither was he here by virtue of his father's name, nor via his poster-boy looks. In fact, all of these factors might have worked against what he actually was – a primal talent utterly enraptured by the phenomenon of music for its own sake. At the same time, this extended into an awareness of *why* he was actually sat in Columbia's offices, storeys above the bustling and grimy grandiosity of Madison Avenue. Jeff was no longer hoofing it down among the smoke and steam of the crowded sidewalk with all the wannabes. He was now part of the music business, and this meant making records. Jeff was a rare breed – both romantic and pragmatic. All of this slowly dawned on the pleasantly surprised Wallace as Jeff spoke passionately of endless varieties of music, well beyond the pantheon of grunge, hardcore, and rock. He raved gently about hillbilly bands, of blues and mondo music, and name-checked the sacred transcendental freak-out jazz of Sun Ra and the spooky lounge sounds of Esquivel – not what Wallace may have necessarily expected from a new Columbia investment during the early 1990s. This was both impressive and beguiling. Wallace also went along with the key suggestion that he do everything for the record. Meaning that he alone would engineer, produce, record and mix the work, keeping the project insular, just as the artist wanted it. The meeting went well for both sides of the table. Jeff and Wallace came away convinced, and so the former gave the nod to Stein and Berkowitz, who in turn informed Wallace's own management. Columbia had no argument with the man who had mixed the *Nevermind* tapes, and thus Andy Wallace got the gig.

The next hurdle towards a completed product (i.e. the finished CD) that Jeff had to overcome was his projected personality and how those around him perceived it. Almost everyone involved in the Buckley cause up to this point seemed to assume that the album would reflect the Sin-é experience; both as it was live and as it would be on the forthcoming EP (which was at present being mixed, edited, mastered and having its artwork completed). After all, Jeff hadn't played with an actual band since the aborted Gods and Monsters. The assumption was that he would record a singer-songwriter album that would be solo in almost every sense of the word. Jeff was no R.E.M. or U2. The most obvious comparisons at this point would have been Chris Isaak, Leonard Cohen, Suzanne Vega, and maybe – although no one let Jeff hear them say it – Michael Bolton. In the final analysis, Jeff's name and portrait alone would grace the album cover, surely?

Yet even as such assumptions made the rounds of the Sony building in the form of faxes and memos, the singer was in the act of confounding them. Jeff now had his hungry heart set upon having a band. The Sin-é experiment had been successfully completed and the recording of the EP had sealed that process. In fact, some argued that it came a little late, just after the very phase it was meant to capture.

Jeff was moving on and, while he wanted his debut album to reflect as many of the facets he had found in himself during those café days as possible (including the chanson singer, the crooner, and the rocker), he now wanted to capture those aspects in the company of living, breathing, sweating musicians.

Wallace was comfortable with this, but almost everyone else at Columbia was immediately taken aback by the idea. Stein in particular was concerned that the subtle nuances of his client's talent could be neutralised by such an approach. Various meetings ensued. It was suggested that Jeff would focus on just one of these traits – the rocker or the chanson or the folk-singer. (Although Jeff himself was not fond of the latter term. 'You get up with just a guitar and they call you a folkie,' he had sneered at the Sin-é a few months previously before launching into a devastatingly comic extract from Motörhead's 'Ace of Spades'.) It was hoped he would conveniently hone one of these qualities into a single marketable niche.

Without making any great show of protest – he could be exquisitely passive-aggressive when needed – Jeff held his ground, and ultimately

Columbia acquiesced. Jeff would do it his way.

The 'Integrity, patience, hands off' mantra had prevailed.

The punch line was that at this point, as far as the 'Jeff Buckley Band' went, Jeff had no specific personnel in mind. What he did know was that he didn't want session musicians. 'Jeff hates the staleness of a session band,' future drummer Matt Johnson explained. 'He's seen a lot of that shit, those pretty singer-songwriters who go and hire the people recommended by the producer or the record people.'

Jeff's philosophy was the antithesis of such methods. He was certainly not prepared to settle for anyone who may prove transient or superficial. If his own musical heroes could find their bands in time, so could he. He would take the organic route. This may have been the nineties, and the final product may have been a digital CD rather than a double vinyl album, but the process remained the same. (Most studios still used analogue tape as their main recording medium.) Whatever the era, Jeff was still a musician and this was still music. That much was timeless, and Jeff reached beyond the trappings of fashion and trends – or so he hoped his as yet unknown and undiscovered band would prove.

Of course, Jeff knew a plethora of musicians from gigging so hard around NYC, but none seemed quite right for his aesthetic. Either that, or fate wasn't on their side. Andrew Goodsight, who had recently worked with Jeff, received a call that he would regret the consequences of for the rest of his life.

'Jeff called me on a Thursday and asked me if I was free to do a gig on Friday, the next day,' sighs Goodsight. 'I already had a gig that night. It was with a band I couldn't give a shit about, but they were counting on me. If I didn't do the gig there was a chance the whole band would miss a payday. I also got a lot of work from them over the year. I told Jeff that. I said I would hang this other band and do his gig if he wanted. I told him I didn't want to blow my chances of playing with him by not doing his gig. Jeff said, "No, no, don't worry. I'll do the gig solo." And that was the last time he asked me to play with him. To this day I feel like an ass for not doing that gig with Jeff. It kills me... man, it broke my heart to lose that gig.'

Once Jeff had decided on letting fate arrange the auditions, things started happening. Over the coming weeks, with strokes of voodoo luck, the players he and his album needed would seem to gravitate towards him. 'I was sending out a pheromone,' Jeff half-joked to a college radio station some months later. 'Rather than have anybody, *anybody* besides me pick my band for me, I decided to stall until I found the right people.'

By 'stall', Jeff meant that he was playing as much as ever. Still gigging guerrilla-style and utterly solo. He finally discovered – or was discovered by – his bass player when the lanky, rangy, Denmark-born Mick Grondahl happened to catch his completely acoustic (the venue had no amplification) set at Columbia University in 'a café made out of a crypt', as Jeff described it. Mick was blown away by 'the real thing' and, not having the slightest idea who Jeff was, introduced himself after the set. The two hit it off, and in the coming days the pair jammed together at the singer's apartment, played pool and chatted up women at local hostelries, and by common assent Mick was 'in'. Although at this stage, ignorant of Jeff's deal with Columbia, Mick had no real idea of what this meant. As for the bassist's style, Jeff loved that Mick was authentically both melodic *and* rhythmic – untypical dual qualities in most rock bassists. The chemistry felt right to all concerned from the off, and for someone as attuned and particular as Jeff, this was all he needed to know. It was not until a few jams down the line that the singer casually mentioned that he had a deal with Columbia and Sony. Mick took it in his stride, and the organic process continued.

To some at Sony, Jeff's meeting with Mick obviously looked like the freak streak of luck that it was. The priority was always the recording of an album, and the momentum of the Buckley buzz and the indie credibility that the EP would hopefully churn up had to be maintained, taken advantage of, exploited and eventually alchemised into money. Not just *some* money either: it had to be enough to recoup the sizeable advance afforded their investment and then some. Sony was in the business to make a profit. An LP was needed as soon as possible, and there were some executives deep in the bowels of Columbia who would not have been surprised if Jeff had wanted to make this much anticipated debut record as part of an avant-garde singer-bassist duo.

'He had started to play with Mickey,' remembered Berkowitz, 'and there was no band. There was him and Mickey and that *was* the band.' Indeed, the two did gig as a duo that summer, surely stirring murmurs in the hearts of those at Sony who had witnessed Jeff's recent Fluxus shenanigans. The thought of causing sleepless nights among the less hip staffers at his record label was something Jeff would have no doubt smiled at. Berkowitz never lost faith, but was nervy nevertheless: 'It started to be August... and it was still just the two of them. I was concerned a lot as to where he would find a drummer.' The true problem, as the more tuned-in Berkowitz and Stein realised, was that Jeff needed to find a drummer on the same wavelength as him (and Mick). Great session drummers wandered NYC in packs, but Jeff needed more than that – he needed a great drummer he had chemistry with, someone he and Mick could hang and connect with.

The missing cog in the rhythm section machine eventually slotted into place when drummer Matt Johnson was delivered via the recommendation of Jeff's sometime girlfriend, Rebecca Moore.

Matt was a Texan-born musician (he wrote songs as well as thumping tubs) who happened to share a star sign with Jeff. The arrival of the lean, blonde-haired, 22-year-old drummer into Jeff's life was so casual and effortless it appeared almost pre-ordained, further confirming the singer's instincts. Following a message left on Matt's answerphone by a 'raspy-voiced Jeff', an audition at the downtown Contact Studios was quickly arranged.

Johnson remembers the audition well. 'Jeff was a clean-cut non-smoker with short light brown hair. He still wore the cute little porkpie hat and denim jacket and he was hanging onto a Telecaster.'

Amazingly, although Matt was the first drummer they had auditioned, the chemistry was instant. The three just clicked, jamming and, in Jeff's memory, ultimately composing 'all night long', although the drummer maintains it was merely a couple of hours. Whatever the time span, Jeff Buckley had found his drummer.

'He [Matt] just hooked up,' grinned Mick. 'He knew what we were up to and he just... laid in.'

'Jeff had a lot on his mind,' points out Johnson. 'And so did I. The feeling of frustration and readiness to move on and up for me was so intense at that time in my life. I was aggressive and ready to try anything to fly. I was also unstable and flammable. Jeff must have picked up on that and probably felt the same. I remember he was searching my eyes, trying to piece a band together under pressure.'

As Jeff, Matt and Mick stomped and roared, sliding and soaring through a sea of sound in the small, grubby room, Jeff grinned his wolfish smile, knowing that his hunch had paid off. His rhythm section had been delivered to him in the space of a few months, although he saw it as a case of him having hunted them down. 'I came in like a whirlwind,' Jeff smiled, 'and ruined their lives. For the better.'

That very first night, Buckley, Grondahl and Johnson's jamming session birthed the music to 'Dream Brother'. The atmosphere was relaxed. 'We just got stoned together,' mumbled Jeff, 'and went to play...'

At the audition's end, the vocalist was happy to have found his band, and just as happy that it was his heart and not the classified ads or a 'fixer' from Sony that had led him to them. Still, he had only just made it. 'Jeff was a procrastinator,' says Johnson, 'who had run out of time. So in a way my audition was a midnight trip to the hardware store. Jeff had to grab what he needed quickly, and couldn't forget any essentials because it was closing – and I resonated with this urgency and singularity of purpose.'

'I went solo in order to get someone like Mickey to come around,' Jeff told MTV in 1995, going on to pay his bandmates a massive compliment. 'I found Matt... And when I met Mickey... it's basically the first really good group I've been in. Ever.'

Ever-aesthetic, Jeff was also beguiled by the drummer's appearance. 'He's very handsome,' he grinned, echoing Miles Davis's maxim that the first thing he looked for in a musician was, 'How he looks – how he dresses.' (Jeff continued to share a lingering love of and fascination with the trumpet player with his late father. 'There was a time when I wanted to be Miles Davis,' he cheerfully admitted.) The visual reference was telling. Where in Gods and Monsters, Jeff had looked like a prince among plumbers (or, indeed, a god among monsters), next to Mickey and Matt he looked like part of a righteous, cool gang. Together, the trio looked like a band.

The studio eventually chosen by Jeff ('suggested by my A&R guy [Berkowitz], who used to work for the Cars') and approved by Wallace (who helped them get a discount due to his longstanding professional relationship with the establishment) was the legendary Bearsville complex in Woodstock, New York. This was a major venue for the conception and recording of Jeff's debut, and was an apt choice on Sony's part for their million-dollar signing. Founded in 1969 by one-time Bob Dylan manager Albert Grossman, the studio offered state-of-the-art recording standards in a rustic setting a short commute from New York. All in all, it was a perfectly located, dream environment that didn't come cheap. As such, most of its clientele – the Rolling Stones, the Band and Dylan himself – were in the 'big league', and this boded well for Jeff, Mick and Matt when they were given a start date of 20 September 1993.

In direct contrast to undertaking recording at such an auspicious location, intensive rehearsals in a cheap and nasty downtown NYC studio were immediately embarked upon. The band were new, young and psyched and would only have been stoked into further intensity by the knowledge that they were soon to be recording for Sony, with a top producer, at a historic recording studio.

As such, during his regular visits to the band, Wallace was often a mite perplexed to find them hyped-up and sounding more like a rock-fusion group, jamming and improvising twenty-minute freak outs. The gentle-looking, grey-haired, bespectacled Wallace was concerned, but obviously had enough faith in Jeff and his own producer's abilities not to worry unnecessarily, and no further 'panic' meetings were held between George Stein and the record label.

Jeff finally, consummately had his band and everyone was thrilled. And nervous. And excited. 'It was very shocking... to go from meeting someone,' exclaimed Matt, 'and to be recording with them three weeks later. It was really scary.'

That fall, as he stomped up the tree-lined gravel road to Bearsville in his army boots, a trademark cup of coffee in hand, keys jangling, Jeff was aware of the history of the place he was walking into and, like the true pop music fan he was, relished it. '[The sense of history] was like ghosts coming down at you,' he sighed. 'Like bees to honey. It was great. It was perfect.'

Like Berkowitz and Stein, Wallace was concerned about how Jeff should come across on the record – how his talent should best be captured, which cell of the prism should be held up to the light.

The approaching Sin-é EP was the most obvious recorded reference point. But Jeff had exploded that particular blueprint by surrounding himself with a band. Wallace understood that Jeff, between stations as it were, needed to get to the next point, and that included recording him as part of a group and not with a *backing* group.

True to the sensitive natures which influenced their playing and which so endeared them to Jeff, the new band were also initially reticent about 'getting in the way' of Jeff's strengths and 'fixing something that ain't broke'.

Jeff had no such reservations himself. 'There ain't nothing like a great band,' he stated simply. 'I really can't stand being on my own all the time.'

The trio, as fresh as they were, were far from being a 'great band' in any way other than potentially. Wallace knew this and, like the professional he was, the producer turned a possible crisis into an opportunity, figuring that the rawness of the inexperienced group was an advantage, giving them all a 'clean slate' to work with, one where 'anything went'.

With this open, progressive attitude in evidence, one of the first things the group did upon arrival at the studio that September was to have the place rearranged to suit their own particular dynamics.

The studio was quite literally a complex, harbouring numerous rooms, zones, atmospheres and spaces beneath its high ceilings. Five weeks had been booked at a cost of approximately $70,000. This was for basic studio hire and would not have included Wallace's fee, the musicians' fees (only Jeff had signed to Sony), daily expenses, additional instrument hire, cost of tape etc. The plan was to record solid backing tracks at Bearsville. The laying down of drums and bass would be something akin to laying down the foundations of a building. These basic frameworks could then be turned into complete songs via overdubs at a later date within some other, less prestigious (and less costly) studio.

At Bearsville the studio staff set up three distinct recording environments. There were two sound stages for the band. One (Studio A – pine floors, concrete walls and high ceilings) was miked-up to capture the boys more or less as a power trio – the kind of noisy, gnarly, sinewy group that Wallace had been surprised to first hear at the downtown rehearsal space. The second space (Studio B) was for softer, more subtly dynamic ensemble playing, allowing the band a jazzier vocabulary. (As a reference, Jeff almost certainly had in mind the sound of Van Morrison's beloved *Astral Weeks* album). The third area (Studio C) was for Jeff alone and was basically a scale (actually bigger) reproduction of Sin-é, although presumably he wouldn't be passing around the tip jar to any studio employees that came to listen.

Such a seemingly elaborate set-up was not merely a theatrical indulgence or wishful thinking. The rainbow of Jeff's expression encompassed all of these styles and sounds. Wallace was merely setting up three subtly different traps to capture three subtly different animals. And 'capture' was a key word. The idea was not to painstakingly record metronomic, pristine and antiseptic layers of sound one on top of the other, but to ensure the band's energy, a feel and a vibe upon which to build. Such recording would of course be perfectly in time – more or less – and would eventually be spiced and sweetened by string and percussion overdubs, but for now, Berkowitz, Wallace and the band wanted to start by setting up a recording space that was always 'on' – an environment that was in perpetual record mode. No one wanted the common studio interruptions – the creatively sabotaging chores of re-miking instruments to suit particular songs, of pulling out boxes of guitar and microphone leads and unpacking FX racks – all cumbersome activities bound to get in the way of the recording of a potentially classic debut album.

Once suitably acclimatised to the somewhat imposing, semi-rural environment, the trio set up in Studio A and let rip in a series of frantic, spunky jams, losing their major label studio virginity in the sonic equivalent of some reckless, tousle-haired fucking. Wallace dutifully recorded every nuance, sigh and howl of this aural sex, but was nevertheless slightly disconcerted. 'They were jamming more than anything else,' he reflected. Concerned, he asked the band, 'Is this song really supposed to be fifteen minutes long?'

Jeff boyishly replied, 'Well… it *could* be, right?'

The trio were working in a legendary studio that had been used by some of the biggest names in rock history, recording for Sony and being produced by the man that had just worked with the globally exploding Nirvana on their *Nevermind* album. It was natural they would want to let off a little steam by say, jamming quarter-of-an-hour-length versions of Big Star's 'Kangaroo'. They were also still relatively new to each other – socially and musically. Although one of the advantages of Bearsville's pastoral setting was that there was little in the way of a city's night-life distractions ('I'm an easily, easily distracted person,' Jeff would confess), by jamming so intensely the three young men were making up for this social shortfall. The fact that only Jeff was actually signed to the label seemed to be forgotten in the pursuit of pure music-making. They were coming together, as Mick would happily confirm: 'I never really felt like, "Oh I'm a sideman," or that I wasn't part of the process… artistically or professionally or whatever. It was just like, "Yeah! We're a band," you know? And it just felt great.'

Johnson concurs. '*Grace* was a great time, although for me it was a very challenging process. But the environment was reassuring and inspiring. The separation from daily domestic mundane environs in favour of an awe-inspiring environment and the quality live rooms in great studios can combine to facilitate something much greater than is possible elsewhere.'

As time passed and the routine became more relaxed and natural, Jeff took to warming up alone in Studio C before a day's recording began proper. There in the dimly lit facsimile of Sin-é, he would run through varying versions of Hank Williams's 'Lost Highway', Nina Simone's 'The Other Woman', and the now ever-present cover of Leonard Cohen's 'Hallelujah'. Sometimes Mick and Matt would rise up and melt-in beside their singer, lending sympathetic and subtle accompaniments. All the while, Wallace kept the tape running, unknowingly feeding an archive that would see posthumous release in the decades to come.

By the end of the first fortnight, between Jeff's morning warm-ups in Studio C, the heavy jamming sessions in Studio A, and the late-night busking sessions in Studio B, the group had found some sort of equilibrium. Recording of the as yet unnamed album had properly begun. As well as laying down the basic skeletons of 'Dream Brother', 'Eternal Life' and 'Lover, You Should've Come Over', two of the songs spawned by Gods and Monsters made the sessions – 'Grace' and 'Mojo Pin'.

Since Jeff's departure the jinxed group had hobbled on with little success, and Gary Lucas was no doubt ecstatic to hear that the hope and faith he had placed in Jeff hadn't been completely unfounded. (The

Jeff Buckley and the Three Ms (from left): Matt Johnson, Mick Grondahl and Michael Tighe.

publishing royalties from these two co-writes would provide Lucas with more future income than all his other works combined.) He was further enraptured when he got the royal pardon via a call from Jeff to come to the studio and lay down some of his trademark atmospheric guitar squalls over 'Grace' and 'Mojo Pin', although it must have stung him to know that he was there in a cameo role and not as Jeff's partner.

As September faded into fall, definite progress was being made at Bearsville. Wallace had been under obligation to send Columbia a weekly DAT containing the previous week's work in progress. Mike Webb had newly started a job at Columbia and been a fan of Jeff's music since the latter days of Sin-é. He spoke for the majority at the label when, on hearing the initial tapes, he announced plainly that, 'It's obvious that this is going to be an amazing debut album… a masterpiece was being created right under my nose.' Rhythm tracks and guide vocals were satisfactorily put to tape in a vibe-drenched, energised atmosphere. However, it wasn't quite the kind of fluid, magical, shamanistic *Astral Weeks* experience that Jeff had perhaps secretly wished for. Wallace would eventually describe working on the album as 'phenomenally satisfying', but did not whitewash the singer in his evaluation. 'Jeff could be very hard. Not that he was an aggravating person... but he could be very scattered at times and difficult to reel in. Anytime you're working with an artist like that you're going to have frustrating moments.'

The self-effacing Jeff agreed. 'He [Wallace] brought focus,' he admitted a few years later. 'Like where sometimes Matty couldn't get a direction from me because I was in a mood, he would go to Andy. He was very receptive to a lot of things. His input kept me grounded.'

Jeff's mind and energies flitted butterfly-like, settling day by day upon whichever particular passion his mood prescribed. There was a heavy pull on those around him to concur with the often disparate directions in which Jeff was moving, because at the end of the day, he alone was signed to Sony and he alone would be accountable for the debts being incurred – in effect Jeff was paying for everything. Despite the guidance of a sometimes erratic compass, the journey was obviously more than worth it. 'Working with Jeff was extremely satisfying,' concluded Wallace. 'You felt you were working with a uniquely gifted artist... it was gratifying to be able to capture that and be part of the inspiration of making it happen.'

The environment and even the era itself continued to be a source of that inspiration. 'The fall breeze was cool,' remembers Johnson fondly. 'And, of course, you have to remember that this was pre-internet, so no one was tapping around on their laptop. There were no iPods. No Pro Tools. No war. No 9/11. Just tape machine, a great producer, a great talent, and a couple of lucky kids. Things felt hopeful. It felt worthwhile to make music... we had a budget and got to make music. That's all we cared about. So we just got completely lost in making that thing for that short time. We were focused. No digital distractions. No drugs, minimal alcohol, no partying. Just music, the occasional coffee break, walks in the forest to digest the emotions and find perspective, Jeff writing his lyrics and notes in the shack behind the house...'

Despite this occasional idyll there was some discussion amongst the band at this point as to what exactly it was they were creating. 'He [Jeff] didn't have enough songs, I think, to make a twelve-song "Jeff Buckley" record,' recalled Matt. The result was evolving as a mash-up of material that drew from Jeff's Sin-é era cover versions, the Gods and Monsters off-cuts, and the songs crudely birthed via the band's heavy jamming sessions. The running order of the still-unnamed album was turning out to be an eclectic mix of songs written by artists including Benjamin Britten, Leonard Cohen, and Jeff and the band themselves. While sounding occasionally powerful and moving, there was always the slight worry that almost *anything* Jeff put his voice to would sound impressive. This only made the issue of quality control even more difficult, not helped by Jeff's need to constantly rewrite and rearrange as the tapes rolled. As a recording artist, Jeff was proving to be fascinatingly eclectic. His debut release (by now scheduled for the forthcoming November) was a live EP half made up of cover versions, and his debut album was shaping up to appear more like the kind of rag-and-bone compilation of covers and oddities that usually comes out long after an artist has ceased to become a creative concern. But there was no doubt, particularly to the tried and tested ear of Wallace, that something special was at work. For now, Berkowitz and company considered the job enough done.

True to W. H. Auden's maxim that 'A poem is never finished, only abandoned,' Sony pulled the plug on the sessions (at one week over their initially allotted five-week stint) on 30 October 1993. Nobody involved considered the album completed at this point, but it was felt that enough groundwork had been laid for everyone to take a breather and reflect on what had been achieved so far.

Back in New York, Jeff and the band decompressed for a few days, surrendering themselves to the pleasurable distractions of the city like sailors on shore leave. The holiday did not last long – by early November Sony, Stein and Berkowitz called Jeff into the Sony offices, where the newly mixed tapes of the August Sin-é sessions were proffered for Jeff's approval.

Only a few years ago Jeff had done much the same thing at Ensign's offices, listening to the ghost of his long-dead father soar and sigh on the *Dream Letter* tapes.

Now it was his turn. After the fresh, full-on sonic assaults of the recent album sessions in Woodstock, the experience of listening to himself so naked must have been disconcerting, and although the sessions were recorded just that summer, Jeff undoubtedly felt like he'd come a long way since those sultry Sin-é days. The mixing of the four EP tracks hadn't taken long. There were only three basic sound sources (Jeff, his guitar and the audience ambience), but there had been a wealth of material to choose from. Eventually four songs were chosen, splitting the material equally between Jeff's originals and covers. Although the tracklisting hinted at the breadth of Jeff's taste – including as it did an Edith Piaf song ('Je N'en Connais Pas la Fin'), and a re-imagining of Van Morrison's 'The Way Young Lovers Do' – the two originals, 'Mojo Pin' and 'Eternal Life', sounded more like works in progress than statements of intent. The EP was just that – a record of Jeff's 'woodshedding' days, a time capsule documenting a period which would from now on only ever be revisited in a live context.

Released on Sony/Columbia and its relevant licencees throughout the world in December 1993 (it was later put out on the Big Cat indie label in the UK), the EP, while not a commercially gainful prospect, was critically well-received and almost all who sought it out were instantly smitten. Yet, true to form, its creator was vocal about having already left his debut release behind.

'At first I didn't even want to record it,' he explained, no doubt causing random sighs among the suits at Sony. 'It was just a way station to something I was getting to. I wanted to go through training... it isn't indicative of what's to come. It's a love note to Sin-é, really.'

Despite having little enthusiasm for the EP, Jeff was of course expected to tour to promote it. Yet there were some who argued that the priority now was to complete the album. A compromise was made, with Jeff eventually heading out on a one-man tour from 12 January 1994, which would be punctuated by sporadic visits to the studio back in NYC and LA.

'As soon as the EP came out I was dying to be with a band,' said Jeff hungrily. 'Bass, drums, dulcimer... tuba! Anything!'

For the next two months he moved between major North American cities with just a tour manager-cum-driver, Reggie Griffith, and the occasional presence of Dave Lory, an industry veteran who had joined George Stein as a partner, finally providing Buckley with the official manager he'd evaded for so long. Jeff packed his notebooks, guitar, amp and boom-box, and hit the road to look for America.

While Andy Wallace continued to overdub, cut, paste, edit and mix in the studio, Jeff had an obligation to get out and take the word to the people. He was no longer merely duty-bound by his muse to play, but under the terms of his contract with Columbia professionally obliged to do so.

This meant that he would have to adapt to a less linear way of life. To the casual observer, Jeff's current situation might have seemed fairly nonsensical. Yet the sometimes confounding and illogical itinerary he found himself committed to was a typical scenario for a recording artist of his generation.

At this point Jeff was three-quarters through the completion of *Grace*, which featured not only his new band, but a gaggle of session musicians and guest players via numerous overdubs. At times, the album sounded massive and symphonic. Yet now, in the midst of a hard and bright

American winter, Jeff was called upon to promote a painfully intimate-sounding EP of four songs recorded completely solo in the broiling heat of the summer just passed. In addition to such a disorientating flux of affairs, having finally found a rocking rhythm section with whom to hang and make noise, Jeff had to go out and play cross-country, accompanying himself with a guitar.

Outside of his beloved New York (the 36-date tour began in earnest on 15 January at the Railway Club in Vancouver) Jeff was still relatively unknown, and the cosy, intimate venues he moved between throughout San Francisco, Washington, Berkeley, Los Angeles, Dallas and Michigan reflected this. Reviews for the EP had been mostly positive, but other than exposure on college radio, airplay was far from ubiquitous. Beyond the borders of NYC, Jeff remained much less famous than even his father. The venues were small enough so that it wouldn't take many bodies (as little as 50 in some cases) to fill the spaces he was playing. As such, there was little sense of disappointment or underachievement at the shows. Quite the opposite.

Free of the cosy confines of Sin-é – and by extension New York – Jeff, his music and his reputation were beginning to rise amidst the endless fields of cafés and bookstores. However intimate the shows were, Jeff could never be underwhelmed by such an experience, and indeed usually sounded confident, even carefree onstage. As in Sin-é he repeatedly flaunted his great comic timing with witty stage banter. 'Being in New York is like being in a big apartment and everyone is your roommate,' he joshed in Toronto, 'everyone just ignores you until they need something.' Jeff simply loved performing, and anyone who happened to walk in on one of these low-key shows was usually instantly enraptured. They arrived as casual passing punters, and often went away as lifelong fans.

'Dave Lory was involved with the Allman Brothers Band for sometime before we worked with him,' states Matt Johnson of Jeff's manager. 'And he seemed well-acquainted with some of the seedy and decadent aspects of those antiquated dinosaurs of the music industry. In this sense, he sometimes seemed as if he'd come from a generation that represented all that was but could never be again. Still, he never did wrong by me, although it was frightening when his lung collapsed and he got up and just kept on smoking. He's a tough person and will probably outlive me.'

Lory accompanied Jeff and Reggie for those initial dates, sometimes acting as a relief driver. He and Jeff slowly got to know each other over the miles of endless highway. 'Just him and me pulling into bad truck stops and buying bad cassettes and talking about music,' Lory remembered. 'The first couple of nights in Vancouver were kinda rough.

He could do anything he wanted in New York at that point, but now we were getting into the general public who didn't know who he was, but this was how he wanted to learn his craft.'

The cross-country mission continued as both an inner and outer journey for Jeff, recalling the endlessly changing homes and bedrooms of his youth. For how many hours back then had he dreamed of taking his music into the world in this way? He was also well-versed in the American mythology of the wandering minstrel, with its tradition perpetuated by such luminaries as Hank Williams, George Jones and Willie Nelson. In addition to these obvious musical references, there existed in Jeff a strong taint and stain from the Beat Generation. This bohemian literary presence swam in his blood, enforced by his love of Burroughs, Kerouac and Ginsberg, so that despite the exhaustion brought on by the inexorable rhythm of the van's windscreen wipers and the grinding monotony of diner after diner after truck stop after diner, some essential part of Jeff still relished every mile.

Travelling with such a skeleton crew and usually carrying both his own amp and guitar, the presence of a monolith like Sony in any capacity throughout Jeff's journey was discreet to say the least, and this meant that – especially to the discriminating 'alt music' fan – he appeared much cooler than he would have had he turned up coked off his face in a groupie-laden limo.

Not that Jeff particularly minded travelling in such a down-home fashion, or playing chic and petite rooms such as Seattle's Velvet Elvis Theatre, Portland's La Luna, and Austin's Cactus Café. As both an audience member and performer, he preferred and felt empowered by small scale places. Night after night of performing deepened rather than diminished his passion for music, as well as enlarging his understanding of it. 'Music isn't really... mine,' he told one journalist in a Syracuse diner that February. 'Just like the air isn't mine. I don't own it, it's free.'

Asked what this particular tour had taught him, his reply was more philosophical than musical. 'People are basically good, but they're easily... distracted,' he opined.

The setlist was by now a flawless mutant mixture of songs from the Sin-é period and those written and recorded for the album, then still a work in progress.

Anyone ignorant of Jeff, as most were, would wander into a gig to find a diminutive pretty boy with a huge voice singing everything from Nina Simone to the Smiths via Leonard Cohen, his own songs poised and perched somewhere in between. Although it was just one man and a guitar, the performances were by no means polite or folkie. Occasionally it sounded like there was a squadron of Jeffs up there, a regiment on the brink of bursting and shattering the corporeal form of the lone singer and his orchestral-sounding guitar. 'Grace' in particular often took on a profoundly symphonic shape, and to hear Jeff joking and riffing with the audience on such diverse subjects as Ian Gillan, John Cage and PJ Harvey immediately after these sonic excursions only added to the sense that weird magic was afoot in the most ordinary of surroundings.

For those who would come to adore in particular Jeff's singing, the *Live at Sin-é* tour was hog heaven. Unobstructed by the noise of a band and unreliant on the variables of PA sound systems, his voice soared and roared in all its natural colours.

Technically, Jeff was a light lyric tenor. His *tessitura* – the range that came most naturally to him, most comfortably – was between E below middle C. Although obviously different stylistically, this was a range he shared with Pavarotti. Yet having a great voice and knowing how to sing is not the same thing. Jeff, however, knew how to use his gift and had been learning to improve it via breath control and phrasing throughout his life.

The proof of this is that no matter how many consecutive shows Jeff played – and there were many – his voice rarely degenerated and never gave out completely. He was a rare breed.

Despite the incredibly intense itinerary (Jeff would often have to do interviews with local press – both paper and radio – before and after the gigs, as well as fitting in the soundcheck and occasional Sony-sponsored meet-and-greets at local record stores) he ate it all up. The fixed smiles, the dead handshakes, the flirtatious girls, the endless coffee, the miles of desert, the stale club sandwiches, the motel nights, the scribbled setlists, the perpetual tuning of his Fender, the brief, lonesome soundchecks and the sparse but appreciative and affirming applause. 'I'm seeing things that I would never see,' he said. 'Like, just driving across the Midwest I'm seeing how America's blood pumps. People's farms and the huge, mountainous piles of sawdust next to paper mills steaming against a grey sky with the people standing next to it. It makes you realise that the whole scope of this music business is very small.'

With every other fourth day off on average, Jeff had little time to do anything other than surrender himself to the experience. The tour frequently entailed extra-curricular activities that were, thankfully, musical. Occasionally Jeff would be called into a Sony-endorsed studio (as in LA) to check in on and contribute to the ongoing process of making the album, and on one occasion in Philadelphia he was presented with various mock-ups for the artwork of the forthcoming LP. (Jeff insisted on the rather ironically glam Merri Cyr photo that was eventually used, despite grumbles from Berkowitz and Columbia.) The whole trip for Jeff was just that – a journey traversing both the roads of his personal mythology and those of urban and rural America. The Kerouac-loving kid in him was on the road in every sense, eating up days made from a blur of snow, dust, pay TV, coffee, car radio and endless motel music. 'Knowing that music is going to come puts me at ease on stage. Being on the road, every show I do is new and will be new until the day I die.'

After a final show in Athens, Georgia on 5 March, a wiped-out Jeff and Reggie made their way back to the Big Apple. Letting himself and his ever-present guitar case into his bachelor apartment, Jeff barely had time to go through the messages on his answerphone, read his mail and catch up on sleep before he was called in for further meetings with Stein and Berkowitz prior to attending yet further album mix sessions.

By now Wallace had moved on to other projects, leaving the LP more or less ready for mastering. But although scheduled for another one-man promotional tour of Europe that month ('My fantasy of Europe is very, very romantic,' said Jeff, "cause it's the old country'), Sony were eager for Jeff and the band to record further material for B-sides with engineer and producer Clif Norrell.

In addition to this, although the next round of gigging was yet again put on the slight shoulders of Jeff alone, the long-term plan was to have a full band tour around the release of the album.

Back in NYC, work had begun in earnest on the basic tracks recorded at Bearsville. No residential studios would be used this time. The plan now was to use a recurring hit-and-run approach, where overdubs utilising both the band and session musicians would be added quickly, allowing Jeff and Wallace to step back and evaluate the song before working on the track again and again. This was not a relaxed situation. Not only had Jeff not yet completed his vocals, in some cases he hadn't even finalised the melody and lyrics. The fledgling songwriter was disarmingly candid about his weaknesses. 'I don't know how to do lyrics yet,' he confessed that February. As a mid-March European tour loomed, Matt and Mick sat waiting for the phone to ring and the album's release date was bumped back to summer. Tensions grew.

The album still lacked cohesion, in part due to the wildly catholic tastes of its author, which were voluptuously reflected throughout the material. Jeff, Matt and Mick were by their own admission aiming for something akin to a hybrid of 'Billie Holiday, Led Zep, Bad Brains and the Smiths.'

'Dream Brother' was one of the rockiest tracks recorded so far, and with its last-minute lyric and evocative vocal it clearly referenced one of the singer's earliest loves. A blood sample at this point would surely have revealed that Led Zeppelin was part of Jeff's DNA. 'I have been a fan since I was five... the sound of Led Zep had more "anarchy" to my ears. Those earliest influences remain very determining.'

His voice on this track blew away everyone privileged enough to hear the initial mix. 'I like to think of the voice as an instrument in itself,' said Jeff. 'Not enough people experiment with it or use it to its full capacity. I like to explore it.'

At the other end of the sonic spectrum was the haunting, hymn-like Cohen song. Rather than affirm its religious qualities, the singer saw 'Hallelujah' as an 'homage to the orgasm'. Jeff sang it purely for the sake of the song itself, not solely out of admiration for its writer, although he certainly was a Cohen fan. (The song originally appeared on the sketchily-produced *Various Positions* album, where it sounds more akin to a work in progress.) Jeff had first heard 'Hallelujah' via John Cale's version, as featured on the French Cohen tribute album *I'm Your Fan*, released in 1992. 'That's my favourite [version],' Jeff would reminisce. 'I just heard it one night before a gig at Sin-é and someone suggested it should be on the album.'

Most would be hard pressed to fit in yet another track that bore little stylistic similarity to any of the other intensely eclectic selections, but Jeff managed it with his interpretation of 'Corpus Christi Carol', a song from his late childhood. He plainly saw Britten's piece – which he had been introduced to as a teenager by his friend Roy, whom he now dedicated it to – as being a fairytale about a 'falcon who takes the beloved of the singer to an orchard. The singer goes looking for her and arrives at a chamber where his beloved lays next to a bleeding knight and a tomb with Christ's body in it.'

Deciding to interpret a piece part-authored by Benjamin Britten (considered by some to be the UK's last great modern classical composer) once again served to demonstrate Jeff's untamed and pure taste in music. 'I love it,' he stated simply. 'I love so much music from other countries that finds its way to my country.'

'Eternal Life' was approaching its finished state, although its title was a quixotic choice, with the song's intent being much more political than it may have suggested. 'What I want to say with a song like "Eternal Life" is: if you're one of those people who thinks he has to spend energy in putting people down and discriminating against others or passing on racist ideas... why waste your time with all that bullshit? Try to see people as people and don't fixate on the colour of their skin, status or sexual preference…'

These four songs alone were coming close to achieving the rare hybrid of the Smiths and Bad Brains that the band had in mind. Yet the recipe for this bedazzling aural cocktail was not yet quite complete. The final gunslinger to join was, however, already in Jeff's orbit. Guitarist Michael Tighe had been on the periphery of Jeff's life since his initial trip to New York in 1990. 'I'd always known Michael throughout that whole time,' said Jeff, 'daydreaming of having Michael in the band.'

An actor by vocation, Tighe had surreally discovered his inherent affinity with the guitar by accident when a character in a play in which he was performing was called upon to use one. He immediately started playing blues licks. Jeff loved this naturally warped approach.

'He'd never been in a band before, and hadn't even been in a garage band, or *anything*,' raved Jeff, clearly delighted by the perversity of such a situation. 'He'd just gotten together with directors in plays. So he had a very, very different idea about music, very different. Usually people come into a band and they're very musically ambitious in a way that they'll be visibly seen doing their musical thing, or that they'll be "We're just gonna get there and rock" or "We're gonna get up there and blah blah blah," which ain't bad, it's just there's so much more to it…'

Although Tighe was an obvious candidate, Jeff still played the game to an extent, auditioning handfuls of other guitar players before selecting him. Predictably, most were typical professional session guitarist types, coming into the rehearsal rooms with gleaming racks of FX pedals and shiny new axes – exactly the kind of characters Jeff had escaped when he left the Los Angeles Music Institute. Tighe, by contrast, had a busted-up guitar and a lead so short that the only way he could plug it into the amp was by sitting astride it. Although they were already firm friends, Jeff re-bonded with the misfit musician in Tighe and the nameless 'Jeff Buckley Band' had its fourth and, for now, final member.

'I couldn't have been more fortunate in my taste,' Jeff said smartly.

Tighe brought more than an attractively eccentric presence to the group. Within a couple of hours of jamming, he and Jeff had composed 'So Real' together (a song that in Jeff's words combined both 'fuck you' and 'I love you' in one sonically abrasive sentiment). It was hastily recorded by last-minute engineer Clif Norrell and the band in NYC, for inclusion on the album that had by this time found its title: *Grace*. The spooky intro, consisting of Tighe's hesitantly played diminished chords, had instantly bewitched Jeff. 'I like chords that have parts of two chords,' he said of the song's eerie opening. 'I like the guitar's mysterious quality best.'

Clif himself was similarly blown away by the last-minute addition. 'It sounded different,' explains the engineer. 'It was written several months after the rest of the songs in a different location, so the band was in a completely different headspace.' Penned at the end of an extended tour, the track was eerie sonic worlds away from any of the band's previous studio efforts. But in the end, this mattered to no one. Clif confirms that, 'Once everyone heard "So Real" and how it came out, they decided that it really needed to go on the album.' The next step seemed natural enough.

After some discussion between Stein, Jeff and Berkowitz, with Jeff playing at his passive-aggressive best, 'So Real' ended up replacing 'Forget Her' on the album. In addition to having a total crush on 'So Real', Jeff's feelings toward the ousted track were ambiguous in the extreme. 'That song ["Forget Her"] came to him at a time when he was breaking up from a very important relationship [with Rebecca Moore],' confirmed Mary Guibert. 'He ended up not wanting to sing it every night of his life. I think he thought it would be a song that he would grow to hate.'

As the record neared completion, it became obvious that Jeff Buckley was now more a band than a solo singer. Yet putting a name to this group still seemed to provide a minor dilemma. He was not without ego and had proved himself *to* himself during his café-playing period. Having signed him up as a solo artist, and by having his name alone already successfully PR'd wherever the EP was released, Sony wouldn't have wanted him to disappear into a band either. Yet it perhaps seemed corny to bill the signing as 'Jeff Buckley and the...' For now, in interviews and socially, Jeff referred to his rhythm section and guitarist affectionately as 'the Three Ms.'

With the album sessions finally deemed complete and the band stoked – '*Grace* was made in the best possible conditions,' reckons Johnson – Jeff left final mixing duties to Wallace and his band in New York while he set off on a solo tour of Europe.

Grace (meaning: elegance, refinement, loveliness, beauty, polish, style and charm amongst other things) was, to all intents and purposes, finished and Jeff was free – wrapped in a fake fur coat with his guitar in hand – to go forward again.

'The only goal is in the process... it's the only thing... it's the life in between,' Jeff reflected towards the end of this, his own personal era. When asked what it was that he hoped people would get from *Grace*, his reply was the only one that mattered. 'Whatever they want. Whatever you like.'

6. IN STATE

'A live experience with people making music for people that are in a place, in a club or in a room… that never really loses its rhythm or its life. We always make it new and sometimes we're forced into… hippy improvising… [Laughs] Sorry. But that's what I got!'

Jeff Buckley, 1995

Leaving Berkowitz to reprogramme the CD's tracklist for mastering, and the ever-patient Johnson, Grondahl and Tighe cooling their boots, Jeff flew into the UK 'with no expectations' for his first show on 11 March at the homely (the venue boasted a roaring fireplace as one of its attractions) Ratner's Bar in Sheffield. Jeff then headed to London for two days of jet-lagged promotion before returning to his ancestral roots, playing Dublin's tiny Whelan's Bar on 14 March. Dave Allen, the then venue manager, recalled fondly: 'I remember the groupies hanging around the dressing room. It was just him and one electric guitar the first time he came in. He filled the downstairs part [of the bar]. The groupies were a surprise. He wouldn't have been that well-known, and yet he definitely had a lot of female admirers.' The next day he was back in the big smoke and on a proper stage again. Journalist Caitlin Moran witnessed his central London debut when Jeff played at the scruffy Borderline venue just off of Soho. He soared and ebbed through most of the forthcoming *Grace*, hauling in the audience with a particularly transcendent 'Hallelujah'.

Moran, like many of the other usually impenetrable industry types in attendance, was instantly smitten. 'Suddenly this *boy* wanders onstage. The way he moves suggests street-level royalty. His hair was rumpled and appealing. How do you get hair styled like *that*? "By fucking wild-eyed on the floor," my friend explained.'

Jeff flew out to Glasgow's School of Art the next day for another typically intimate showcase attended by future singer-songwriter Fran Travis, who remembered: 'It was amazing. I thought his voice wasn't

'Music should be like making love,' said Jeff. 'Sometimes you want it soft and tender, other times you want it hard and aggressive.'

something of earth, it was fantastic. It was uplifting...' Having impregnated the seeds of future bands into a handful of Scottish teens (Jeff had a habit of inspiring audience members to form their own groups – ensembles such as Travis, Belle and Sebastian and Geneva would all cite Jeff gigs from this era as inspirational), he returned to London once more, hanging out in the capital for a further four days, plugging away in full interview mode before a live Greater London radio session, and playing a set upstairs at North London's Highbury Garage.

The small portion of London in the audience that night were enraptured, including tennis champion and amateur guitarist John McEnroe and Pretenders frontwoman and 24-carat Tim Buckley fan (she had even interviewed him as a teenage journalist) Chrissie Hynde. 'People my age flocked to see Jeff,' said Hynde, sounding the tiniest bit embarrassed in hindsight, 'because we wanted to hear that [his father's] voice again. All these toothless hags hanging around the stage door saying, "I knew your dad!" '

McEnroe – a perennial pop music fan who once, on finding that David Bowie was booked into the hotel room next to him, cajoled the bemused singer into personally teaching him the 'Rebel Rebel' riff – was stunned by Buckley to the point where he offered to lug Jeff's amp down the stairs and out into the waiting taxi after the show.

Jeff ploughed on, barely sleeping or eating as he rode the wave of a glorious London buzz through various radio sessions and after-gig celebrations at all-night drinking clubs.

The following day he was roused to put in two more live performances at the Rough Trade record shop in Neal's Yard during the afternoon, where recently departed Suede guitarist Bernard Butler remembered that he 'made sure I got in. I stood on the stairs six feet away from him at eye-level. He did "The Boy with the Thorn in His Side" and smiled all the way through...'

That evening there was another intimate show in a tiny, albeit mythical (Paul Simon and Bob Dylan had played there in the sixties) venue called Bunjie's, a short stroll from Rough Trade. Writer Mark Brend was one of few at the now-legendary Bunjie's show, and claims that some were there purely because of the inevitable nostalgic curiosity invoked by the Buckley name.

'There was about him the distinct aura of the man on the rise, but he was not yet a star in any mainstream, commercial sense,' remembers Brend. 'In those pre-internet days he was a connoisseur's choice, known to devout readers of music papers, and of interest to most of those mainly for the fact that he was Tim Buckley's son. This is where I – a keen Buckley

Senior fan – came in. I was there that spring night out of curiosity more than anything else. I hadn't yet heard any Buckley Junior music.'

Few in the audience had, the numbers being made up mostly by in-the-know journalists, staff from Sony and Big Cat, and the occasional old-school fan of Tim. Nevertheless, the tiny venue didn't require legions to swell it to haemorrhaging point.

'I don't know what the official capacity of Bunjie's was,' recalls Brend, 'but it must have been exceeded that night. I remember that the room was packed beyond comfort. I sat on one of the school benches towards the back, facing Jeff. The audience extended to his right and left, almost surrounding him. My recollection is that he picked his way through the crowd to the small space where he would play. I'm pretty certain there was no dressing room or backstage area. Nor was there a PA. He sang unamplified, for the most part backing himself on a blonde Telecaster plugged into a little amp. He started *a capella*, with what was probably "Corpus Christi Carol", though I can't be sure. I can't be sure about what else he played that night, as I wasn't then familiar with any of his songs, though I am almost certain that "Hallelujah" featured. What does stick in my mind is the shock I felt at how closely he resembled his father, both in appearance and as a singer. The hair, the bone-structure and the multi-octave voice. For me, by then a Tim Buckley devotee of some years standing, it was eerie and uncanny. Listening to the son's records later I realised that he was much more than a copy of his father, that he was his own man with his own artistic identity. But nonetheless, the dominant impression I went away with that night was of the similarity between father and son.'

It's hard to illuminate how untypical Jeff's impact was in London at the time. Although mostly limited to fellow industry types – PR officers, TV and radio pluggers, managers, journalists, DJs, and other celebrities and musicians – the audiences at Jeff's shows were truly moved. This is a rare phenomenon in a social and professional scene where every other audience member is non-paying (guest list) and has to ask his or her colleagues to tell them how they feel about the latest 'buzz' artiste.

That said, Jeff often seemed to slip into 'messianic' mode and some there that night did have reservations. 'There's no doubt that he was a charismatic, mesmerising performer, and that he delivered a compelling show, but for me there was one false note,' states Brend. 'With so many people packed so tightly underground, the room soon became unbearably hot, and Jeff made, for me, rather too much of a deal of asking for jugs of cold water to be bought in for everyone. I'm sure his concern was real, but I remember sensing even at the time that he was revelling in the adoration of his people a little too brazenly. I think he even said "the people need a drink", or something like that.'

Such a gig did not end – it merely paused while another venue was prepared. Once Bunjie's reluctantly began emptying its tills and mopping up, Jeff was forced to stop singing, albeit momentarily. 'Everyone spilled out into the night air to cool down,' continues Brend. 'After a while Jeff himself emerged, too, and I recall him going off into the night leading a crowd of people down the dark street. There was talk that he was going to put on another impromptu show somewhere else.'

This was indeed the case. Emma Banks, an assistant to Jeff's UK live agent, had hastily arranged for Jeff to continue at another tiny venue off Charing Cross called Andy's Forge. Jeff not only led the throng to the new venue through the rain (although he could influence the emotional climate of any audience, the weather outside, alas, remained beyond Jeff's control) but also waited for everyone to get safely in, even going as far as to hold the door open for any bedraggled stragglers.

Jeff did another 90-minute, looser set that lasted into early morning, until exhaustion and the joints passed up to him by audience members eventually brought him down. Finally satiated, Jeff collapsed into the back of a black cab, and was driven away through London's early morning rain.

Outside of the almost religious, womb-like environment of Jeff's gigs, the besotted Caitlin Moran was one of a score of journalists who got some one-on-one time with the exhausted but satisfied singer. 'So, what noises do you make when you come?' she asked him cheekily.

'*Whaaaaat?*' exclaimed Jeff, simultaneously shocked and amused. Moran explained that his 'baby scat singing' evoked for her and her friends the language of orgasm. 'It's very flattering that you think I *can* imitate the sound of orgasm. However, some of the pictures that have been taken of me onstage have brought back a couple of happy memories when I look at them. Y'know, head thrown back, jaw locked, sightless eyes…'

The sound of orgasm was subsequently heard in the exotic locales of Wolverhampton and Stevenage (where, ever-generous, he did two shows; one lunchtime set at a local pub and a later one at a youth club where he played third on the bill to some local punk groups). Jeff then more appropriately took his sonic *petite mort* to the actual sex capital of Europe, playing an engorged upstairs room at Amsterdam's smoky Paradiso Club.

The week after Jeff's victorious trip, *Live at Sin-é* was released in the UK via Big Cat records. The EP did not trouble shops for long, and on the back of positive reviews (although little radio airplay) it sold out its first pressing in its first week. ('Jeff Buckley – young and electric with the kind of fanny-moistening good looks only a Hollywood surgeon could chisel... a voice that sounds like a choirboy singing from the rafters of a whorehouse. Buy it and melt,' ran the then typically lurid prose in *Melody Maker*.) This was a worthy success for a pretty much unknown act debuting in an atypical format, even if most of those sales were London-based.

Jeff flew from Amsterdam into JFK airport on 22 March 1994. To say that the European promotional trip had been a success was a tetchy understatement. Short of healing the sick or turning Evian into Rioja, Jeff could not have 'gone over' any better.

Flushed with success and confidence (if the public loved him alone, the impending impact of the full band and album could be imagined with no small amount of excitement) Jeff, only partially rested, was sucked once more into a round of meetings and discussions at Columbia.

In his heart, he could have continued work on the album forever and, as it was, Columbia had been rarely indulgent of their utterly commercially unproven signing, but there came a time when tracklistings and mixes were final. Buoyed by his recent trip, Jeff let it go, and as the album moved a step further toward being pressed, the next preliminary round began.

Now they had a physical product, Columbia had to decide on the best way to sell it. The marketing plan for *Grace* and Jeff himself was long-term and richly detailed, its content and strategies drawn from the collective efforts of almost all who were involved with and had invested in the young musician. Stein, Lory and Jeff himself contributed to the minutiae of the brief, which was actually printed up as a multi-page booklet. (Jeff would deny knowledge of such a manifesto. 'I have no idea... I do not adhere to any plan. It's not like I have to turn out yoghurt.') Such a document did exist, however, and one particular angle was especially shrewd – some would say cynical. Columbia intended to market Jeff as an 'indie' act – in effect, as someone too cool for the actual major label that was funding and promoting him.

With the ripples caused by the *Live at Sin-é* EP finally ebbing into stillness, and with the album itself scheduled for a summer release, Columbia released *Peyote Radio Theatre*, a three-track promotional CD that was never sold, but circulated as a tool for radio play only. The tracklisting was typically untypical, featuring the straight-down-the-line classic 'Mojo Pin', an instrumental version of 'Dream Brother' and a rollicking version of Big Star's 'Kangaroo'. While this curio did the college radio rounds and was eagerly snapped up in second-hand shops by fledgling Jeff completists, the source of all this hullabaloo rested as well as he could, listening to new releases by Smashing Pumpkins and catching up on his reading. (*The Fairy Tales of Oscar Wilde, The Writings and Drawings of Bob Dylan, Hunter: The Strange and Savage Life of Hunter S. Thompson*, and *Keeping the Rabble in Line* by Noam Chomsky were all recent additions to the Buckley bookshelf.)

Meanwhile, one of Andy Wallace's former colleagues suddenly committed suicide. Kurt Cobain died on 5 April 1994. Jeff was, like much of the Western world, aware of Kurt and Nirvana's growing myth, and like any pop-rock fan loved and appreciated the hits, but the two had never met and his response was refreshingly pragmatic. 'I have no knowledge of his life or of "him",' he said. 'People who want to die will kill themselves, that's something I know for sure.' Jeff was more passionate in response to the comments made by ageing rocker and gun-freak Ted Nugent, who on hearing of Cobain's decision to take his own life, labelled the grunge star 'a pussy'. Jeff's response was visceral. 'Who's more of a pussy?' he raged. 'Someone who has the guts to end their own pain or someone who shoots a deer with a twelve gauge? Eat my dick, Ted!' More soberly, Jeff reflected that 'It's not within anybody's judgement to judge Kurt, alive or dead… hell, I can't even judge Ted Nugent.'

Life went on, with a major tour booked for the coming summer, employing the full weight of 'the Three Ms' – Mick, Matt and Mike. Roused by the frontline stories of Jeff's European and North American one-man shows, the group went about the last few months of their civilian lives repeatedly listening to their advance cassette copies of *Grace* and discussing possible setlists and choices of equipment – all ammunition for the forthcoming campaign. Although the Three Ms were on a Columbia-funded salary, a further advance may have been taken from the 'tour support' budget in order for the group to invest in new equipment. (All such monies would have to be repaid by Jeff from his future record sale earnings.) Jeff's main guitar of choice, which replaced his Sin-é era silver Fender, was the 1983 issue customised Blonde Fender Telecaster that he had borrowed seemingly indefinitely from his friend Janine Nichols. 'At some point I suggested to Jeff that he keep the guitar since he had gotten so attached to it and buy me a Gibson Robert Johnson model acoustic instead. He then bought a Gibson for himself and kept the Tele…' remembered a candid Nichols. 'If there were no Telecasters,' reckoned Jeff somewhat romantically, 'there would be no James Brown, no Elvis, no country and no Prince.'

Jeff put the Telecaster through a beige two-channel Mesa Boogie 2x12 Amp (as favoured by Gary Lucas). Other than an Alesis Quadraverb effects unit, he used few effects, relying instead on technique to supply a wide sonic palette of shades and colours. The guitar was always serviced prior to the tour. 'He was very particular about the [guitar's] action,' said Mary Guibert. 'The voice, he didn't care if it was pretty or exact. But the guitar had to be right on... he was all about precision.' A classic Rickenbacker twelve-string was provided for the occasional more acoustically inclined band member. Jeff's guitar of choice was a sunburst guild semi. Mick's was a classic Fender jazz bass guitar played through an Ampeg amp. Matt played Slingerland drums. Michael used more or less the same combo as Jeff. With the obvious exception of the drummer, all used custom-made 'Jeff Buckley' plectrums, something that the little Scotty Moorhead inside of Jeff would have inevitably got off on.

Summer came to the city again and at noon, 1 June 1994, Jeff and his group, augmented by their two tour managers Reggie Griffith and Gene Bowen, set off in their newly-hired bright red tour bus for Asbury Park. For three days they rehearsed at the Springsteen-sanctioned Stone Pony practice studios of New Jersey, where, rather than simply focus on reproducing *Grace* as accurately as possible, the group emphasised improvisation in rehearsal. In this respect they were preparing in the style of a jazz band rather than that of a rock group – an approach Tim Buckley would have approved of.

Their leader was amped-up and more than ready to go out into the wider world with his gang of gunslingers at his side, but was also aware of the potential problems in how the Three Ms may be perceived. After all, the tour went out under one name only. 'It'll be a great day when someone asks them about their musical journey and their opinions on things,' stated Jeff diplomatically. 'They're quite fascinating. Yeah, I've got a group of hot-blooded young men!'

His group were under no illusions. 'Jeff was the artist. He was signed. He had a stake in the project,' states Matt Johnson pragmatically. 'We were hired on salary, rarely on retainer, and the money was stupidly low. We were ass-poor and Jeff wasn't rolling in dough either. It was a bit hard to wait to go out on tour after we finished the record. But I was always chomping at the bit to play.'

The adventure – entitled the Peyote Radio Theatre Tour – began officially on Saturday 4 June at the Rochester, New York. The group were vibing and crackling but far from polished, and Stein and Lory got Berkowitz to agree that no Columbia staff or press would be invited to the first two weeks of the tour lest untactful criticism dent the fledgling band's confidence.

Despite the press embargo, with Jeff's blessing, friend and photographer Merri Cyr joined the group throughout Florida and Texas. She remembered that, far from feeling insecure, 'Jeff allowed me to photograph him in an uncensored way: while he was being interviewed, playing, at dinner, at rest – everything. He wanted people to see his authentic self as opposed to a rock icon. I photographed him when he was angry, tired, pissed off…' One recurring motif that was sure to irritate Jeff was the questions from the press about Tim. 'People think that my father and the EP is all there is to talk about,' he moaned, perhaps righteously.

Offstage, when not being drawn into Leonard Cohen-baiting by uptight Canadian journalists (having stated during an interview that he found pessimists 'immature', Jeff was then asked by the interviewer if he believed this to be true of self-confessed pessimist Cohen), Jeff tried his best to include the other members of the band in interviews and photo shoots, with predictably underwhelming results. Onstage was a more level playing field, where the group were rapidly finding both their feet and each other as musicians. But while fresh, they were far from completely musically unformed. And although it was no pyrotechnic blockbuster, some thought had gone into the tour beyond the music. The very line-up of the band on stage was unusual, with the musicians being in a row and Jeff ahead of and to the left of the drum kit.

The schedule was intense, ultimately involving 48 shows reaching from New York to Philadelphia, with every major city taken in between. Given his upbringing, such a roaming lifestyle came naturally to Jeff. At their meeting earlier that year journalist Caitlin Moran had observed, rightly, that 'he's had a restless, rootless upbringing and wants to feel part of something, a member of a gang. When he talks about his band he speaks of them in the way that would one a brother, a sister, a lover. He obviously enjoys the camaraderie and the closeness, the in-jokes and the we're-all-in-this-togetherness.'

Ticket prices for the shows were kept artificially low – five dollars to begin with – and as such, those early gigs sometimes sounded and looked more like public rehearsals, not that this wasn't beguiling in itself. But as the band themselves found, sparks eventually spluttered and spurted into life, and the group began to cook. Even though Merri was at the shows principally to work, to photograph and to document, she still occasionally found herself lapsing into the role of awed fan. 'He could give of himself completely when he was on stage,' she stated, going on to shrewdly point out the inherent personality flaw in such a talent. 'This was a position

'When he sang he was gorgeous,' said Wanda Phipps, a friend from Jeff's Sin-é days. 'It was like some channelling of the divine.'

wherein he felt very much in control. And I think that for him this was a very valid way of experiencing love. In a way that didn't threaten him in the same way that personal interaction with people did.'

By the time the group returned to New York's Fez Club for a three-night residency from 17 June 1994, Jeff Buckley and the Three Ms were, it was obvious to all, serious contenders.

The tiny venue was packed (guests included U2 guitarist the Edge and actress Winona Ryder) and the performance was an unmitigated success. Even the somewhat jaded Sony executives who were at last allowed to come and see Jeff were suitably impressed.

Dressed as he appeared on the cover of the forthcoming album, in his spangly gold old lady's jacket, Jeff was obviously confident and proud of his band. The bulk of their Fez set was typical; most of the songs from the forthcoming *Grace*, plus live favourite 'Kangaroo' and the occasional goof-off – as exemplified by Jeff's rendition of the theme tune from TV show *Land of the Giants*. Matt Johnson was so enraptured by the experience that in a way he became both band and audience member.

'The Fez for me was singular,' he remembers. 'It may sound strange or deluded, but I will assure you here, I felt for one second on that stage a very definite and potent electrical shock of synergy and inspiration, mixed with awe and fear, run through my whole body. I am not bullshitting. That kind of spiritual power is fucking awesome. You don't see it coming. Your attention is absorbed into the music, as the music winds along, so winds your mind. And before you know it, you see the design from above that each man's intuition and instincts have woven. A shock of recognition ensues. Implosion, explosion... whatever. You're looking at yourself in a truer light. And the stage just explodes with energy... people create this. JB knew this. When those moments hit, he was always right there, ready to catch that current and take everybody to the next fucking level.'

In the aftermath of this seemingly near-shamanistic experience the group and crew were out on the endless highway again, with show after show after show through Montreal, Detroit, Chicago, Saint Louis, San Francisco... If the Three Ms had been previously frustrated by Jeff's solo sojourns, they were sure as hell making up for it now. Even on the road, Columbia heckled for more new material. In Vancouver, the group, somehow finding time, manage to mangle out a new instrumental entitled, appropriately enough, 'Vancouver'. 'We played in Vancouver,' explained Jeff, 'and there was this incredible pressure to record a B-side. We were working on an idea of Michael's. But the song has no definitive form, we change it every night. I don't really have much time for writing while touring... only little pieces of melody, riffs, texts, when I can get enough time alone. But I find travel inspiring.'

Along the journey, friends were made. Jeff and his band, unlike many other groups in similar positions, nearly always got on with their support acts, a fortunate dynamic born of shared understanding. 'We had good friendships with people. There was always a climate of respect,' states Johnson simply. 'I personally didn't get to be a musician by being a fucking judgemental entitled asshole who thinks he's great. I had to, and still have to work fucking *hard* to progress. So these bands were good and I wanted to check them out, enjoy and learn. JB, I think, respected musicians for their uniqueness. These bands had real creative individuals. So he dug them. And emulated them, in fact.'

Two bands in particular – the Grifters and the Dambuilders – would go on to share a special relationship with Jeff and his band. Of the former, bassist Tripp Lamkins clearly recalls the bands' first meeting.

'We ended up in Iowa City playing a place called Gabe's Oasis,' he remembers. 'When we got to the club we saw the posters for the show which showed the Jeff Buckley band headlining with us, and the Dambuilders in small print below. So at first I'd say our collective professional pride was bruised ever so slightly, and we all swaggered about somewhat. This *was* the first time we'd heard of Jeff, and at the time we thought we were hot-shit. We decided we would let the Jeff Buckley band find out just how hard it could be to follow a Grifters set. In the hours leading up to the show we all got friendly though. I recall Scott [Taylor – Grifters guitarist] and myself taking Jeff out to our van to smoke out. So peace was made before the show started really. Not that was ever any danger of anyone actually being standoffish. We were all kindred musical spirits, I suppose.'

Dave Derby, lead singer of the Dambuilders, would be similarly impressed when he finally got around to meeting the headliner. 'I had heard a lot about him, but actually missed his set for some reason. I think I was doing something stupid like eating dinner.'

Although immediately friendly toward Jeff, Tripp remained eager to compete musically. 'We *still* wanted to put our best foot forward and deliver as rocking a set as we could muster,' he says. 'Which we did. Back in the day, when we wanted to, we could pull off a pretty good rock show. Our shows were loud, chaotic, veering into moments of improv and always delivering hard, weird rock. I can't speak for anyone else really, but I was feeling pretty self-assured. Then Jeff started. Just him. He started out with some sexy vocal styling and a little atmospheric guitar, and before the full band had even kicked in Jeff had pretty much erased all memory of our set minutes prior.'

The show that night saw Jeff and the Three Ms on particularly fiery form, perhaps inspired by such high-quality support. At the end of the night, a celebratory atmosphere pervaded.

'It was fantastic and afterwards all members of all the bands were in a state of drunken revelry,' says Tripp. 'I think everyone had realised a new standard was to be attained by everyone present. We became huge fans of Jeff and co, and vice-versa.'

Dave Derby confirms this: 'We were all hanging out after the show and he struck me as totally down-to-earth, low-key and really funny. I had heard that he was a magical performer, as I was to find out later when I finally saw him play.'

'By the end of the night' Tripp concludes on a less musical note, 'we had all noticed that Jeff and Joan [Wasser – Dambuilders violinist] seemed to be hitting it off a little extra.'

Despite the tour's growing momentum, fuelled by press, radio and simple good old-fashioned word-of-mouth, the shows were far from sell-out events and tickets were still usually available on the day of the gigs. Apart from the fact that Jeff and the band were still simply new on the scene, they also didn't want to play run-of-the-mill venues.

'We go to places where people go to listen... or places where we've never been before, so we all pay more attention to each other,' explained Jeff, referring to himself, his band and their audience.

When asked if he saw himself and the band as a contemporary version of groups like Genesis from twenty years previous, Jeff let go a disgusted 'Ugh, no!' before moving the conversation along by defining his taste and direction. 'I'm more like... the garage band is what I grew up doing but... I love Duke Ellington, he's my hero. And I loved Miles Davis. *They* were singers.'

Although Jeff was progressing in every way, these were early days, and the shadow of Tim Buckley still cast itself in subtle ways. As with the early UK shows, Jeff's family name remained an initial draw for some. 'I chose to see him at the Hot House in summer '94 based purely on the fact that I'm a Tim Buckley fan,' remembered one anonymous audience member. 'I took a date, and while I wasn't sure about his originals, his singing was transcendent, as were his covers of Van Morrison, Big Star and Nusrat. My date was practically drooling, and I probably had the best sex of my life at that point after the show.'

The Peyote Radio Theatre Tour would climax on 16 August, back where it had begun, with a raucous farewell gig at New York's Wetlands (Jeff would soon leave for Europe with his band close behind). Across the States, the setlists would change only subtly. Surprisingly, considering the jazz-like nature of rehearsals, for the most part the group – now locking into one another – kept to the bulk of *Grace*, with an extended jam of 'Kangaroo' left in place to let off steam at the end of each set.

True to his morphic personality, Jeff took what he needed from touring. He did not dismiss the often-gruelling monotony of living in city after city, day after day, as being inherently worthless or of getting in the way of the mystical art of recording and writing. The experience of being a band member seemed to him, for now at least, to be possessed of wholeness, and he embraced it for what it was with good humour. 'I'm not uninspired with the situation,' he declared, from the typically seedy pit of his actual tour bus. 'Being on the road offers up some great gifts which more than make up for having to live on bad buttery ham sandwiches that I detest or endless slices of flabby pizza. I guess the worst part of being on the road is not having good nutrition or a regular bath life. Because there *is* no bath life.'

With a few days off before Europe, Jeff briefly re-entered the world of regular ablutions, while over in the UK and Europe, one week ahead of its American debut, *Grace* was finally released in three formats – CD, vinyl and cassette.

From the self-mythologising cover image to the finely finessed sonics of the production, there seemed to be little that was 'indie' about Jeff now. The whole package was of high quality and higher commerce, as befitted a million-dollar investment.

Those already seduced by the live experience and the EP, and indeed by the hype, rushed out to their local record stores, and rushed back home to their hi-fis just as quickly. Flicking through the sleeve, some would be slightly disappointed. Jeff was an artist who obviously had an interest in words as poetry, and as such there were fans who questioned why there were no lyrics in the CD booklet.

Even on this usually rudimentary detail, Jeff had a typically headstrong approach. He had initially asked Sony to press up two versions of the CD – one with lyrics and one without. Predictably, the idea was rebuffed. Jeff wasn't particularly bothered. In fact anything beyond the basic process of making music seemed to bore him. Still, he justified Columbia's prudence eloquently. 'It's better just to garner your own interpretations of the song. You know, just to get your own picture of it and having it happen to you as much as possible rather than having a blueprint to go by.' The press release in itself verged on the lyrical, with the seemingly nihilistic Jeff comparing the recording of his music to disc as 'like dying'.

The opening of the album was the sound of a group very much alive, kicking off as it did with the powerful and dynamic duo of 'Mojo Pin' ('a song about obsession') and 'Grace' ('it's a song about my death but not fearing it'). From the whomp of the bass drum to the stratospheric firework splinters of Jeff's voice and Lucas's guitar, this already sounded a light year away from the music-under-a-microscope aesthetic of *Live at Sin-é*.

The album as a whole reflected and refracted the wealth of material and its disparate origins. Buckley had co-produced the last-minute addition of 'So Real', and its mangled car crash of guitars suggested that without Wallace as the dominant producer, the album might have steered closer to the garage-stained *frisson* of Sonic Youth rather than the slick pseudo-heaviness of Pearl Jam and Soul Asylum.

One Columbia staff member, Mike Webb, reckoned at the time that 'Wallace's final mixes of the songs took away some of the intimacy of the recordings. He's a hit-mixer and these weren't necessarily hit songs... it's not really an album that was ever made for radio.'

Jeff's one-time bassist Andrew Goodsight reckons: 'It's a great mood record. He was trying so hard to write a great song. It was as if every song he wrote had to be as good as "Stairway to Heaven", and to me that's the wrong way to go about it. His musical talents were off the hook, but as a songwriter he was still struggling. *Grace* is really good... but it is not a fun record. He was just testing the waters in my view. Trying not to fall on his face; as if he could. The label wanted a crooner CD, not a rock band. Jeff wanted *Grace*, and you have to respect that.'

Jeff was not averse to crooning. He *loved* to croon. 'Lilac Wine' and 'Hallelujah' would sound almost naked next to the more highly-embellished tracks on the album, and it's these that have dated best, sounding simultaneously massive and intimate. To hear just the voice and guitar together after the symphonic explosions of the other tracks is akin to being whispered to in a cathedral. Jeff would comment on the spiritual presence in his debut album in his own colourfully oblique way. 'I like a spirituality with a God that knows how to drive a car,' he told *Rolling Stone* that summer, 'that knows how to take his girl to the dance club, dance all night, have a little drink, kiss the kid when they come back in and go to sleep. God doesn't need a chauffeur – he needs to drive himself.'

The album effortlessly found its niche in a UK press then dominated by the first gentle waves of the approaching tsunami of Britpop. Amidst the pages of Blur, Pulp and Oasis, Jeff struck a peculiarly alien and high-sheen Hollywood presence with his seemingly carefully tousled hair, dead-rock-star-dad credentials, and a pair of porcelain cheekbones steep enough to ski down.

The UK reviews, true to the style of the time, were almost as poetic and lyrical as the record they were reviewing.

'...after a series of desperate but sadly unsuccessful attempts, he finally realised that it wasn't actually possible to carve lyric poetry into the night sky with a 300-foot flame thrower, so Jeff Buckley became a singer,' babbled journalist Caitlin Moran's then other half, Taylor Parkes, in *Melody Maker.* 'Buckley uses his voice, drawn out like a slow stretched bolus of heavenly bubblegum... a massive, gorgeous record... the point at which others are struck dumb with rapture is the moment Jeff Buckley finds his voice and starts singing.'

Mojo magazine was slightly more apprehensive, at least to begin with. 'The questions remain, however: is Jeff Buckley merely wearing the emperor's new clothes, or his father's hand-me-down, or is he a truly major, emergent new talent? Somewhat tantalisingly, the answer on the strength of this, his first real album, appears to be all three.' The reviewer concluded positively: 'When you're this good you don't need to be told. You need to learn how to live with it.'

Grace was, in a way, an expensive alternative to the alternative; slightly left of leftfield, indie and alt rock, and yet in some ways oddly closer to the intensively-produced Mariah Careys of the world. Truly enigmatic, Jeff was in the rare position of having heaps of mostly positive criticism thrown his way, whilst also being an increasingly viable and popular live draw without actually making much of an impression on the charts. Daytime radio play and major TV exposure, however, remained elusive. The singles were deceptively radio-friendly, chicly recorded and produced, but too deep and sweet-sounding to steal onto playlists in the manner of grunge, or straight-ahead pop-rock. Jeff's voice had the mixed blessing of making whichever other singers came before or after him sound horribly ordinary, and thus he just didn't fit in as far as radio programmers were concerned. As a consequence, while healthy, sales were relatively modest, and the debut album did not significantly chart. (Had it been released on Big Cat rather than Columbia, the album would have no doubt topped the indie charts.)

Such reports, coming as they did from thousands of miles away in the shape of blurry faxes and photocopies, were vague and exotic enough to be nothing but exciting. A long-time reader of the British 'inkies' – Jeff was well aware of *Melody Maker* and *NME* – he was quietly and privately ecstatic to be in the hallowed pages previously graced by the Smiths ('Jeff was a huge Smiths fan. He thought Morrissey was a living legend,' affirmed Mary Guibert), the Cure and the Cocteau Twins. The lead singer of the latter band had actually covered Tim Buckley's sublime 'Song to the Siren' during her stint as guest vocalist for Ivo Watt-Russell's This Mortal Coil project. This association did not flummox Jeff at all. He loved the Cocteau Twins: 'They carried with them this unexplainable... thing, this spirit. They let their deepest eccentricities be the music itself. Everything I love and have heard about music – I want to leave it all behind and go someplace else. There's so much more, so many more ways of saying "I love you" or "where the hell do I fit in?" And it's nothing arty, nothing lofty, just fucking different. I'm just trying to do my thing.'

On 19 August 1994 Jeff actually flew ahead of his band to the UK to meet the Cocteau Twins. He had been a fan of the FX-saturated trio since the early nineties, and this admiration would soon be reciprocated. The band had originally been introduced to Jeff while on tour in 1991. They had hung out again in 1994, on the US leg of their Four Calendar Café

Tour, when Liz Fraser and bassist Simon Raymonde went to see him perform at a bar in Atlanta.

The band Jeff introduced himself to that August were in rocky shape, and for their singer in particular, he acted as a kind of balm. 'He was just so spontaneous, it was just so exciting,' recalled Liz Fraser. 'He wanted to experience... everything. I was going through a hard time with the band I was in, and to me Jeffrey was like being given a set of paints to play with. He just brought so much colour into my life.'

Jeff had apparently 'idolised' the singer before meeting her, which is usually a bad starting point for any relationship, except in this case his fervent admiration was reciprocated by a successful and established artist who admitted that with Jeff even she sometimes felt like 'a groupie'. 'I just couldn't help falling in love with him,' she cooed. 'He was adorable.'

Their mutual affection was consummated on record, with the two recording the Jeff-penned 'All Flowers in Time Bend Towards the Sun'.

'It was really only one little session, through the night,' recalled Fraser. 'We just got an engineer to come in for a few hours. He [Jeff] was very free, so it was very easy for him to do those things. It was nothing for him to do that stuff, it was like breathing. He just had to do it. It was just something you did. And I wasn't like that. I'm *not* like that, so... you can imagine what it sounded like! But it was the makings of something fun if I'd been more chilled out.'

The result was sadly underwhelming and indulgent, replete with giggles and studio banter, sounding curiously (for such a usually overproduced group) incomplete.

On 23 August Jeff then flew back to Dublin to begin a handful of solo shows before planning to join his band in London for what would be the start of a brief tour of Europe. At the gig that night in Dublin's Whelan's Bar, his old Sin-é colleague and friend Katell Keineg performed a duet with him.

While Jeff celebrated after the show with a Guinness or five, back home, *Grace* was finally released in the USA.

Although initial sales were respectable if modest, *Grace* was in the main an instant critical – if not commercial – hit, although there was a note of ambiguity in many of the US reviews, perhaps reflecting the patchwork content of the record itself. The most negative review would come almost incidentally. *Streetsound* magazine played devil's advocate, but indeed spoke for some when it said, 'It is possible that Buckley is... a pathetic weeping sap who is entirely dependent on your indulgence to smile on egomaniacal yodelling as impassioned art... but if you give him the benefit of the doubt, unmitigated pleasure is yours.' Others found the singer-songwriter a little too sensitive. 'Sounds like an album by a young man who as a kid frequently had his lunch money stolen,' claimed the *Jerusalem Post*. But such critiques of Jeff's image rather than the music were as about as bad as it got.

'...ends up pulling off things no other young singer-songwriter guitarist in his right mind would even try,' reckoned the hugely influential *Rolling Stone*. 'But sometimes his arrangements sound too meticulous; too ornate... the vocals don't always stand up: he doesn't sound battered or desperate enough to carry off Cohen's "Hallelujah".' Time would prove this particular critic wrong, and most of the other reviews were positive and encouraging. 'He displays a remarkable gift for expressing the inexpressible,' reckoned *Stereo Review*. 'Watching Buckley develop from this audacious starting point will be a pleasure and the sky's the limit for a talent of his magnitude.'

Jeff appeared to remain charmingly aloof to much of his press. 'I keep my perspective about it,' he told a UK TV show. 'I always ask my management not to give me press. "*Pleeeeeeease* don't give me my press." But they do. 'Cause I think they want me to see something. So I read it through, and then I just throw it away in the garbage.'

Mark Geary, a frequent punter of the kind of small-time cafés Jeff loved to play, had a slightly different take on Jeff's attitude to reviews and press in general. He remembered vividly that on his return from the UK tour, hanging out at the Sin-é, someone brought Jeff in a review of his Dublin gig from the previous March. 'He was incredibly anxious about the review,' recalled Geary. 'I think he went into the toilet and had a little peep and then he let me see it as well. He gave a shit about what people thought of him and he gave a shit about how his gigs were reviewed or whatever.'

Jeff played Belfast's Limelight on 24 August, before jetting to Holland's Lowlands Festival the next day, flying back to Britain to perform a set at the Reading Festival, and then taking off to Scotland for another solo gig at Edinburgh's La Belle Angele.

Despite a major label release and feverishly positive reviews, particularly in the UK, Jeff was still very much a cult concern outside of London and New York. Yet those individuals who were clued-up enough to catch him at these intimate gigs would relish the subsequent memories.

Lorna Goldie was one such witness. A classic eighteen-year-old indie kid, she had heard the *Live at Sin-é* EP via a promo cassette in her capacity as a part-time writer for a local Strathclyde newspaper. She and some friends took a train into town in order to attend the shabby subterranean venue.

'I knew of his dad but not his material,' she remembers. 'So my interest was piqued because of that – his dad. Plus, I think I'd seen a tiny piece on him somewhere, a really small thing. Anyway, I took the tape home and really loved it. I thought it was really... charming. A Piaf cover? Wow. And he sounded like the Cocteau Twins sometimes, when he sang, and I loved the Cocteau Twins. I didn't think his original songs were that good but the cover versions were really, really charming. He was just starting to get written about, but I think a lot of people were intrigued by the name, you know? "Ooh, I wonder if he's like his dad?" So a bunch of us went to the show together.'

A friend of Lorna's, university lecturer Iain McDonald, attended the same show. 'La Belle Angele was a small underground – literally – venue in Edinburgh,' he recalls. 'A perfect setting, small – but packed – and intimate; the stone walls, dim lighting, and just the sense that you were somewhere quite special all added to the atmosphere of the gig. There were candles involved – the whole place had a sort of church-like feel to it.'

Jeff was by now a seasoned and confident performer and little concerned with public ceremony. 'He walked by me,' says Lorna, 'on his way to the stage. He put his hand on my shoulder and said "'Scuse me m'am." That was it, I thought, I was never gonna wash my shoulder again! He was very good-looking. I was young. I thought, "Oh, he's so beautiful and sensitive and tragic!" You know, all that bollocks.'

Iain remembers him 'appearing on stage with little sense of ego, no grand arrival, and tuning his guitar. He was a pretty short guy but extremely handsome. The combination of looks and talent has always seemed a bit unfair to me.'

Jeff played his seamless mix of originals and cover versions – combining the legacy of Sin-é with *Grace*. By now the songs came on and off like a second skin, and Jeff wasn't afraid to let the joins show occasionally. Iain recalls 'the technicality of his performance – lots of tuning between songs to get the chords he needed – there was a sense that everything had to be just right. "Lover, You Should've Come Over" was amazing, but it's difficult to distinguish particular songs as the quality overall was extraordinary... he invested so much in his performance of these songs, and "Mojo Pin", with that dim intro and his voice just crooning as the song builds – gorgeous.

'The one downside from my point of view was an extended jam of – I think – "Kangaroo" by Big Star? This easily clocked in towards the ten- to fifteen-minute mark and came very near the end of the set – desperately seeking a melody. That was perhaps the only part of the set where it really just seemed about him pleasing himself rather than simply performing. Overall, he just sang, powerfully and really passionately – it was odd, really. The performance almost had to be because the audience was there but it was, at the same time, the kind of performance where the audience just *happened* to be there – he was just incredibly involved in his own performance. Our presence might be the reason why he was there, but it wasn't the reason why he sang the way he did. There was just this incredible commitment to what he was doing. What was also odd was that he had this chanteuse quality about him. Like a female torch singer. It was amazing.'

'It was special,' concludes Lorna. 'But then each time I saw him after that, and I saw him about four or five times… it was a law of diminishing returns. He just seemed to get less interested in that particular material every time I saw him after that.'

Jeff made it back over to London where, on 1 September, he was reunited with the band. The quartet played downstairs at North London's Highbury Garage to a hyped audience that included chemically eccentric Lemonheads singer Evan Dando, who heckled Jeff surreally throughout the set. Things had changed since Jeff had last played at the venue's smaller upstairs room, and the event now had all the ambience of an avant-garde boy band concert, with shoals of screaming girls in the audience and Jeff stripping down to his waist.

Jeff and the Three Ms ultimately silenced everyone there that night. As a sonic 'fuck you' to those critics who bemoaned *Grace*'s 'wimpiness', to the occasional bitching executive from Sony, and perhaps even to the abusive Evan Dando, the group ended that night with a monstrous cavalcade of sound in the shape of a behemoth-like, heaving and burning version of 'Kangaroo' that lasted for over 30 minutes.

Guitarist Bernard Butler was once again in attendance. 'It went on forever and I thought it was great,' he said. 'I was willing him on, hoping it would go on all night. It inspired me.'

Jeff concurred with Butler. 'I hate the songs to really end. Sometimes they don't need to be just three minutes. Sometimes they need to be four or fourteen.' Or 30, as the extended jam had proven, much to the displeasure of some in the audience. (Jeff, however, maintained that 'every fucking person that was in front of me at the beginning of the show that I saw – and I'm aware of my audience – was still there [at the end]. The place was silent while we were playing.')

It's hard to know how much of the audience's reaction Jeff could have gauged from within the squall of that night's version of 'Kangaroo', but what was indisputable was that once again, this roaring take on the Big Star classic signified the end of an era for Jeff. '*Grace*… it's just a bunch of things about my life that I wanted to put in a coffin and bury forever so I could get on with things,' he said, adding decisively: 'I don't want to do any more covers. It's good to learn to make things your own, but the education is over. *Grace* is putting a lot of things to rest.'

7. SUMMER WINE

'I like low stage volume. I want the idea and the sound of the idea to intoxicate – not the voltage… Once you have stacks of Marshalls you need stacks of people to take care of them. Plus you have to jump around and get nipple piercings.'

Jeff Buckley

Although he was not prone to long bouts of navel-gazing, Jeff undoubtedly had a healthy ego. Being famous, even in the select and cultish way that he was, was a delicious and secret surprise that still excited his inner geek. Back at his mother's house in Orange County, stacked among the boxes of old notebooks, fanzines, high school gig setlists and magazines, was a copy of *Musician* from the late eighties. Astride its cover stood Jimmy Page, poodle hair blow-dried and dyed bible-black. The mythical axe warrior had been cast somewhat adrift since Led Zeppelin's dissolution almost a decade earlier, but Jimmy could still throw the iconic rock god shapes. The cover photo showed him wrestling with a Telecaster in the manner of renowned satanist Aleister Crowley fending off the devil himself. *'Has Jimmy Page still got it?'* demanded the cover line's howling blurb. On the same page, in comically tiny biro'd black print, the teenage Jeff had inked: *'Will Jeff Buckley EVER have it?'*

Now, less than a decade later, those same magazines were affirming just that. Yes, young lord Buckley did indeed have 'it'. Jeff was still close enough at this point to his bedroom-bound teenage self – the boy who subsisted on guitar scale exercises and the vinyl grooves of *Physical Graffiti* – that he was able to enjoy this acclaim from both sides of the mirror. Jeff was still the reader of such magazines, and yet increasingly he was their subject too. It was if he were sat in the stalls watching the movie of his life unfurl on the silver screen – as he lived it.

Besides the growing sales of and fecund market for the glossy magazines and inky, blurry fanzines of that period, by the mid-decade yet

Jeff onstage with his red Rickenbacker guitar at the Nighttown in Rotterdam, Holland, February 1995.

another media was blooming, spreading inexorably across the planet like the red Martian weed in *The War of the Worlds*.

The internet was a phenomenon slowly but surely gathering visibility in the 1990s. Record companies – typically the smaller, independent labels to begin with – were hip to the marketing potential of this digital medium. Inevitably, dinosaurs like Columbia were also slowly cottoning on, and Jeff often stopped by the offices of either his label or manager to access the Usenet groups and crude Geocities pages dedicated to Jeff Buckley that were sprouting up across cyberspace with increasing frequency.

As early as March of 1995, Jeff was publicly pissed off at the availability of bootlegs which were then online, particularly those that he considered 'terribly lame. Very, very sucky... One can't avoid having one's dreck smeared all over the computer waves by curious net-surfers,' he moaned in a primitive blog posted on his label's site. He was aware that he was not always running at full-speed and was often unable to make peace with the flaws evident in these uploaded live shows. 'I can only cover three octaves at the moment,' he admitted that spring. At his best Jeff could cover four.

The prospect of such unconditional piracy was, however, ultimately positive. The very real possibility that every sonic emission that Jeff or his group happened to omit could be filtered, edited, EQ'd to CD-standard and made available for trade or free via the internet within a few days of the gig had the perverse result of pushing the quartet towards an even more refined ideal of perfectionism. Disappointed by the occasional show he heard via the online fan recordings (most commonly found on a site labelled the 'Mojo Bin'), Jeff vowed that there would be no more 'off nights'.

'This time I'm making sure that *all* of our shows rise in quality in a *radical* way,' he promised his audience and himself.

This very audience did not necessarily include the employees of his label. Jeff seemed indifferent to the fact that by sometimes riffing on 'Kangaroo' for up to half an hour at the end of each show, he was pissing off the more conservative suits at Sony, to the extent where official memos were written up prissily complaining of such sonic indulgence. When informed that Jeff was growing increasingly inclined toward the harder, more 'prog' side of his musical nature, one Sony executive is said to have barked, 'What the fuck is Jeff Buckley doing?'

In upsetting the 'squares' at the record company in this way, Jeff must have realised – even unconsciously – that in some ways he was mirroring trajectories once mapped by his father's career. His dad came back to haunt him in other ways too. It was an obvious and inevitable truth, but somehow Jeff had never considered it until wandering into his local Tower Records shop. Now that he himself had two records out, they would obviously be stacked next to the other Buckley; Tim, the obscure folk-jazz prog-rocker who died young. There in the racks, *Grace* and *Live at Sin-é* nestled before *Starsailor* and *Happy Sad*. Jeff was momentarily spooked by this queer reunion, but soon found a kind of acrid solace in the irony of it, musing that he and his father were 'separated all our lives and now I'm right there in the bin next to him'.

As the tour progressed through Germany, Sweden, Norway, Italy, Belgium and France, Sony's displeasure toward Jeff's occasionally indulgent side became so pronounced that one executive actually phoned Jeff in his hotel room to complain. The singer's indifference now turned to indignation. This was the first time that Sony had not completely accepted Jeff and his – as they saw it – whims. What they didn't understand was that for Jeff, *Grace* was already behind him, and the cacophonous extended carnival of sound that was 'Kangaroo' was the soundtrack to a changing man. But this particular evolution was incremental.

While Jeff had no intention of recording a 'Grace II', he had no clear idea of exactly how his next album would sound. What was apparent was that his interest was turning toward the noisier elements of his music – as in the mangled middle-eight of 'So Real' and the propulsive dissonance of the Big Star cover. Increasingly, this was at the expense of Jeff's inner 'diva', as evident in the frosted elegance of 'Hallelujah' and 'Corpus Christi Carol'.

Whatever the clash of taste and philosophy manifested between Jeff and Sony, both knew full well that the occasional overlong live encore was hardly a deal-breaker. Jeff was signed to Sony/Columbia as an artist, not as an employee. Knowing this, Jeff and the Three Ms turned the amps up to eleven and the extended excursion of 'Kangaroo' stayed.

Arriving back in New York from Europe on 23 September, an exhausted but strongly bonded group collapsed into their civilian lives whilst their singer was roused for the final solo show of the Peyote Radio Theatre Tour, at the annual CMJ festival. According to fan and critic Gina Arnold, this last gig of the fall saw Jeff as 'the toast of the CMJ convention' (alongside Courtney Love's abrasive grunge-rockers Hole). Jeff played seated, and while this meant that many could not see him, they could most certainly hear him. 'Buckley was golden that night,' affirmed Gina. The golden boy would barely have time to cool his boots before the next round of meetings and promotional duties began – all preliminaries to yet another tour scheduled to begin in late October.

In the midst of this claustrophobic routine, Jeff was aware that it was important for him to have a life that reached beyond music. Although he found it superficially new and thrilling, he was not ready to use life on the road as his source material for new songs quite yet.

During his time off, Jeff did what any other 26-year-old Manhattanite did – he went to movies, played pool, ate out (angel pasta was a favourite), read and wrote in his journals. Yet even these everyday activities seemed to revolve around the core element that made up his centre of gravity – music. 'I'll always be a slobbering idiot for people I love,' he admitted happily. 'The Grifters, Patti Smith, the New Ginsberg Box, MC5, Sun-Ra, Kiss…' Where Jeff differed profoundly from other pool-playing, angel pasta-chomping New Yorkers was that he was now actually entering a phase in his life where he would come to be working with some of those very musicians he name-checked, including two from the previous list in the subsequent year alone.

With *Grace* showing only moderate, albeit steady, sales in the US – it was selling a few thousand a week – another month-long tour of the States kicked off unofficially, with a 'secret' last-minute show at the legendary CBGB's venue on 19 October. Sony sent out the requisite promo materials to all the relevant regional press along the way.

The press release for the tour featured Jeff's characteristically lyrical musings:

> *I'm really into flying. I don't care about being a gospel singer or a blues singer per se, but elements of that music are keys to my subconscious. When I sing something like that – if I do it right – it's like a weird snake that will get in you and unlock something. If I wasn't able to do this, I think I would really lay down and die.*
>
> *Music comes from a very primal, twisted place. When a person sings, their body, their mouth, their eyes, their words, their voice says all these unspeakable things that you really can't explain but that mean something anyway. People are completely transformed when they sing; people look like that when they sing or when they make love. But it's a weird thing – at the end of the night I feel strange, because I feel I've told everybody all my secrets.*

The fact that Jeff and the band were able to play many of the same venues – sometimes twice over two nights – that they had played only a few months previously on the Peyote Radio Theatre Tour showed that despite the lack of a *Billboard* chart placing for his debut album, there was a definite demand for and growing interest in Jeff and his music.

As the opening act for this jaunt, Jeff chose fellow label-mate and friend Brenda Kahn. With enough to worry about as the headliner, there was no need for Jeff to involve himself in this particular tour logistic. Sony would have happily arranged their own opening act of choice, or the venues themselves would have provided local bands as support. His pro-activeness in this regard demonstrates that he was both willing to act on his taste, and aware of and concerned for his musician friends' own lives and careers.

'I think Jeff and I had a mutual admiration for one another's music,' Kahn confirms. 'I have an idea that he felt himself more of a musician and singer than a lyricist, and I was always the opposite. I have always loved words and the music never came as easily, so I think we looked at each other and sort of said, "Why can't I do that?" I remember after one show in New Orleans, I walked off stage and Jeff hugged me and was going on and on about what a great songwriter I was. Which always amazed me, because he was phenomenal in all those ways.'

What was also phenomenal was the condition of Jeff's voice. Despite almost relentless touring it held up remarkably well throughout the year, rarely sounding husky, parched, fatigued or strained.

The group continued to grow, evolve and compose, adding a new instrumental to their set in the shape of 'Vancouver' – the true sign of a band in musical motion. 'I met Jeff and here was a person who just wanted to fall into the abyss and trust that he'd land on his feet, much like a cat, which we're still pursuing, and I love that,' explained Mick Grondahl.

The tour saw other modulations too. Previously, the group's hedonistic indulgences were kept to the confines of the luxury tour bus and backstage dressing rooms, yet in Chicago's ornately-decorated (velvet and hardwood) Green Mill venue on 8 November, Jeff very publicly dived to the bottom of a tequila bottle.

After an exhausting day of promotion that started first thing that morning and included a TV appearance and various interviews for local papers and radio, the inevitably less-than-straightforward soundcheck, the fake-smile fiesta of a 'promo party' at the venue, and the usual mild hassle from a smattering of fans, Jeff headed back to the relative sanctity of the tour bus to prepare for the day's *raison d'être*: the actual concert. But before he could even check his messages, undress, shower and change, Sony demanded to speak to him immediately. His road manager handed the stressed-out singer a phone. An exhausted and severely tried Jeff had to listen as a distant Sony executive lambasted him about recent disparaging remarks the singer had made in a *Rolling Stone* interview concerning MTV.

This was neither the time, the place, nor the subject. Right now, or at the best of times, Jeff couldn't give a fuck about MTV or promo videos. But he was, after all, signed to a major company who ultimately designed his art, his music, his songs, and his voice as a product. The trade-off was the beautifully produced and packaged CD bearing his name that was – as he stood there being more or less told off by his 'boss' – available to buy in mainstream record outlets the world over. The exchange for having to listen to Sony tell him what he could and couldn't say about what was basically a TV channel that advertised their wares for 'free' was that they paid for the band he was playing with, the tour bus he was standing in, and the very phone he was holding.

'That was a difficult time for Jeff,' sympathises Kahn. 'He was a rising star at Columbia and he resisted all forms of falseness. And of course the music industry is filled with image-conscious folks who have a terrible time telling the difference between art and ego... I remember him saying he didn't *want* to be a video jock on MTV.'

Once the call was done, Jeff swiftly grabbed one product to hand not endorsed or owned by Sony – a bottle of José Cuervo tequila provided by the local promoter as part of the backstage rider. Hassled and fatigued and deeply pissed-off, Jeff retired to his bunk to get drunk. Outside, it started to rain.

By 10:30pm Brenda Kahn had started her opening set and Jeff, having made his way through most of the bottle, was now propping up the bar in the club itself, piling on tequila slammer after tequila slammer. He mingled easily with fellow audience members and drinkers, accepting the offers of shots from appreciative fans and slugging them down into his slight frame while Kahn etched through her low-key, lyric-driven set.

Towards the end of her performance, she invited Jeff up to play with her, perhaps in an effort to get him to walk away from the bar while he was able. Still wearing his overcoat – the rain had been hammering down outside all evening – Jeff somewhat reluctantly slouched from bar to stage, where he sat behind Kahn with his back turned to the audience. This was seen by most as an effort not to draw attention away from Brenda, although for some the crumpled back-view of a drunken Jeff Buckley was more than a tad distracting.

By the time Jeff and band took to the stage at around midnight, he was reeling. A gaggle of photographers crowded the front of the stage, illuminating Jeff's tragic, James Dean-esque face as he bravely attempted to undulate his voice into the solo introduction of opening song 'Mojo Pin'.

His distaste for the photographers was apparent, but even when this distraction had receded during the *a capella* opening, Jeff could not seem to find his place. For some in the audience the spectacle was agonising to watch. Kahn confirms that 'he was terribly drunk that night... by the time he was onstage he was toast. I remember he was rambling on and on in very graphic terms about how drunk he was and how he was not really in any condition to perform for people... all this onstage. And he was chewing gum the whole time. I never saw him like that any other time onstage or off.'

Songs the group had played a thousand times – 'Grace', 'Mojo Pin', 'Eternal Life' – had trouble starting, and when they did Jeff would break them off and begin rambling monologues. 'God that sucks... let's start it over again... I suck... I'm so sorry... I just suck...' The audience were not afraid of vocalising their own opinions either. 'Just shut up! Sing the song!' was a typical refrain that Jeff, who was strangely and painstakingly courteous in the super-deliberate way that drunks sometimes are, did not directly engage with. Rather than heckle back, or argue with any disgruntled punter individually, he instead repeatedly apologised to the crowd en masse, berating himself rather than the hecklers. 'You guys... I am so sorry... I am drunk! *D-U-R-N-K!* I want to give everyone their money back... I am so sorry... I suck so bad.'

Occasionally the band would get off the ground, and the voice would take the songs to an altitude where they were temporarily free of the tequila-forged shackles. A second attempt at 'So Real' and a liquidly mesmerising 'Lilac Wine' both managed this, but others – 'Hallelujah' for instance, where he riffed on the line 'it's a cold and it's a broken hallelujah' alone for over five minutes – crashed and burned.

The band seemed supportive and patient, if slightly amused. 'Jeff was talking shit about Bob Dylan and getting fucking wasted,' says Matt Johnson. 'He was just being a punky little douche... cute and funny and naughty. He did stupid shit sometimes.'

'That was a pretty funny night, you had to laugh,' recalled Grondahl.

They somehow made it in a zonked-out fashion through a set of sorts, still occasionally lifting the roof off of the small club. Aside from a few random albeit loud hecklers, the majority of the club that night were, for better or worse, spellbound.

Some of the more perceptive audience members saw beyond the amusing, bemusing car crash spectacle of a pretty drunk boy spooked by the oncoming prospect of fatal fame, sensing something darker, more tragic. 'There was wildness in him,' remembered freelance writer and audience member Sheila O'Malley, 'a potential for unhinged grief – you could sense it.'

Coming to in his bunk the next afternoon, Jeff must have been gripped with a hungover sense of self-loathing accented by the reality that *his* asshole shenanigans of the night before had been acted out very much in public.

Sufficiently recovered in time for the second scheduled show at the Green Mill that Wednesday night, Jeff sought to put things right with a demonically energetic set that, although impressive, was somehow less enthralling and less honest than the previous night's Bacchanalian theatre. Much to Jeff's displeasure, only the first of the two Chicago shows was reviewed.

This particular road trip again and again put a heavy pressure on Jeff alone. As well as the more traditional band performances, the singer was often required to play radio sessions and turn up at local record stores to perform solo. It was his name on the advertising, on the record and in the listings. It was – for some – a disconcerting fact that although on the road the four players strived to be a very real band, a Jeff Buckley show without any of the Three Ms was still very much a Jeff Buckley show. As such, Sony would often require him to go out alone.

On the last leg of the fall tour, Jeff played an in-store at his own neighbourhood's Tower Records at the stroke of a freezing December midnight.

He was now practically playing to his neighbours. Such appearances were short but deep. The different and potentially uncomfortable dynamic of these shows – record stores are built to sell recorded music rather than host it live – was something Jeff took in his stride. A denizen of the East Village at the time, wearing a white T-shirt and with straggly tousled hair falling into his face, he joked about how weird it was to play where he shopped. Such settings provided another strange duality, Jeff was also playing 'amidst the bins' – among a forest of vinyl and CDs that included racks of Buckley product by both father and son. The presence of such ghosts would have been troubling, as was the occasional in-store mishap. While he worked effortlessly through his album, about halfway through the set an audience member clumsily upset the CD racks, sending waves of albums tumbling to the store floor. The show momentarily stopped and Jeff looked annoyed, perhaps unable to modulate the musical key of such a disturbance. (While he was adept at playing in tune with cappuccino machines, falling plastic was another challenge altogether.) Across the floor lay strewn CDs by Jeff's heroes, villains and contemporaries: Van Halen, Suzanne Vega, the Velvet Underground, Loudon Wainwright III, and Dionne Warwick. Buckley coughed, gave the offending fan the evil eye, and resumed playing. His nerves were no doubt soothed by the skimpily dressed groupies who could be found stood on the stairs after the show.

Jeff did enjoy his fans. As serious and committed an artist as he was, he could also be a shameless player of the game. He loved to perform and he loved the idea of being a successful, adored rock star – up to a point. He regularly corresponded with his fans, both personally and via newsletters and Sony-facilitated internet mail-outs. In a Christmas 1994 message to the fans via mailing list that year, Buckley wrote:

Hello... um... how overwhelming can something be? Just tell everybody for me that Mickey, Michael, Matt and I LOVE YOU ALL SUPREMELY! This has been the most surreal year of joy and utterly satanic bullshit mixed together... your support and your love has completely inspired us to go on with the tour with more patience and energy... it's a massive task, my tour... we play sometimes six out of seven nights a week, sometimes three gigs in one day. In-store gig in the afternoon, radio show pre-gig, then on to the big mama... Believe me we fucking FEEL you out there... it helps us so much and I just wanted to tell you that I love you, too... NO MORE CUERVO NIGHTS! DON'T WORRY CHICAGO!

Harking back to the second Green Mill gig in particular, Jeff was often pissed when shows weren't reviewed: 'The stinking journalists didn't show up... that's okay... there'll be plenty of articles for them to write in hell,' he raved in the same mail-out.

No sooner had Jeff and band staggered from the treadmill of incessant promotion and touring than Sony started making noises about another album. But rather than free-up his songwriter's muse, life on the road had instead stunted it. As Christmas came and went it, so did the emergence of the unspoken fact that Jeff was at the beginning of a two-year period of writer's block.

Over the New Year holiday, Jeff played a short solo set at Sin-é on New Year's Eve, (filmed by Merri Cyr) and performed by reading a poem at a New Year's Day 'happening' at St Ann's Church before rehearsals began in preparation for the Mystery White Boy Tour, which kicked off in Dublin on 14 January. Two more UK dates followed, with Jeff selling out an Astoria show in London; a major progression for someone who was playing to 50 people in the same city less than two years ago. Jeff was also becoming an official 'heartthrob', drawing an increasingly female audience initially enraptured by his appearance and – more often than not – seduced by his voice and songs.

In London, Paris and New York, Jeff was becoming downright famous, and this led some of his more sophisticated female fans to adopt increasingly devious methods of interception.

Excerpt from the journal of Cressida Johnson, January 1995:

I first heard Grace *at the flat of journalists Taylor Parkes and Caitlin Moran in 1994 when I was nineteen-years-old. I was a massive Tim Buckley fan and didn't expect Jeff to be anywhere near as good. I was blown away by his voice and his brooding, angelic and devilishly good looks.*

In early '95 Caitlin was going to see him live at LA2. I was desperate to go, but couldn't get tickets. Bored by my complaining, Caitlin cooked up a plan. She knew where he was staying in London and suggested I call him up, say I was a journalist writing for a fanzine and that I had interviewed him when he was in London the previous year. So I did. When I got put through to him, he said 'hello' in the sexiest groggy husk I have ever heard. Weak at the knees, but determined in my mission, I went through my spiel. I was terrified that he would catch me out and quite rightly tell me to fuck off, but he didn't. He was charm personified. He apologised for not remembering who I was and confessed that he had been asleep. (Cue Technicolor fantasy of Jeff lying naked in crisp hotel sheets, eyes half-open and hair artfully mussed from having been torn from sleep.) God knows how I managed to continue speaking. He said he remembered me and thanked me for my message wishing him a happy new year – result!

I said that I really wanted to come to the show and that I hadn't been able to get tickets. He said no problem, you'll be on my list. I thanked him (not too profusely – I needed to play it cool) and gave him my number to confirm. He called later that night.

'Hey Cressida, it's Jeff.'

I could barely breathe, let alone think… Needless to say, I muttered some crap. He said he looked forward to seeing me and my ticket would be on the door.

The fateful day came a Wednesday, 18 January. I arrived fashionably late at LA2, trembling with excitement and fear that if Jeff saw me and didn't recognise me, I would be booted out. I strode up to the ticket office,

Jeff slumps for the camera in Chicago. Over his shoulder, a Charlie Parker-inspired porkpie hat can be seen.

confident and proud that I was on Jeff's list.

My name wasn't there.

'Check again,' I implored. 'Cress…'

Still not there…

'He promised!' I whimpered – to myself.

I slunk off, utterly defeated and ashamed. As I fought my way out through the fans, I ran into Caitlin. She was sympathetic to my humiliation and determined to get me a ticket. She located Jeff's press officer, who apologised on Jeff's behalf and promised to tell him off for forgetting to put my name down. She got me in.

The show was absolutely, unforgettably, tears-streaming-down-the-cheeks amazing. The best gig I ever went to, by a mile. Jeff didn't turn up to the after-show and so I went home.

When I got in there was a message on my machine.

'Cressida, it's Jeff. I'm so sorry about what happened tonight. I promise your name will be on the list at Shepherds Bush when I return in March. Hope to see you there. I'll make it up to you…'

There was further, more substantial proof that things were on the rise. Increasingly, the occasional show was being recorded for radio or television, sometimes for both mediums, in almost every country. This was a sure sign that Jeff and the band were becoming accepted by the wider media and starting to infiltrate the pop consciousness of the public at large. The group were certainly photogenic, and were also naturally dynamic on stage. But this was no forced theatre, merely an honest projection of their growing chemistry.

'It's about listening,' explained Grondahl, 'and I'm watching Michael too – he's a melodic instrument. And I can look at Matty and see these white sticks going and that gives me information. And I can see Jeff and that gives me other information. I don't really look at Mike that often… only when I'm really comfortable, like in "Kangaroo" or something. And then it's just a free-for-all and it's very fun.'

'Yeah, I loved to play,' affirms Johnson. 'I needed to play. I sucked and had to gig and gig and gig until I stopped hating myself and finally let go for the music and the moment to take over. So I wanted it to go on.'

Sony obviously wanted to take advantage of the visual aspect of their product, and so the group flew to a Paris warehouse on 22 January to rendezvous with friend and photographer Merri Cyr. Here a video was made for 'Last Goodbye', but again, as far as Jeff was concerned, this was an appendage to the art form – not an art form in itself. Or at least not one he was interested in. 'Videos are a tyranny,' he moaned. 'There's no invocation of any kind. It's just, you know, toothpaste, pimple cream, Eddie Vedder, Green Day, burgers, the grind, Pepto-Bismol... it's like, commercial, commercial, commercial...' The video, while no minor artistic breakthrough, was pretty and efficient. It served its purpose, garnering modest but effective airplay on MTV, making 'Last Goodbye' a bona fide 'alternative hit', however nebulously that term could be defined.

Another American tour was scheduled for that spring, this time to be shared with indie babe Juliana Hatfield. But outside of America, Buckley was growing beyond cool cultdom, and in new territories such as Japan and Australia, the bigger venues included in the itinerary were hard evidence that while *Grace* had been no *Thriller*, it was a slow and steady seller more than returning its investment in kudos alone. After a predictably hectic and hysterical sojourn to Japan, where the polished sheen of his recorded music and Jeff's natural class and photogenic looks instantly translated into sales, the band returned to Europe.

Jeff seemed dazed by the trip (he would later write 'Woke Up in a Strange Place' about it): 'Japan was a crazy weird wacky kind of town,' he said. 'A real adventure.'

Things seemed cooler in Europe. 'We usually spend more time in America because it's bigger,' explained Grondahl. 'In Europe it seems a lot wilder... and more festive and patient.' The audiences were also more appreciative; especially compared to the arguably less sophisticated US audiences. 'You get a lot of gabby people in the States,' said Grondahl, 'it's really very curious why people want to come to a show and talk about their dead cat.' Jeff himself could be chatty onstage, often taking his time with wandering monologues that ended where the next song began. Introducing 'Lilac Wine' at the Roskilde Festival that year, Jeff was actually beginning a kind of transcontinental conversation with himself. 'So let me tell you a story,' he told the audience in their thousands, 'this is for all the men in the tent, for all the men that fuck up with their women and have to drink. I know you've done it, said the wrong thing, didn't say the right thing, looked at somebody funny, criticised their favourite TV programme, something really really stupid, that you know you shouldn't have done, and so you get messed up on lilac wine.' A few months later in Australia, he would tellingly introduce the song again, providing a kind of punchline to the comments in Roskilde, confessing, 'This is a song that I find myself singing to myself a lot.'

Jeff was particularly beloved by the French and his concerts in France that winter saw increasing displays of crowd hysteria in the medium-sized venues that he and the band would never play again. Jeff seemed to stir something in the French, as if he were fulfilling a need they had been hitherto unaware of. The hybrid of movie-star looks, uncommon musical chops, and poetic sensibility contrasting with his unabashed Americanism all added up to something peculiarly affecting for the French psyche. The myths concerning the tragically deceased father that Jeff had never known only added to this seduction. In Lyon on 10 February, the media interest was such that it was deemed best for Jeff to give a press conference. At 3:00pm he took his place at a long table, from which bloomed a small bouquet of microphones.

Q: What does Grace mean to you?

JB: It's nothing religious, it's nothing mystical. It's quite ordinary. It's this kind of thing which makes people divine. That's a quality I admire enormously in somebody. Especially in men, as it's so rare.

Q: What do you think about critics who found that *Grace* is overproduced?

JB: There is a journalist in New York who adored me when I was a solo performer at Sin-é and suddenly as *Grace* was released, he declares, 'I was mad to appreciate Jeff Buckley! His album is totally overproduced! Blah blah blah!' He thinks I have betrayed him because I've evolved. When I'm creating in the studio, I have the opportunity to experiment with all the ideas I have in my head. I can say, 'I need this. I don't want that.' That's a fantastic feeling – to be able to give life to sounds, to emotions that you have inside of you.

Q: Most of the songs on the album express the difficulty to manage a romantic relationship and the damage brought by the inevitable split. What experience do you have in this regard?

JB: From my romantic experience and from what I'm expressing in *Grace*, I learned not to count only on somebody and not to live through a person.

Q: In Europe, the media are unanimously favourable, and in the US it seems to be different. How can you explain that?

JB: In America, a very influential rock critic, who writes in most of the music magazines and is well-known, has straight out insulted me. He thinks I'm all over the place, that I don't know where I'm going, that I spread myself too thin. He is not able to define me, to classify me, and due to that he throws me out with the bathwater. I'm not... crazy! [It's] just that I feel different emotions and I express them through different ways, with different sounds. Because that's the way it has to sound! People have many different personalities inside themselves. They can be serene or tortured. Everybody has in himself different states of being and contradictory feelings. And music reflects these paradoxes. Each art form does this. But in music especially, there is something special with the medium of music which makes people respond powerfully when they listen to it. They may hate it or love it, but music gives rise to more reactions than a movie, a sculpture or a painting does. It's a weird art... the one which is the nearest to dreaming. I cannot explain or define a sound. I would like to but I can't...

Q: Who are the artists that influence you most?

JB: I believe that the artists who made the biggest impressions on me are those I listened to as a child... like Led Zeppelin, Joni Mitchell, MC5, Billie Holiday, Nina Simone, Patti Smith, John Lennon and later Siouxsie (I have much of her influence in my voice), Nick Cave (especially when he was in the Birthday Party), the Smiths... I'm a fan of thousands of people. Listening to them, they remind me of all the different possibilities of expression. *That's* the inspiration! Today, there is still a lot of good shit around but it's more underground. Musical evolution is an important thing. That's the reason why the sixties and seventies were so fantastic. There were the Beatles and everybody said 'Ooooouaah!' then Jimi Hendrix: 'Woooh! Is this possible?' and then James Brown, the Stones, the Beach Boys, the Doors, and so on...

The journalistic interest easily spilled over to the public and the small venues were routinely packed. 'The audience is young (except the "old" fans of Jeff's father) and already knows *Grace* by heart,' wrote one French reviewer of the band's Toulouse show at Le Bikini Club that February. Jeff strolled onstage exhibiting 'huge charisma' with 'dishevelled hair, a possessed look in his eyes, a disarmingly natural smile and an airy ease... he resembled the young Jim Morrison.' As usual the show finished with the hypnotic 'Kangaroo', but the audiences rarely let Jeff off lightly and encores were more or less mandatory. 'All that I can expect from the audience is that they smile, that they cry... And then, I'm grateful and I believe in them... totally,' said Jeff.

In France even the heckling was more sophisticated: 'Get your soul out!' shouted one existentialist fan in the crowd that night. Jeff was happy to oblige – even if his knowledge of French didn't allow him to translate each and every crowd request. Jeff wasn't put off by language barriers and continued to apply elaborate introductions to songs in whichever country he played. 'It's not the bottle. It's not the pills. It's not the face of strangers who will offer you their lines and hot needles,' he told the audience one night, introducing 'Hallelujah'. 'It's not the time you were together in their place. So perfect. Like a second home. And it's not from the Bible. It's not from angels. Not from preachers who are chaste and understanding of nothing that is human in this world. It's for people who are lovers. It's for people who have been lovers. You are at last somewhere. Until then it's hallelujah.'

They continued throughout Germany and Italy, where in Correggio, according to Jeff, the band performed 'the weirdest gig we ever did... it was at an open air festival and usually at festivals you get a million bands... but we were the only band there. The whole thing was just us... so everyone gets fooded up and beered up and comes to see us and... we didn't know this until we turned up but... er... we were actually there raising money for the Communist Party. So that was an added bonus. There are some awesome commies down there in Italy.'

'That Italian festival was fucking sweet,' concurs Matt Johnson. 'I think we played in shorts and shirtless. We looked like assholes but we were super-cool. Jeff kicked ass and screamed and cranked the distortion. What a rocker. We didn't speak Italian so we didn't know what the hell was going on. But I say, at this point, if the commies are paying, I guess we'll work for them too. They're no longer a threat, right?'

The adventure moved on throughout the Netherlands and Belgium with a punishing schedule of TV, radio and stage work. All the while Jeff's voice held up under this massive strain, never losing its higher registers.

Mid-tour, some complimentary news came in. Robert Plant and Jimmy Page (who actually attended a future Jeff Buckley show in Australia) had offered Jeff and his band the opening slot on their forthcoming tour. Elated, Jeff nevertheless declined. 'I'll never perform in stadiums,' he explained. 'Can you see me singing "Lilac Wine" in front of a hard-rock crowd? No, it's impossible. But still, it's an honour and an incredible thing that I was asked.'

The group's return to the UK that March saw them playing even bigger venues than two months previously, both within and beyond the capital. The band's appearance at the Shepherds Bush Empire – a significant benchmark among London's venues – was awaited hungrily by many fans, male and female alike. But particularly by one individual female.

Excerpt from the journal of Cressida Johnson, March 1995:
In early March 1995 I excitedly schlepped down to the Shepherds Bush Empire. This time my name was on the guest list and I had a

pass for the after-show party too. The gig was terrific, but lacked the intimacy of LA2.

It was a very strange night for me. The after-show was teeming with music's great and good. Everywhere I looked there were famous faces. Caitlin felt ill and wanted to go home. She left me in the care of James Dean Bradfield from the Manic Street Preachers. It was just after Richey James had disappeared and he seemed quiet and low. He politely batted off endless well-wishers, but obviously wanted to be left alone. I was nervous and overwhelmed and had no idea what to say to him.

Eventually Jeff arrived, smaller and more fragile than he appeared onstage; he was surrounded by chaperones who whisked him around the room, presumably getting him to speak to the assembled bigwigs and hacks. I was struck by how shy and uncomfortable he seemed.

And finally, he was stood next to me at the bar. He was barely taller than my high-heeled five-foot-four and heart-stoppingly beautiful. All jutting cheekbones and wild, dark hair. I was utterly transfixed. I stilled my beating heart and shook his hand.

'Hi, I'm Cressida.'

His face lit up when he smiled. 'It's good to see you, how've you been?'

We chatted for a bit, he apologised some more for missing me off the list before. He said he was exhausted and that being on the road was taking it out of him. He said it wasn't like him to forget things. He seemed genuinely mortified and I felt bad for tricking him. We were constantly interrupted and he said he'd had enough. I suggested a drink elsewhere, but he declined, saying he couldn't wait to get some sleep. He offered to walk me out and we struggled through the crowd out into the street.

He put his arms round to me to hug me goodbye and gave me a long, luscious, passionate kiss. When he broke off, he quickly retreated and I stood, astonished, as he waved to me from the window of the tour bus.

And then he was gone. I never heard from him, or saw him again.

Clearly, the Jeff who was appearing hassled, distracted and trailing an entourage was not the happy-go-lucky minstrel who had charmed tiny audiences at minute clubs a mere eighteen months previously. But then how could he be? A year alone is a lifetime in the music industry, and Jeff was surely getting what he had dreamt of all those years ago in Anaheim. The hassle of touring and promotion came with the territory. At least in Europe they were (usually) too polite to shout out requests for Tim Buckley songs.

Touring North America yet again that spring, with Soundgarden as support, 'Tim's son' was occasionally affronted by old deadheads who would call out requests for songs by his dad. Jeff's response was initially caustic, but he tempered his put-downs with good humour. 'Fuck *off,*' he drawled gently at one such request. 'The sixties are bullshit... the seventies – bullshit! The eighties? I don't even need to tell you! Except for the Smiths maybe... get out of it! Shit's happening *now*! Now, now, now...'

Not waiting for any audience comeback, Jeff would then snarl into song, seemingly rejuvenated by such a *frisson*. (Admittedly he had caved the previous year and given the Tim Buckley stalwarts a soothing, if half-remembered, rendition of 'Once I Was' in Denver.)

Although relief was not a word one would associate with relentless touring, Jeff and the easily audience-irked Grondahl must have been glad to finish the shared North American tour with Juliana Hatfield that May and return to Europe for scores more live shows and festivals that summer.

Part of Jeff's blessing and curse was that he could do so much, as the wide panorama of *Grace* – which straddled both 'Lilac Wine', 'So Real' and the valleys and oceans between the two – proved.

When his band was in full flight Jeff could easily move into the edges of a hard rock festival, but he could also sing 'Corpus Christi Carol' at Elvis Costello's tasteful Meltdown Festival in London that summer. Jeff beguiled the mix of classical and rock musicians in attendance.

'I was amazed when he did Meltdown,' remembered Costello. 'I asked him what he'd like to sing and he said he'd like to do one of Mahler's *Kindertotenlieder* in the original German! Absolutely fucking fearless.'

Instead Jeff ran through an equally audacious mix of 'Corpus Christi Carol', 'Grace', 'Dido's Lament', and the Smiths' 'The Boy with the Thorn in His Side'. 'My last memory of him,' concluded Costello, 'was at the little party in the green room afterwards. There were all these people sitting around him... a classical pianist, some jazz player – all talking and laughing about music. He charmed everybody.'

Anyone capable of uniting fans of both modern classical music and Metallica could only end up exhausted. At some point it was apparent that Jeff would have to make a choice – and making choices was not his strongest characteristic.

The circus continued with Jeff and the band playing Northern France's Tourcoing on 27 June. The group were by now gaining status, particularly in France. After-show dinners were extravagant, the hotels – when the luxury tour bus was put out to pasture for a night or two – were five-star and the venues were aesthetically pleasing. The interior of the

Municipal Theatre in Tourcoing was Italian-style art-deco, shrouded in wall-to-wall red velvet embroidered with years of dust, red wine and ash – an accurate parallel of Jeff's voice that night, which was finally beginning to show some strain.

Those in the stalls expecting the often smooth digital sonics and polished textures of the *Grace* album would be pleasantly, albeit abruptly, surprised by both Jeff and his band. Very much *live* in concert, the group – now a well-oiled machine – rocked the material in their catalogue, adding sinew and gristle to the songs whilst still somehow retaining their subtle and ethereal qualities. Compared to the sometimes polite FM radio dynamic of the album, the live result was a much more kinetic, heavy and masculine performance that remained both hypnotic and enthralling in its femininity. In a way, this perhaps mirrored more accurately the true qualities of the band's singer, as opposed to *Grace* itself, which leaned subtly towards his more feminised, castrato side.

For all the noise, each song still came out of a definite, loud silence – the audience were almost always rapt and some audience members commented on being as enthralled by the quiet between the songs as the songs themselves. Such elements only added to the dynamic when the band heaved both gracefully and powerfully into each piece on the plush stage, like leopards bringing down bison.

As the gravitational centre of all this kinetic activity, Jeff was a subtle and playful showman. 'He came on stage with a huge glass of wine,' said Tourcoing audience member Oliver Ansel. 'In the kind of glass that you have in America for iced tea – definitely not the kind of wine glass that we use in France!'

Despite the vino, the show started with Jeff and the band fully focused. They saw themselves as a self-contained unit of serious musicians, perhaps in the style of the progressive Miles Davis quintets of the 1970s. As the gig began to marinate – easing in with 'Dream Brother' and 'So Real' – and the love from the friendly French audience became obviously apparent and sincere, Jeff's demeanour mellowed accordingly. At one point, smiling that boyish smile, he asked the audience – in passable French – for a cigarette. The result was a blizzard of Gauloises that showered the band in fresh cancer sticks. Jeff gratefully inhaled his in three drags, stubbed out what was left on the body of his guitar, and fell smokily into 'Hallelujah'. Even as a singer onstage in France, however, Jeff rarely abandoned his guitar. (A characteristic he shared with his father.) For someone who loved Nina Simone and Edith Piaf as much as he did Miles Davis and Led Zeppelin, Jeff rarely struck the chanson-crooner pose, despite his newly acquired nicotine habit. As a performer and musician he seemed happily rooted in his combat boots, planted solidly on stage. From this usually sedentary position he allowed his voice and guitar to fly out fountain-like, rising and falling according to some unseen inner pressure. Jeff's guitar playing was in the main seemingly basic and workmanlike, often deceptively so. Jimmy Page, on first seeing Buckley live, had wondered what 'weird tunings' the boy was using. When he found out that in the main Jeff actually tuned his guitar to the standard pitch, Page was gently gobsmacked. 'Oh, he really is clever.'

In Tourcoing, on a song like the sprawling 'Lover, You Should've Come Over', Jeff exhibited none of the finger-on-fret pyrotechnics that had enthralled him so as a young buck. Rather he seemed to revel in basic strumming that set up a kind of looping drone, a harmonic web which meshed and bound with the group whilst his singing voice sprouted wings and coasted over and beyond the assembled throng. Anyone unfamiliar with Jeff's muso past would have seen him as just another shoe-gazing artisan.

Gary Lucas, himself a supremely competent axe wizard, had instantly recognised Jeff as being 'simply, a great guitar player'. Jeff partly credited the tool itself for his talent. 'A guitar player has an orchestra in his hands,' he shrugged. Andrew Goodsight, the NYC bassist who had worked with Jeff for three consecutive weeks back in the spring of '93, points out: 'He was an amazing guitarist. I don't think many people know this about Jeff. *Grace* was no reflection of his guitar playing unless you listen real close.' Ex-Suede guitarist Bernard Butler was in agreement. 'Yes, he had a fantastic voice and was very sexy, but he was a fantastic guitar player as well... which nobody ever mentions. He used a lot of open tunings, jazz and blues.'

'Musicians are a childish bunch in general, so it's no surprise that it does not get acknowledged,' continues Goodsight. 'He could play anything on the guitar. And not just play anything but really play it – with feeling. He had a certain touch that is hard to explain. Many people can play a Muddy Waters riff, but few can really play it like Muddy. Jeff could.'

Jeff would have been aware of and perhaps even amused by those who saw him as a mere common-or-garden rhythm guitarist, but rarely did anything to counter such pedestrian perceptions. He enjoyed, above all, being part of a group. 'A lot of our shows just seem like huge, pleasurable, messy kissing sessions, where you're so filled with passion that every move you make on the body... sends it into pleasure,' Jeff would claim. Evidently, he saw music as a shared and communal sensual experience rather than the equivalent of jacking off his ego in a lone spotlight. Thus, at this stage, any solo diva posturing was kept locked in the closet. Even in France.

Nina Simone and MC5 songs followed the spiralling 'Lover' (What other band could encompass such extreme poles in a single live set?), along with a version of their own 'Eternal Life' that sounded, according to Oliver Ansel, like 'they had to play it for the last time ever'. Despite the lack of Bono-buffoonery and pantomime moves, 'Jeff gave all he had that night,' concluded Ansel. 'It was such a physical performance. He was totally wet, and had to dry himself off with white towels.'

Although there were reports of Jeff dabbling in heroin on this tour (French journalist Julien Wautier interviewed him in Tourcoing and remembered that 'he was totally high, like a zombie... it was a complete waste of time interviewing him'), Jeff did not need such self-medication. Music was the drug itself, the ultimate rush – he was chasing a natural high that lesser performers would have turned to narcotics to supply. 'I'm completely chemically altered by the end of a performance,' he said, 'due to the places I have to go in my head for the songs.'

Jeff finished the European tour with a typically elegant and dignified solo performance at France's La Veille Classical Festival in St Florent on Tuesday 18 July. He was then flown home, utterly spent and noticeably worn, bedraggled and exhausted.

Back in New York that August, Jeff met up with one of his major musical loves at Electric Lady Studios on East Eighth Street. Jeff had fallen for Patti Smith as a kid when he chanced upon her stoned appearance on MOR-crooner Mike Douglas's TV show during the late seventies.

Patti was at Electric Lady recording her *Gone Again* album, and it was okayed for Jeff – now a respected name in his own right – to be there. After hesitant and polite introductions via mutual friend and engineer-producer Lenny Kaye, Jeff soon became part of Smith's session, ultimately contributing a redemptive high choral part to the otherwise typically dirge-like 'Beneath the Southern Cross'. Like many other musically inclined human beings in the Big Apple, Kaye already knew Jeff from his Sin-é days; the two had spent mellow evenings hanging out in bars, talking about old doo-wop bands, favourite bootlegs and the nature of music itself. He had also worked with Jeff already, recalling: 'I met him through Tom Clark when he played on his demos. He did these incredibly meticulous four-part harmonies which really impressed me... We [Patti and I] thought he'd sound good as the boy on "Beneath the Southern Cross".' Fired up, Jeff cabbed to his apartment and back to retrieve a rare Egyptian instrument – an essrage, a kind of mini-sitar – in order to add texture to another Patti song called 'Fireflies'. Jeff admitted that he was no master of the instrument, but nevertheless, he managed to get a complimentary melody out of it.

'One thing that struck me about Patti Smith,' recalled Jeff, 'is that she has either developed or always had a great deal of compassion for herself... [she's a] great band leader. I was there, at this one jam that they were going to edit down and turn into a song. I had never met Patti before and she was fabulous, fabulous... I felt very embedded in every second that went by.'

'He was very emotional,' Kaye continued. 'A great guy to hang with in a bar... a very soulful human being.'

Jeff seemed like a raw wound during this session, so into and open to it as he was. When Smith told him to 'shut up' at one point – his basic essrage chops were, in his own words, 'putting a strangle on something' – Jeff actually broke down and wept. This one-off session seemed to have a profound effect on him, and as such showed that he was perhaps shedding layers rather than toughening up at a time when a thicker skin may have helped him survive the journey into fame that lay ahead. On a practical level, Jeff met another individual who would play a significant role in what future was left to him. Jamming along with Patti and her band was legendary Television songwriter and guitarist Tom Verlaine.

After months of passive deliberating, something clicked, there in the room. Jeff suddenly decided that he wanted Verlaine to produce the next album.

At this point Sony had invested approximately $2.2 million in Jeff Buckley. *Grace* had performed healthily, but hadn't done enough business to silence the money men. It had not even cracked the *Billboard* Top 100. Territories in Europe and Asia had gone well, but apart from Japan these were seen as minor – ultimately secondary. Yet Jeff had done all that was asked of him by Sony so far as promotion went, whilst somehow managing to retain his ethics, vision, voice and sanity. He had not succumbed to any wholesale addiction aside from music – and apart from the odd off-night, as in Chicago – he was not swimming at the bottom of a glass on any regular basis. The success, as relative as it was, seemed to wash neutrally over the acclaimed singer. 'I'm glad they like it,' he said, referring to *Grace*. 'I'm glad people like music in general. While I'm happy about the accolades and about any acceptance or any liking of the music, it needs an ongoing dialogue.'

In many respects Jeff was tired of talking.

As the end of summer came on slowly, Jeff was not only utterly exhausted by the year's touring, but was at a loss as to how he would follow-up *Grace*.

Tom Verlaine offered a cool possibility, but at this stage it was just that. While Jeff's people talked to Columbia's people and Sony's people talked to Verlaine's people, Jeff and the band were taken to rehearsals in preparation for yet another tour. This one scheduled for the other side of the world – in Australia.

As he unpacked his Strat for the hundredth time, he could only surrender once again to the oncoming whirl.

'Life,' he would profess, 'is chaos.'

8 HELLO AND GOODBYE

'The thing that really shook my world and got my mind thinking about what was true is issues of truth. Like living in this life as a public person now, which I never ever, ever, ever used to be... it's an amazing alternative universe. Just the way people base their beliefs and their decisions on the things they hear about other people but not things that they actually find out for themselves... and you feel like you're surrounded by absolutely non-trustworthy people and that can really kill you. And it did. It killed me.'

Jeff Buckley, September 1995

When Jeff Buckley had moved to New York in 1990, he was to all intents and purposes just another anonymous face in the hustle and bustle, one more John Doe. His 'image', such as it was, was linked steadfastly to his physical presence. He was not perceived, in any exaggerated sense, outside of who and where he was at any given time.

If Jeff was at home in Harlem reading the funnies in the *New York Times*, that was where he was. But in another very real sense, he also existed in the memories of friends, lovers and family members. There were fragments of him in letters, figments of him in photographs, songs – and even in the scrappy, fuzzily photocopied flyers advertising his performances that had eventually circulated around the dives and cafés of lower Manhattan. But in the first year of the new decade, if you wanted a piece of Jeff, you had to go to the source.

This had changed. Within a few years of his escaping LA, Jeff's state of being was in flux. By 1995 Jeff Buckley and his various shades existed as countless diverse images and impressions across the world. While he sat in a Canal Street diner enjoying eggs over easy, a schoolgirl in Tokyo was checking out his latest photo spread in *Rockin' On* magazine. Simultaneously 'Last Goodbye' was leaking from a radio in a kitchen in Cologne, while in France his voice and visage were being smeared across TV screens daily.

Famously uncomfortable at having been voted one of People *magazine's 50 'Most Beautiful People', Jeff eventually sought to downplay his striking good looks. He described his own features as 'generic'.*

People he had never met and would never meet took what they wanted from a lyric, a song, a photo, a video – or more likely an amalgamation of all four – and filtered and refracted these fragments through their individual needs, tastes and prejudices to suit their own subjectivity. Jeff now had little control over how and where his identity was used. In short, Jeff Buckley had become famous. He now existed beyond his immediate self and was by degree becoming other people's property. This was an unsettling and abnormal new reality, and one that he would never have enough time to become accustomed to.

While he was no Elvis Presley, or even a Kurt Cobain, Jeff Buckley and his music were successful on a global scale in a very competitive market. Many countries seemed to take him to their heart in their own particular idiosyncratic terms. Earlier that year, on 13 April 1995, France announced that *Grace* had earned him their prestigious 'Grand Prix International du Disque – Académie Charles Cros – 1995'. This was an award given by a jury of producers, journalists, the president of French culture, and music industry professionals that had previously been awarded to Jacques Brel, Yves Montand, Georges Brassens, Bruce Springsteen and Jeff's own personal favourites, Edith Piaf, Leonard Cohen, Bob Dylan and Joni Mitchell. A gold disc for the album soon followed.

In Cool Britannia he was regarded almost regally by a fierce few. In all the major markets – the top three being the US, Japan and Germany – he did well, the album sales and concert revenue coming close to justifying the expense of both. This was notable, particularly in a music market then dominated by the afterglow of grunge and the new wave of Britpop. But arguably, Jeff embodied a strange amalgamation of both of these genres, one infused with a piercing and baroque chanson element. It was as if he and Sony had forged a new niche in which Jeff Buckley could reign. Jeff himself, when pressed, humorously referred to his own particular style of music as 'degenerate art-fag chamber core', or when further pushed, settled on 'rock'.

He seemed sincerely modest in defining the worth of his success to himself, curious as to why he wasn't more moved by it. 'It's odd, I didn't write "Anarchy in the UK" or "Won't Get Fooled Again" or "The End"… I don't know. I'm just whining, I guess…'

As well as a being a committed musician, permanently intoxicated by music no matter what, Jeff worked hard at pleasing Sony in his professional capacity as their 'product'. He was aware of their investment in him and his attitude toward the money being spent was not a reckless one. On some levels being 'in debt' bothered him, but he acknowledged it as part and parcel of the righteous struggle. 'Everything is a fight,' he would say that year, 'everything... even fighting to come... fighting... against physical fatigue to have an orgasm with the one you want. That's a fight... I need the fight just like the needle needs to be on the groove, or else there's no music.'

So he toured ceaselessly, promoted incessantly and answered the same old questions repeatedly. An average day on the road included waking up exhausted to face interview after interview with little respite or time for true reflection. As photogenic and articulate as the Three Ms were, at this stage few journalists wanted to interview anyone but the man whose name was on the record. Within the structure of such days, music was often consigned to a marginal activity, and throughout these duties Jeff had to use his main instrument – his voice – for the duration. This instrument was then expected to hold up for each night's performance and for each taped TV and radio show. 'I'm pretty well-suited to this life, I think,' mused Jeff, 'it's very adventurous.' Yet even someone raised in transit as Jeff was must have found the constant grind of driving eventually debilitating. Sleeping in the bunk of a bus is no long-term substitute for a night's sleep in one's own bed, or even a hotel room.

Constantly beleaguered by a fresh PR person in each town, denied the time to write new material or to properly rehearse, frustrated, tired and irritable, and never allowed to feel as if he could ever 'switch off', being trapped in such a state of constant motion – all of this meant that no one would have begrudged anyone in such a position the relief of the occasional bottle of tequila, toke on a joint or gram of blow. Jeff did draw the line, however. He refused the main TV chat shows as then hosted by David Letterman, John Stewart and Arsenio Hall. This was quietly radical. Even 'outsider' artists like David Bowie and Tom Waits did such shows when they had a film or CD to promote. But even so, to the casual observer it must have seemed as if Jeff's PR people were still operating in the era of the legendary Nashville radio programme the *Grand Ole Opry* and the days of personable country-and-western crooners like the early Hank Williams. A quick glance at Jeff's itinerary would have given the impression that Sony wanted their boy to go out and actually meet every one o' those good ole folks who had bought his record *personally*. Faced with such remorseless pressures, Jeff began to soften in his attitude toward promotional videos and other such endeavours that he had initially held in vague contempt. In Europe and Canada, where the set-up was more 'workplace', he agreed to appear on TV – as a purely musical guest – with no reluctance at all. 'I just choose wisely,' he said. 'I don't want to be overexposed too soon... I hate the way TV kills stuff. Cobain would write a good song and they would just *kill* the fucker, until you didn't want to hear it anymore… because they'd played it so much.'

Further negatives came with the growing success and minor fame. *People* magazine had voted him one of their 50 'Most Beautiful People'. This was a drag. For anyone who wanted to be revered solely as a serious musician and songwriter, such a label was an annoyingly capricious tag that had the potential to drain credibility for years down the line. Jeff would often be heckled and teased at gigs about this dubious honour. 'It's bullshit,' was his usual curt response.

There were other drawbacks – in public Jeff noticed a loss of anonymity and privacy, depriving him of the simple pleasures of a quiet afternoon beer in a local bar, or of sitting on a park bench and scribbling in his journals. Last but not least was the skewed celebrity stalking. Other, often deranged 'celebrities' wanted to welcome Jeff 'to the club'. The most distressing result of this was a horrendous date with the recently widowed Courtney Love, who invited Jeff to a Broadway production of *Hamlet*. Outside the theatre the pair were besieged by paparazzi, and lurid tabloid stories about their supposed 'affair' flooded the gossip columns. Another high-profile run-in had occurred before *Grace*'s release in November 1993, when – the night after he was introduced to Bob Dylan by Steve Berkowitz – Jeff did a light-hearted impression of the living legend during a Sin-é gig, unaware that members of Dylan's entourage were in the audience. The *Blonde on Blonde* singer subsequently called Sony to voice his displeasure, and a mortified Buckley was coerced into penning a letter of apology.

Jeff was particularly disturbed by his brush with the strange Love, but fortuitously, while he and Columbia haggled over his next single release (the label desired a Christmas release of 'Hallelujah', Jeff wanted them to put out 'So Real') the other side of the world beckoned. A series of dates awaited in Australia. Initially the journey was planned as a showcase tour, a kind of engorged promo and marketing trip, or a series of 'dog and pony shows', as Jeff called them. But this time the Three Ms would accompany him, and he would be relieved to have the full firepower of his band backing up this exotic occasion.

The trip, starting on 28 August and ending on 6 September, would take in seven shows at small theatres consigned exclusively to Sydney and Melbourne. There would be the usual squadron of promo-related duties slotted in between sleep, soundchecks and performances. Ever-hungry, Sony arranged for a promo video to be filmed for 'So Real' prior to rehearsals and departure. The result was endearingly goofy and borderline surreal – the band hammed about in gorilla suits while Jeff simultaneously stripped and ran down the deserted streets of his neighbourhood – but despite the somewhat tacked-on catchy chorus, the song itself was far too enchantingly minor-key and esoteric to become a hit. Still, by granting the release of Jeff's favoured song, both Sony and their signing had reached a compromise. But by the time Christmas came around, 'So Real' had come and gone, selling even less than 'Last Goodbye', and subsequently any interest in releasing 'Hallelujah' fizzled out.

When the band departed for Australia that late summer; their debut album had shifted close to 700,000 units worldwide. But financially they were yet to recoup the money Sony had invested in them. The income allotted to Jeff from these sales would be split between him and the label in the latter's favour, and his share would first go to paying off the countless extra-curricular expenses incurred during the venture thus far. As well as the obvious recording and manufacturing costs, Jeff had to pay back the wages Sony had advanced for his band, crew, and videos. As such, while it was unlikely he would see an actual royalty cheque from sales any time soon, he would at least receive some money from publishing revenue, in particular from his songs being played live, and on TV and radio. That said, he had co-authored only a handful of the songs on *Grace*, and Gary Lucas would justifiably be pocketing as many royalties from 'Mojo Pin' and 'Grace' as Jeff was. Leonard Cohen (or more accurately his manager) would ultimately receive more for Jeff's version of his song on the album than Jeff would for his share in a minor hit like 'So Real'. Although he worked ceaselessly, Jeff was a long, long way away from being rich.

Still, at least while touring, Jeff and the band didn't have to worry about the day-to-day expenses of living, each member being allocated a lump of money – a *per diem* for the duration of the tour. Promoters usually always provided a meal, and a group as easy on the eye as Jeff's were never going to be short of dinner invitations.

'I don't lose myself on stage,' Jeff admitted, 'but I lose my concerns for yesterday or what's gonna happen tomorrow.'

Spirits were further buoyed on the transatlantic flight when it was reported that the Australian shows had sold-out in minutes. Arriving furiously jetlagged almost a day later, the Australian arm of Sony could barely wait for Jeff to recover before shunting him out to an eager press.

Although physically tired, Jeff and the band were energised mentally and spiritually by their arrival in Australia by dint of the whole place looking, smelling and feeling so new to them all. Touring had certainly taken its toll. 'I was getting tired of it in the last moments of playing in Europe,' Jeff told his first Australian interviewer, 'but it's entirely new here and I've had time to convalesce.'

After a further smattering of interviews and not quite enough sleep, the band performed their much-anticipated debut show at Sydney's Metro Club on 26 August. Enthused by the strange new climate, the quartet aired most of the album, adding rocking, incandescent versions of MC5's 'Kick Out the Jams' and perennial favourite 'Kangaroo' to their usual *Grace*-heavy set for good measure.

The tour support was a well-regarded Australian band by the name of Crow, and their then tour manager Jen Brennan recalled that 'there was high anticipation which was rewarded tenfold when he played. He just moved a lot of people. It was quite extraordinary. It's not often that you get a crowd at the Metro that's so silent and still. It was serene and very powerful.'

Buckley tour manager John Pope momentarily dropped his professional guard, ceased being a part of Jeff's road crew, and metamorphosed into a fan. 'He held the audience in the palm of his hand. He'd take you on the ride with him,' he recalled breathlessly. 'He'd lift you and take you down. He paced his gigs with finesse. When he walked on to a stage, he felt a responsibility, but it wasn't to the audience. It was to something else. God knows what.'

The critics were in love too. Australian *Rolling Stone* writer Bruce Elder reckoned that Jeff was 'Mind boggling. You just stood there and you couldn't believe that there was this person whose voice was just pouring out of him... there was so much power in that performance.'

Despite the predictable chat throughout the gig from the industry-types at the bar, many recalled the first Australian show at the Metro as being a mercurial, perfect musical moment in their lives.

A weary but game-sounding Jeff – 'I was in bed from 10:00 to 10:15 and then I got my wake-up call' – was heard the very next morning on ABC's Triple J radio show, answering questions that ranged from what music he liked to 'bonk to' (Henryk Górecki and Disney soundtracks, as it turned out) through to misjudged mentions of his father. Discussing their regular 'Top Ten Tunes to Bonk to' poll, the female radio host made a serious misstep.

JJJ: And so. I get to the point here that [Tim's] 'Sweet Surrender' and 'Get on Top of Me' consistently make it into this Top Ten list. Does that surprise you? [That] Tim Buckley songs... consistently make it in the list of songs to make love to?

JB: [Tense pause] Interesting...

JJJ: Obviously not your preferred choice?

JB: [Longer, tenser pause] Not... really...

When he wasn't being asked how he felt about strangers getting horny to the songs of the father he never knew, Jeff's mood on this first Australian tour was generally upbeat. John Pope was assigned by Jeff's live agent to be his tour manager throughout the trip and the two got on well. He noted that Jeff swung to extremes in his moods when confronted by his public, a boy still struggling with the disorientating new gravity of fame. 'Someone on the street might say, "Are you Jeff Buckley?" ' Pope recalled. 'And one day he might say, "No, he's over there, I saw him just go around the corner." Or sometimes he might go, "Yeah, I'm him," or "Leave me alone." Then they might say something funny and he'd open straight up to them and talk to them like they're long lost friends.'

Still, no matter how fatigued and spooked Jeff was, he never lost his essential joy of life, nor his sense of humour. For instance, the singer was upset when he found out that Pope hadn't made his birthday public knowledge. Jeff promptly organised a penis-shaped cake and presented it to his tour manager on stage in Melbourne before shoving his face into the gift.

The brief tour continued in good spirits for the most part, although the weather occasionally let them down, bringing unseasonal rain for the second show of the tour at Melbourne's Australia Lounge, which was broadcast live on local radio and preceded by an interview with Jeff. 'Damn this precipitation,' he mock-cursed as he took to the stage, back-lit by gas heaters that gave the whole scene a foggy, diffused and eerily romantic air. Although the sun had failed, Jeff's good humour persisted as he teased and joshed with a local DJ prior to the gig.

Excerpt from RRR radio interview, 31 August 1995:
RRR: You're in Australia now – are you aware of many Australian musicians? Nick Cave, have you heard of him?
JB: Oh sure, of course.
RRR: Yeah, he comes from this town, this is his home town. Any other performers that you're aware of here?
JB: Well, in the States everybody's aware of... actually, nobody, hardly, in comparison... nobody really knows about Nick Cave. People know more about Nick and the Bad Seeds and the Birthday Party.
RRR: Are you a fan of those works?
JB: Yeah, and of the Bad Seeds. But people mostly know about AC/DC, Men At Work, Air Supply, Olivia Newton-John.
RRR: Please, please, please...
JB: Rick Springfield...
RRR: Yes, Little River Band, Men At Work, yes, please, we love

that shit...
JB: We don't. [Laughs]

With another 'dog and pony' in-store show taking place the following day, and four more full-band shows pencilled-in before they were due to return to the States (all confined to the boundaries of Melbourne and Sydney) Jeff and the group cemented a special relationship with Australia, evident from the manner in which their sets there were longer than any performed previously. Before flying out Jeff and the Three Ms promised to return as soon as possible.

On his return to America, many friends commented on a subtle and disturbing change in Jeff, but this was somewhat inevitable. Who could tour the globe and not come back worldlier than when they went away? The Scotty Moorhead in Jeff was taking a back seat to a new Jeff – both the day-to-day version and his magazine-adorning, MTV-featured doppelgänger.

That September, Jeff was asked by *Rolling Stone* for a list of his favourite albums. (The choices were charmingly eclectic, running through Styx's *Pieces of Eight*, Isaac Hayes's *Hot Buttered Soul*, Adam Ant's *Dirk Wears White Sox*, and including his friend Nathan Larson's *Mind Science of the Mind* LP.) This was the kind of promotional duty that delighted the fan-boy in him. Fame itself was a looking glass he had already walked through, and the phenomena of celebrity could never compare to the intensity he found in music, but it was a hassle he would have to learn to live with. Speaking of 'fame' in general, Jeff reckoned: 'People are really, very, very, very misguided. The fame thing isn't what people think. I heard it from Ray Davies most eloquently. I think he said there are two myths about people. One is that you're rich and the other is... er... I forget what it is.'

Back at home in New York, the pressure to tour was almost instantly upon him again. Further North American dates had been arranged, but, exhausted, Jeff instructed his manager to cancel them. Just as he caught his breath, this anxiety was inevitably and instantly replaced by another – Columbia's demand for a new album. While the 'Tom Verlaine for producer' campaign inexorably continued, Jeff, unable to adapt to civilian life again so quickly, drifted back into playing a clutch of local shows during November and December. Perhaps it was a hangover from his single-parent childhood, but Jeff often made a point of gigging on New Year's Eve, and during the last hours of 1995, he performed at the Mercury Lounge. His set there was confident, strong, celebratory and much more focused than many previous solo performances. It also saw

Drummer Matt Johnson's (second from right) eventual departure from the band after a fraught Antipodean tour signalled the end of the Grace era.

the premiere of a brand-new song 'that I just wrote today', the brooding, simmering 'Moodswing Whiskey'.

'You going to Sin-é later, Jeff?' called out one jollied audience member.

He was. Jeff ended the year with four songs played at his beloved café, also reading a Beat-infused poem from his scrappy notebook.

Obviously unable to decompress to the wondrously hectic climate of New York, it was just as well that it had been decided prior to the Australian trip that on their return the band should up sticks and relocate. The plan dictated that the band regroup in a neutral space, far from the distractions of both touring and the city.

'We have this house in Long Island,' stated Grondahl, 'and I'd imagine that in two weeks we'll be cooking, kicking out the jams, getting things together.'

His prediction erred on the optimistic side.

Jeff, Mick, Michael and Matt made camp in an old Victorian house (owned by the Grondahl family) in Sag Harbor, Long Island. The place had been recently refurbished by Jeff's record label; floors sanded, doors replaced, and the whole house cleaned in anticipation of the band's arrival. The thrift shop-loving bass player had actually wanted the place decked out in authentic olde worlde junk, but there was no budget for such a makeover.

With Sony (ultimately Jeff) paying a monthly rent of $1,600 from 1 November 1995, Jeff hunkered down, initially with only Michael Tighe and Mick Grondahl for company. There had been a growing distance becoming apparent between drummer Matt Johnson and the rest of the group, and it was more or less common knowledge that they would replace him, if not before the next Australian tour, then definitely before recordings for the next album commenced. Wary of burning his professional bridges, once he had announced his doubts about continuing as the 'Third M', Johnson agreed to stay until a replacement was found.

While Jeff took the second floor for himself, Mick, Mike and he – now sporting greasy pimp moustaches as a badge of solidarity – began to jam, usually drummerless, in the low-pressure environment of the converted attic space.

There were visitors. A friend of Grondahl's, a drummer by the name of Eric Eidel, came to audition at the house. The session was encouraging, if not definitive. In the final week of January 1996, Steve Berkowitz, Jeff's longstanding A&R man, came to check-up on their progress. Rather than find a band rocking out a brand-new set of 'Grace II'-type songs, Berkowitz was distraught to instead discover Jeff in bed, from where he played the puzzled A&R man tapes of swirling and undulating Brian Eno-esque guitar loops and effects. Berkowitz left bewildered and disappointed. His confidence would not have boosted by hearing a recent Australian radio interview in which Jeff had casually admitted that 'the reason you think my writing had been "epic" is because... I don't know how to write songs.'

Adding to the growing sense of disharmony, the increasingly disillusioned Matt Johnson turned up, contributing ideas and songs that, in his own words, 'fell into a black hole'. 'JB was slow to write new material,' states the drummer, 'and this bugged the shit out of Mickey and me. We would try to get Jeff to make our jams into something closer to songs and start playing them live. We wanted to play in a band in a much more traditional way.'

This continual stop-start lack of progress failed to raise the mood. The atmosphere at the house was far from coherent. Ideas and tunes and fragments were thrown back and forth with little chemistry or ignition. Much of any given day was spent in a beer- and grass-infused fug. Jeff didn't feel like being a 'musical director'. But he didn't much like his drummer's songs, either. His own writing was occurring in fits and starts. 'Moodswing Whiskey' and 'Woke Up in a Strange Place' were evolving, and there was the new group effort 'Vancouver' – but musically or otherwise, little was happening. At one point not so long before, the four had seemed to be able to promise so much to one another, as Johnson sadly remembers. 'Jeff seemed to want us to explore the songs and come up with our own stuff, and he did help to write the drum part to "Vancouver". He was a good drummer. So I welcomed and learned from his perspective. The band was always trading ideas in sound. Michael had a very unrelenting, focused style. He really provided a backbone for the band. Mickey was in a parallel universe to me. He always saw things from a wider perspective, and had a gentle overall nature, whereas I was aggressive in some ways, sensitive in others. It all made a cool psycho-soup gazpacho. I guess we all shared a special capacity for imagination.' Sadly this communal state of mind was not helping bring the bigger picture into focus at Sag Harbor.

At one point, from amidst the fog of pot smoke and incense, Jeff announced that he wanted to ditch the Jeff Buckley moniker and release the as yet unwritten, unrecorded and untitled second album under the group name of the 'Two Ninas'. While this was perhaps never meant completely seriously, Jeff's naturally goofy humour had certainly been further perverted by the constant touring and pressure. He had been so recently confident: 'I think the band will really become a band through the material on the next album because... because we're gonna be going through a creative process together.' Considering that they were on the brink of losing their highly distinctive drummer, this was perhaps wishful thinking rather than a statement of fact, but Jeff so wanted to believe it.

Whatever, the idea of the Two Ninas was balked at by both his label and management, and Jeff relented without too much fuss. Columbia gave their (still potential) golden boy leeway, but stopped short of ditching the Jeff Buckley brand-name altogether. At the end of the day, Jeff was not signed to an indie label. With a fifteen-date Australasian tour looming on the horizon (such was Jeff's lack of enthusiasm for further touring that he considered cancelling the tour and being sued), the Sag Harbor house workshop was abandoned, and the band moved back to their respective apartments in New York.

Jeff used what free time was left before jetting off to catch up with his family and non-musical friends. (Lyrics to new songs, such as the eerie 'Moodswing Whiskey', would often allude to fictional sisters and presumably factual cousins.)

For some reason, those who had not seen Jeff for a while attributed his apparent conversion to tequila and cigarettes as being purely a side effect of his new rock'n'roll lifestyle, rather than the newly acquired habit of a boy catching up with his lost childhood. Once again, just as Jeff started to relax, Sony informed George Stein, who in turn let Jeff know, that they were disappointed by his lack of new material. Momentum was an important facet in a career like this, and there was not the merest sign of a follow-up to *Grace*, just a series of sketchy solo songs, some incoherent group jams, and a few tapes of endless guitar loops and feedback. Yet considering Jeff and the band's recent activities, and with another tour forthcoming, exactly when Jeff was supposed to have found time to write the album was a mystery. The impending trip to Australia and New Zealand at least provided an alibi. After a series of refresher rehearsals, and with Matt Johnson still in the band, on 4 February 1996 Jeff and the Three Ms flew to Auckland for the beginning of a two-month series of shows in New Zealand and Australia, entitled The Hard Luck Tour.

The trip began in fine style, with Jeff and Tighe getting slaughtered on rum before their flight had even left the States. When Jeff puked somewhere over the Atlantic and one of Matt Johnson's shirts was hastily confiscated as a replacement for the drunken singer's vomit-spattered own, it only accentuated the tension between the two, a tension further exacerbated by the fact that Jeff and Johnson were set to share rooms on the tour. 'I was roommates with Jeff,' confirms Johnson. 'We were cool with each other. But the money was shit and everything was being done on a small budget. I just felt ripped-off after a while.'

This must have seemed poignantly ironic considering that by now Jeff and the band were perceived in Australia and to a lesser extent in New Zealand as bona fide rock stars, and regularly played to full, broiling-hot 2,000-seater halls. Although the imminent departure of his drummer and friend was a constant thorn in Jeff's side, his mood was buoyed by being able to once again choose his support bands – these being the Dambuilders and the Grifters. There was the added bonus that the former act featured his current girlfriend Joan Wasser (later to reap critical acclaim recording and performing as Joan as Police Woman) on violin. The support acts on this tour never picked up any particular tension from the Jeff camp, soaking up only good vibes – an atmosphere aided and abetted by Jeff's naturally freaky sense of humour.

'He was a master at doing accents and voices,' recalls the Dambuilders'

Dave Derby. 'He would go off on crazy tangents. I remember him doing this hilarious thing where he would pretend to be a Puerto-Rican super and complain about young hipsters in the East Village. I also remember one night in Australia he did a bit onstage where he was showing off a new guitar pedal and did these hilarious mimicries of Neil Young and the Smashing Pumpkins – he would screech [Billy Corgan's lyric] "despite all my rage, I'm still just a rat in a cage". He had a fantastic, quick and wickedly smart sense of humour.'

Jan Hellriegel, a soft-rock, chanteuse singer-songwriter, joined the group from Melbourne onwards. Her first impression of Jeff was of someone as in awe of his own talent and luck as anyone else.

'He was just a guy with a guitar and amazing voice and the ability to transform the mundane into something magical, but didn't quite get what it was that he did exactly,' she observes, adding: 'And his band were phenomenal. They were so completely *with* him – onstage at least.' Their first show together at the Melbourne Palais was a memorable introduction for Hellriegel. 'All I remember is this incredible silence from the crowd when Mr B set foot onstage. No one talked, no one moved, no one went to the bar, there were no chinking glasses. Everyone was just absorbed in the concert. I vividly remember not moving from my spot for his entire set. I was incapable of doing anything except being sucked into this music – this incredible music.'

As The Hard Luck Tour found its momentum, good reviews and word-of-mouth fed an ever-growing interest in Jeff and band. Audiences were now turning up with the highest of expectations and the venues were getting bigger. With increased ticket sales came the groupies, but Jeff – fully committed to violinist Joan – could never take this aspect of rockdom seriously. 'By the time we returned to Sydney,' recalls Hellriegel, 'suddenly everyone wanted a piece of him. It happened that quickly. He thought the whole thing was hilarious, and because this "thing" called stardom hit him in Australia first he was stunned. I remember sitting backstage between sets laughing with him as the Sydney folks – mostly blonde babes – started clambering to get backstage. He was so turned off by the whole thing they had no idea how funny/ugly he thought the whole scene was.'

Disappointed groupies could have been forgiven for getting the wrong idea if Jeff's stage banter on this tour was anything to go by. Introducing 'Eternal Life' in Melbourne, he was in a horny mood. 'Lots of people like to be kissed all over the neck. And then be fucked like an animal from behind! We all have our knight-in-shining-armour fantasy, and we have our classroom-rape fantasy, and they go together... and you can come here and experience it all vicariously through my show.'

While to outsiders the tour appeared to be going well, Matt Johnson had, at least in his own mind, already left the group. 'I was very unhappy in that psychological environment,' he states, perceptively adding: '[But] I did help create it... So I needed to unravel my own issues from those around me.' To do this he would definitely have to leave the group upon their return, and as a result of this knowledge there was occasional on-tour friction, with Johnson going walkabout after one particularly rapturous show, returning just in time for the encore. To compound these internal pressures, Jeff was always conscious of the need for new material. On arrival, when he was asked if there was anything specific he'd like to do whilst in Australia, his rather sorry reply was: 'Work on stuff between the gigs. See how they work... get stoned with the other bands... and don't get in trouble... I love pot... you got any?' Jeff had little time to take advantage of the other 'natural' pursuits Australia had to offer him, and not much of an inclination, either. When asked if he planned on surfing his reply was typically laconic. 'I love the sand and the water, but it's the beach-goers that irk me...'

Although the audiences didn't seem to notice, the group were disillusioned with the first clutch of shows, but eventually began to cook, often quite literally when the balmy local climate combined with the inevitable heat of the stage. By the time they hit Sydney for their first round of dates there (they would return to close the tour in the capital), the band had introduced Jeff's new songs 'Moodswing Whiskey' and (the Japanese tour-inspired) 'Woke Up in a Strange Place' into the set, as well as a further refined version of the instrumental 'Vancouver'. Occasional cover versions included the ever-present 'Kangaroo', as well as some Edith Piaf cuts and Bob Dylan's 'If You See Her, Say Hello'. While there were no new group compositions to rival 'Eternal Life' ('Vancouver' remained an instrumental at this point), Jeff enjoyed taking his new songs to the Three Ms.

'It deepened my scope as to the life of a song,' he acknowledged mid-tour. 'From when you make it up and then give it to the band and then take it on the road... it's elastic by nature, it changes with your every feeling.'

Occasionally this elasticity irked Jeff's fans. Some audiences who had expected the live show to mirror the airbrushed confines of the record made their disappointment vocal. 'Stop playing that heavy stuff!' screamed one frustrated punter. Jeff's response resonated more than the usual heckler put-down, providing a personal insight that many in the crowd would have wanted to experience first-hand. 'Music should be like making love,' he said. 'Sometimes you want it soft and tender, other times you want it hard and aggressive.'

The new, raging and rampantly luminescent version of 'Eternal Life' – now sounding more like Motörhead than the polite *Grace* version – certainly alluded to the latter scenario. Speaking less metaphorically, offstage Jeff pointed out another simpler reason for people's occasional disappointment. 'When we made *Grace* we were a really new band,' he said, 'and I was just like furiously trying to get them together and focused. So after seven months of touring things are just completely different.'

Referring to the 'softer' side of his muse, he clearly wished for a harder, rockier edge to his music. 'I wish it would go berserk. I wish it would go insane and stop being the middle-of-the-road rock everybody knows it is.'

As the tour progressed throughout Sydney, Brisbane and the Gold Coast the group sometimes appeared more and more fragmented onstage, veering between highs and lows (each show was 'hit and miss' Jeff amiably admitted), with Grondahl by now singing his own compositions each night. Offstage, tensions between Grondahl and Johnson, and by default the rest of the group and crew, became increasingly strained and blistered. 'We were all assholes sometimes,' admits Johnson. 'Sometimes I wish we would have just gone out and played some Frisbee together. A little sunshine and exercise. But those days are gone.'

The band were also unhappy with the sound (at the end of the tour, sound engineer Paul Wilke would be dismissed), and, of course, promotional duties carried on unabated. (One major radio station hosted a 'Jeff and Tim'-themed evening, which the living singer could only have had mixed feelings about.)

Yet Jeff retained his good humour throughout and was always supportive of his friends in the support bands, as Dave Derby remembers. 'Obviously opening for him and being a lead singer was an intimidating thing. I remember one time I was trying to warm-up by singing a song of ours – "Down" – before a gig in the corner of the backstage, and he played the song on piano, doing my bass line as well as Joan's violin line just from having heard us play it. He was insanely musical. Aside from being yet another example of his incredible gift and his ear it was a really simple and sweet gesture of support, I thought.'

The shows were for the most part rapturously received, even as a sense of subtle disintegration pervaded behind the scenes, although some who had witnessed the first mini-tour in 1995 were slightly disappointed. One listener called into the Jeff and Tim-themed radio show stating that 'I saw them last year... and just the energy in that dark and grimy place... and he was right in your face and it was incredible and this time...well, I dunno. Maybe because he didn't play many club circuits [this time around], you were stuck in this huge theatre, sat on vinyl seats and...

there was an atmosphere missing. I mean, I still came out with a smile on my face but... it was different.'

Bruce Elder, the respected Australian critic who was also a fervent Tim Buckley fan, commented: 'That tour, late last year really has to be one of the most remarkable tours I've ever seen, and I think a lot of people who saw that were somewhat disappointed that when he came back this time it wasn't quite as good. And I don't know whether that was venues or, "Gee, they've been playing those songs a couple of years now and they really need a new album and some new material." '

There was a growing, if muted, disappointment at the lack of new songs and Jeff was distractedly aware of this. He found it very hard to concentrate on writing between shows, exhausted as he was, and distracted by inner-band frictions, day-to-day hassles and not least by the presence of his girlfriend. When he did have downtime, he ended up watching low-grade Australian TV in his room until all hours, something else that only agitated his room-sharing drummer, whose main offstage activity now mostly consisted of meditating whilst standing on his head. Tensions were eased a little when the group attended the annual gay and lesbian Mardi Gras in Sydney. ('Insaaaaane,' according to a gleeful Jeff.)

To the numerous Australian musicians who made up the various guest support bands on the tour, the experience was, in the main rare and positive. Many who worked with Jeff on these dates comment that however hassled he may or may not have been at any given time, he always seemed utterly enraptured by music, both on and offstage.

Joe Giuseppe, then drummer with local support group Cactus Child, recalls his own personal highlight from the final Australian show: 'I remember the night at Selina's [Coogee Bay Hotel Sydney] where, upon completion of our opening set, I was lugging my drums and congas back up the stairs toward the dressing rooms, which in those days were just crappy pub hotel rooms. Jeff was sitting on a bed jamming and warming up when he called to me to come in and bring the congas and jam with them. I remember Matt Johnson the drummer was there and we must have played grooves for about twenty minutes before they were called to the stage... That was a definite highlight of my life.'

Dave Derby adds: 'He was very supportive of other musicians. He knew how hard it was to be one and he knew what kind of pressure we were under. He absolutely loved music of all kinds and he consumed it in the way most people consume food. He was inspiring to be around because he reminded me how important it was and is to make music.'

For Jeff there seemed little distinction between the onstage and the off.

'There's music in everything,' he believed. 'There's music in semis going down the street. There's music in school being let out, music in Old Milwaukee beer cans rattling around in a garbage bag. It's everywhere.'

Jeff even found the kind of music endorsed by Stockhausen and John Cage in the 'shittiest' bars. Speaking of a female singer he had heard one night, he explained with awe that she 'sang this Gaelic song to the key of the air conditioner that was in the bar. So there was this long drone. I assure you that this was completely unintentional and natural and she had a voice that was divine and I was sitting there with some very nice people, pleasantly stoned, talking about *Perfume* – the novel – not prepared for what was happening. That woman was amazing. She had a real pure voice, a real pure delivery, a really pure soul behind it. I hadn't seen that in a long time... this woman was divine.' In this regard, Jeff was more than justified in seeing a direct relationship, as he did, between a church and a bar.

There were other highlights of a less divine nature. 'Three cool things happened,' Jeff recounted slyly. 'Jimmy Page came backstage one night. The other was we got to play four songs with the Grifters, and during the encore someone took a shit in the seat and left – either they couldn't control it or they wanted us to die! So they took a shit in the balcony... it was this total Rite-of-Spring loss of control!'

The tour wound up on 1 March 1996. Most of the group had lost weight. Through venues being so full and hot (photographers reported that the lenses of their cameras were fogging up in the heat), Jeff and the Three Ms were sweating away pounds every night. Among the audiences, voices of dissent were in the minority and mostly belonged to those who had already been dazzled by the first mini-tour in late 1995. As such, expectations were high. For those who were seeing Jeff in Australia for the first (and final) time, the concerts were usually nothing less than an epiphany.

Jeff was already feeling at home here, finding it 'beautiful and clean – my impressions of Australia are really superficial'. But, listening to Jeff talk and perform in Australia, one got the impression it was a place he could have lived. (His step-father's dad did in fact live there, but it's unknown whether Jeff and he met up.)

The band flew back to JFK, literally to face the music. Sony was by now insistent that definite work be done on the second album. Jeff was still struggling with finding the time to write new material, but despite the official resignation of Matt Johnson, the mood was one of hope and accomplishment. Jeff and the Three Ms had found a unique warmth and love in Australia, and no one would have believed then that they would never return.

9. ENDGAME

'That's the very first struggle: Should I live? Must I live? Must I do this living thing? Is there a place for me? Does anybody give a shit? Do I? Why should I?'

Jeff Buckley, 1996

A blizzard blanketed the Big Apple that New Year. It snowed so hard that New York had already had its normal seasonal snowfall before the end of the first week of January. Jeff and his group had flown to the warmer climes of New Zealand and Australia soon after, and in their absence, as 1996 slowly budded through the snowdrifts, New York continued as it had done for decades, to simultaneously evolve and devolve. It grew backwards and forwards, down and out, expanding geographically, becoming not only wider and taller but deeper, dirtier and denser. Sociologically it was an overflowing, drone-heavy beehive, the daily grind and bustle hustling through a constant cornucopia of neon, sirens and traffic noise. The buildings and their advertising hoardings, the theatre billboards, the store fronts, the fly posters and the very textures of the city itself changed. As the snow dissolved into a grey mucus slush, the rudiments of the city re-emerged, its walls and sidewalks defaced, spray-painted and weather-beaten. Bars opened and closed, plays folded on Broadway, pop groups, schemes, dreams, and aspirations came and went, Jeff Buckley's story blinked as one among millions that winter.

From the other side of the world, Jeff, Mick, Matt and Mike returned that early March to much milder weather. Once his fatigue allowed, Jeff took to the familiar streets, and amongst the pristinely grubby, choking metropolis he strolled, himself a microcosm of the very city, a walking orchestra of vice, virtue, struggle and contradiction. He was a deeper, richer, more used-up and mutated self than the boy who had arrived in this city some six years ago. Geographically, he had made changes too –

The idol in search of an idyll, 1995.

in recent months Jeff had relocated to Brooklyn. His appearance reflected his journey, mirroring the inner and outer weather. Clean-shaven and modestly bequiffed at the beginning of the year, his look now took on a grungy, eccentric air. As well as freely experimenting with facial hair – Jeff had sported a moustache in recent months – he also claimed to have dreadlocked his pubic hair. He was often unshaven, with long greasy hair that thinned and parted in the middle, and he frequently wore the same nondescript clothes day after day. This was, in part a reaction to the 'Beautiful People' poll results printed in *People* magazine the previous year, after which 'he started uglifying himself', reckoned his mother. 'He dyed his hair black and started parting it down the middle and not washing it. He wanted to be taken seriously as an artist.'

An old friend of a friend, Antony Fine, literally bumped into Jeff during one of these wanderings. 'I ran into Jeff on the corner of Broadway and Houston on a hot and crowded Saturday afternoon,' he recalled. 'He had let his hair grow long and dyed it black – it was odd, and it looked stringy and he looked a bit pursued. He lit up when he saw me and as I was saying hello, still recognising him through the changed hair, he surprised me with a big bear hug. Then we chatted briefly and separated. My impression was that he was troubled, pursued, worried, under some cloud.'

Whilst never by any description either an alcoholic or a drug addict, Jeff continued to dabble with intoxicants when and where the urge took him. Far from the days when, starving, he would hungrily eye a dumped pretzel in the trash, he now not only had easy access to a wide world of narcotics if he so wanted, but as a bona fide if still cultish and coltish rock star, he was also often offered them *gratis*. Yet Jeff seemed too self-aware, too painfully conscious to ever yield completely to the numbness of addiction. 'I believe he was doing some kind of drugs,' says Nicholas Hill, 'but he would make a bad junkie because he couldn't pull it off. He couldn't be devoted to something that much.'

Penny Arcade confirmed that 'Jeff was far too erratic a personality to sustain any kind of drug use. He was too erratic to do the same thing two days in a row. His main thing was alcohol.' Although he never did give into it, the deep and utter – if temporary – absence of pain that smack offered must have sometimes seemed tempting. His system had been re-jigged by the constant touring and adulation. His inner compass was temporarily mangled, skewed, busted. By touring so exhaustively, by filming so much TV, by doing so much radio, by talking about himself day after day, Jeff had in effect been away to a strange and faraway place – not only literally, but metaphorically.

On returning to his neighbourhood, many of his old friends had in his absence been busy simply continuing within the linear strains of their own – comparatively ordinary – lives. No one, least of all his civilian buddies, could ever properly appreciate what Jeff had been through when he disappeared for months at a time. On returning, like many musicians he had a hard time adapting. In some ways he was suffering a kind of post-traumatic stress disorder. Few were aware of this. To them, Jeff just seemed strung out. Old Sin-é regular Daniel Harnett remembers Jeff from this time.

'I hadn't seen him in two years – he'd been on the *Grace* tour. Now he was back and starting to gather his new material, and I saw him at a party. I hadn't seen him in two years, so I wanted to say, you know, "Hey, how are you? How's the music going?" – you know, catch up. But Jeff was never conventional in that way. I walked up and when he saw me, he gave me a big smile, big hug, and – I remember, we were standing in a courtyard, this was a party in Brooklyn – and before I could ask him how he was or anything he sort of looked around in the darkness and said, "Do you smell, like... air freshener?" I sniffed and said, "Yeah, I do, actually." Then he walked away, wandered over to some other group, and I was like, "Uh... oh, okay." '

Columbia were exerting as much pressure as they could – primarily through Jeff's managers Stein and Lowry – for the singer and his band to begin a work on a new album. Much to Sony's chagrin, the word came back that the signs were not good. Rather than having an artist who was raring to go with a tour-taut band and twelve new songs primed to be alchemised into platinum-selling sales by a top producer, the reality of Jeff Buckley in the first half of 1996 was somewhat unexpected. Jeff and the Three Ms had returned from touring not only exhausted and pissed off, but partially alienated from one another. Matt Johnson had actually left the band, and his departure was no small decision for a freelance musician so involved in a set-up as successful as the Jeff Buckley crusade. 'My friend the drummer decided he had to leave,' said Jeff sadly. Yet for the now relatively clean-living drummer, the choice was as good as made for him.

'I can only say that in terms of personal development, quitting the JBs was as good for me as was having the opportunity to play with them,' he states philosophically. 'More than ever in my life I had to face my choices alone. It helped me develop independence, 'cause as a drummer, you really need to be able to stand on your own.' In some sense, his quitting the band was for the *good* of the band, as he saw it. 'If a singer senses fear or reticence in a drummer, they're distracted by it, and can't find their way into the heart of the music.'

Unfortunately, Matt's absence didn't mean that the remaining three were by default particularly 'tight'. As recently as late the previous year, within the communal vibe of the Sag Harbor house, the singer had been explicitly verbal about wanting the next album to be much more of a group effort; even to the point of abandoning his trademark name and encouraging the others to write and perform their own songs. But Jeff was no longer enamoured of this idea. 'I cannot sing Grondahl's songs,' he had admitted. Yet despite this turnaround, he did not have enough strong material of his own for a complete album. And the option – as utilised so well with the debut album – of including cover versions was a *non*-option. Jeff had vowed as much when they were finishing up the *Grace* recording sessions back in Bearsville Studios almost three years previously. To compound this fractious state, Sony wanted – *needed* – the next album to clean-up commercially. *Grace* had not been particularly expensive in relative terms compared to other acts on the roster, but it had still not recouped its costs, at least not globally. Sony had given Jeff his arty freedom, allowing him, in many ways, to treat their multi-global set-up and vast money-oiled machine like a laidback indie label. While this had paid off critically, kudos was not a priority for Sony's multitude of faceless shareholders.

Jeff, while still regarded by Sony as a prestige signing, was, as far as the market place went, still very much a niche artist, albeit (and this made Sony ache so) with the potential to cross over in a very real major league way. Jeff's label-mates Mariah Carey and Michael Bolton (whose sales were effectively funding his own musical ventures) were both going platinum, while Jeff was barely bringing in silver and gold. Even with a lack of new material and a fragmented band, Columbia believed that the right producer could rally the forces, focus the outfit and, in Berkowitz's words, turn Jeff (for better or worse) into 'the next U2'. So one can only imagine the frustration and downright resentment the suits at Sony felt when Jeff continued to stubbornly insist on Tom Verlaine for producer.

The name of Tom Verlaine did not imbue confidence within the hallways and boardrooms of Sony. And while hipper and more pleasantly empathetic than your average multi-national record company's A&R man, Berkowitz had never been sold on Jeff's latest stipulation. Although well-regarded, Verlaine was a cult figure, to put it politely, and his production credits were underwhelming and limited mostly to his own solo records. Since the break-up of his first and most famous band, Television, way back in 1978, Verlaine – identified primarily as a guitar player – had continued a committed but patchy solo career whose critical notices always outweighed sales. He was, however, as supernaturally cool as the French poet from whom he'd borrowed his surname, and although his being a candidate to produce the follow-up to *Grace* may have seemed perverse in the extreme to some, for Jeff – who's fear of actual fame had only been heightened by his recent brushing up against it – the prospect of using such a cult, commercially unproven NYC hipster made perfect sense. Berkowitz and Sony did not buy this. As far as they were concerned, to date they had been more than indulgent of Jeff's idiosyncratic aesthetic, and had been rewarded with disappointing commercial results. Berkowitz spoke for the majority when he told Jeff that he didn't think now was the time for their signing to be going all esoteric on their asses. The A&R man instead suggested more obviously commercial producers with predictable names like Butch Vig, Brendan O'Brien, Steve Lillywhite, Brian Eno and, most obviously of all, Andy Wallace.

Jeff was not impressed by such suggestions. 'In the end, I'm the one who really knows best about the work,' he stated simply. Columbia still tried to insist on another producer – anyone but Verlaine in fact. The singer stood his ground, non-aggressively. His reaction was classic Jeff: hardly any reaction at all. Berkowitz was forced to repeat himself. Sony had major, long-term faith in their signing and as such the company had agreed on Jeff's wishes pretty much down the line so far. To be fair, in return Jeff had played the game and had fulfilled all of his obligations, each and every 'dog and pony show' they had asked of him. His perspective on his place within a massive company like Sony was exceedingly astute. 'What it is, is that people don't exactly know what it is they're selling,' reasoned Jeff, referring to Columbia and major labels generally. 'But they still have to sell it… [so] you have to know your own value… and you have to communicate as to how it should be done. The people I do business with… it's only pretty much five people out of the huge religious cult that is Sony worldwide.'

Yet even among his staunchest supporters at Columbia, and even within his circle of friends, there was the consensus that Jeff had done it his way with *Grace* and it hadn't exactly worked. At least not as well as it *should* have. Regardless, Jeff stuck to his guns, and while the debate slowly simmered, he went about the more practical activity of breaking in a new drummer. Having made first steps toward the drum stool late the previous year, and with Matt Johnson now officially out of the picture, Eric Eidel was a fully-fledged band member. That March he Jeff, Mick and Mike began rehearsing mostly new material (thankfully no new tours had been booked) four days a week. Jeff now tried his hand at the role of band director, instructing the musicians and directing the arrangements to such an extent that often he wouldn't even be singing during these sessions. 'He'd bring in songs and we'd work out arrangements,' recalled the at-the-time fairly inexperienced Eidel. 'Sometimes the songs had words, sometimes they didn't. It didn't fall neatly into a style. But there was a conscious decision not to do any more covers. I think he was growing as a writer, deliberately focusing more on his own compositions.'

Jeff was not tempted to use this diversion to rethink the band on any larger scale. Although much of his recorded work featured numerous overdubs and textures, he seemed to want to stick to the purity of bass, drums, two guitars and voice, although Johnson never recalls any discussion of this subject taking place. 'There was no band philosophy that I'm aware of,' he confirmed. Jeff admitted that the set-up of guitar, bass and drums was 'a natural thing, because that's the way I hear music, through the guitar. I remember teaching myself to learn the ranges and the transpositions of saxes and violas and oboes... orchestration. I loved it. I still haven't applied it, though, but I will.'

When Steve Berkowitz got to hear the new tunes, they meanly dashed his U2 fantasy. These new Buckley compositions were far from the bombastic sermonising of his favoured Irish troupe. Although some of the songs did, within a band arrangement, ripple, rock and flex dynamically – such as the now modified (with words and melody) 'Vancouver' and the esoterically titled 'The Sky Is a Landfill' in particular – the overwhelming tone of the new songs, especially 'Moodswing Whiskey', 'Morning Theft' and the freshly rearranged oldie (dating back to 1993) 'You and I' was one of intimacy and reflection. This was no surprise when one considered Jeff's essential nature. He himself admitted that 'my life is my fuel for my poetry... my lyrics.'

Compared to Jeff's previous recordings, these songs were closer to 'Hallelujah', in the main, as opposed to the bright jingle-jangle bombast of 'Grace' or 'Last Goodbye'. As far as the U2 comparison went, while Bono often sounded as if he were bellowing to the back row of an overcrowded coliseum full of counterfeit human currency, Jeff sounded as if he were singing into a cracked shaving mirror on the moon.

Yet despite such promise, the practice sessions did not have the spark and fire of the original line-up. Jeff was not happy. Increasingly, it became obvious that his musical path was blocked. Bugged by the constant Verlaine debate, and suddenly claustrophobic in a town where he could no longer drink in his favourite local bars or pool halls without being bugged by fans, Jeff did what he always did – he took to the road. This time, he went in the role of bass player, along with girlfriend Joan

Wasser on violin, for four dates in North America with his friend Nathan Larson (of indie art group Shudder to Think), who was promoting his solo album *Mind Science of the Mind*. The tour was just what Jeff needed – low-key, low pressure and amenable to him melting into the background onstage when he needed to. Singer and multi-instrumentalist Mary Timony was also part of the band. 'Jeff was friends with Nathan Larson, who was the principal songwriter in Mind Science. Also, Jeff was the boyfriend of Joan Wasser who played violin. So it all made sense, and he thought it would be fun to join us for that tour, since Nathan was looking for a bass player. He played a baritone guitar instead of a bass. We recorded a song at a WGNS studio which used to be next to the Black Cat [nightclub] in DC. The tour was pretty short. We just played on the East Coast...'

Outside of music, Jeff began to diversify into other extra-curricular activities. Although he continued to turn down endorsements for products such as Gap clothing ('I don't wear Gap,' he reasoned) and still had no intention of gracing David Letterman's sound stage, he did take up the occasional journalistic offer. As well as interviewing the quixotic Mexican composer, Esquivel, that January Jeff sat down with one of his own personal musical gods, Nusrat Fateh Ali Khan.

The interview with the elderly Esquivel was conducted by telephone, and although the maestro's rich Mexican accent was sometimes hard to decipher over the scratchy line, Jeff was clearly delighted to be speaking to such a hero, frequently sounding like a giggling teenager and audibly marvelling at the idea of employing fourteen sets of bongos. Interestingly, whilst Esquivel professed a knowledge of groups like Stereolab and the Tindersticks, he was clearly unaware of who Jeff Buckley was. At the end of the interview, although Jeff had never mentioned his own work once beyond introducing himself as a 'musician and singer', Esquivel, clearly impressed by Jeff's vibe, enquired, 'Can I ask you a favour? If I give you my address can you send to me something that you write?'

During much of his lifetime (he passed away in 1997), Nusrat Fateh Ali Khan was considered one of the biggest stars of *qawwali*, a form of Islamic devotional music prevalent in Pakistan. A vocal art over seven centuries old, *qawwali* was traditionally passed down orally from father to son by Sufi masters, Sufism being a Muslim philosophical-cum-literary movement originating from the tenth century. As a progressive mystical order, Sufism, through *qawwali*, promoted the union of the soul with God through poetry and symbolism.

In Jeff's opinion, 'Nusrat Fateh Ali Khan... [acts as] a living testament to music's power to link all humans, unashamed of emotion, to the divine. At once soaring and penetrating, these sounds seem to rip open the sky, slowly revealing the radiant face of the beloved. *Qawwals* don't sing, they are born to sing, and the men who accompany Khan in his ensemble do not just play music, they become music itself.'

Such a statement could almost apply to Jeff's more transcendent shows.

Although geographically and stylistically, the trio of Jeff, Nusrat and Esquivel seemed galaxies apart, they were in fact all bound by the same goal; the manifestation and pursuit of joy and becoming through music. In addition, there was the obvious parallel between the Sufi traditions of father to son inherent in Jeff's own relationship with Tim. Jeff must have been irked by the irony of this when earlier that January at an NYC hotel, Jeff spoke (via interpreter) to Nusrat for *Interview* magazine. In photographs of Nusrat and Jeff taken at the meeting, the younger singer seems ecstatic, his Hollywood smile threatening to crack his visage in half. Jeff had come some way since that cold winter's day in Harlem six years ago when his drummer roommate had first played him the music of Nusrat on a battered boom-box. But despite his outward success, Jeff remained unchanged so far as his devotion to music went.

His appreciation of the Pakistani singer was sometimes embarrassingly earnest. Jeff would occasionally play extracts from Nusrat's songs live. The audience were often initially shocked to hear Jeff's eerily authentic sounding rendition of 'Yeh Jo Halka Halka'. Such alien-sounding music caused many to assume that Jeff was in one of his 'jokey moods', perhaps pulling off an elaborate riff or a Peter Sellers impression. But by the end of such renditions, Jeff would often have the audience clapping along. ('This is what they do in Pakistan!' he shouted encouragingly at one gig). Parts of the printed conversation that ended up in the perennially-hip *Interview* were, to anyone with knowledge of Jeff's personal history, sometimes unbearably poignant.

JB: You once had a dream that is now very famous. Can you describe it to me?
NFAK: My father [the *qawwali* singer Ustad Fateh Ali Khan] died in 1964, and ten days later, I dreamed that he came to me and asked me to sing. I said I could not, but he told me to try. He touched my throat, I started to sing, and then I woke up singing. I had dreamed that my first live performance would be at my father's *chilla* [funeral ceremony], where we would all sit together again and read prayers from the Koran and so on. On the fortieth day after his death, we

Jeff and his idol, Pakistani qawwali *singer Nusrat Fateh Ali Khan, whom he met for the first and only time when the two recorded a conversation for* Interview *magazine.*
(© Jack Vartoogian/FrontRowPhotos)

held the ceremony, and I performed for the very first time.

JB: What was life like before the dream?

NFAK: I was just studying with my father, a very difficult task for me since he was a great, great *qawwali* singer. He didn't want me to become a musician; he wanted me to be a doctor, because he said singing was too hard…

...When did you start? [Performing]

JB: My first performance was at about age fourteen. And I also hid from my father. He had died by the time I started, but I hid from him a gift that I was born with. There was a period when I was frozen for about three or four years, starting when I was eighteen. In my dream at that time, the ghost of my father came smashing through the window. It doesn't take a dream to make a singer, but yours was a beautiful gift...

Jeff had empathised with Nusrat as soon as he'd learned about him. 'I just identify with his story,' he would admit. 'I identify with his androgyny and his lack of age and his contradictory existence... he was laughed at as a kid, laughed at by his father's pupils. And that's very, very, very... really cruel and very heartbreaking to be laughed at when you're a kid. And it's in front of his father. And he must have wanted to please his illustrious father. He must have.'

Although the experience had been nothing less than wonderful, Jeff would come to regret his approach to this particular journalistic endeavour. 'I wish I had been... prepared when I interviewed Nusrat Fateh Ali Khan,' he sighed a month later. 'My thought was, "Go in cold, don't prepare." Big fucking mistake. I had tons of questions to ask him, all for my own gain. The magazine-oriented questions were shot back to me from his interpreter. On the tape, the only English quote from Nusrat was a misunderstanding. I was saying something about writing all the poems by heart, because all the *qawwals* are sung by heart. Nusrat said, "Without heart, you cannot be a *qawwali*." I said, "No, learning by heart." And he said, "Oh yes. Sing them every day." He was amazing. He was a fucking cafe-au-lait-coloured Brando.'

By the time Jeff had returned from the Mind Science of the Mind tour that spring, Columbia had finally and somewhat begrudgingly accepted Verlaine as being involved in the next step.

As it was generally agreed that Jeff and the band were not yet ready to go ahead with full-on album recording sessions, Sony allowed Verlaine to book into a local studio for what was at worst to be considered 'demo recordings' and, at best, sessions from which at least an EP could be salvaged. Thus, on 15 June the band set up in Studio A at Sorcerer Studios – one of Verlaine's favourites – in downtown Manhattan, north of Canal Street. The modest budget reflected Sony's reticence – less than $15,000. This was ample, as far as Verlaine was concerned. He would later self-deprecatingly say of these sessions that he 'just turned on the tape recorder'. Sorcerer Studios was a world away from Bearsville, where

Grace had been recorded, but it was a fine studio in itself, held in high esteem by such musicians as Iggy Pop and Tuxedomoon. But although it had a funky, grimy, down-home reputation, it was in fact an impressive, well-appointed space laid out in teak and hosting a grand piano within its fourteen-foot-high main room. It also had the other advantages – or disadvantages, depending upon your perspective – of being within minutes of local bars, restaurants, clubs, and dealers.

Whatever the perceived pros and cons, the sessions did not flow; with drummer Eric Eidel in particular having difficulty finding his place, both within the dynamic of each song, within the band itself and even in the studio. He was not used to playing out of the natural sightlines of the rest of the guys. (He was of course shut up in his own drum room which, although it boasted a fine widescreen view of Studio A, would still have seemed alienating to a young drummer.) Such factors did not relax the nervy Eidel, throwing his already shaky gravity and screwing up his timing.

Despite their drummer's weaknesses, Mick, Mike and Jeff managed to put down rough versions of 'The Sky Is a Landfill', 'Vancouver', 'You and I', and Jeff's solo rendition of the achingly spooky 'Morning Theft'. As with the rehearsal sessions, there was throughout a nagging sense of something not being quite right. Verlaine himself was well beyond the point of having anything to prove or needing to impress anyone. He hadn't even bothered to meet with Jeff's 'people' in person once he'd been appointed as producer. He'd also been under the false impression that he was there to simply document a band ready to go, in full flow. As it was, each song sounded slightly different each time they played it, and it was obvious to Verlaine that the group were all over the place. Attempting to mould individual takes, parts and tempos into some kind of shape within the short space of time that the budget allowed, he often came across to the band as being a tad too dominant and on occasion even a bully. At one point, in neutral tones that suggested a carefree attitude to life and beyond, he suggested that they simply sack Eidel and find a new drummer before proceeding further. While Verlaine may have been on the money, it was hardly tactful, and Eidel's nerves crumbled further, the blood icing up in his already frigid veins.

After six budget-dictated and musically mediocre days, the initial recordings were deemed finished. Jeff returned to attend the mixing of the songs for a further five days, but by 26 June the plug was pulled, leaving all concerned with far from satisfying results. Rather than compress the shaky band and songs into a solid, focused prospect, the sessions had achieved the opposite, serving to highlight their shortcomings and flaws. And although Jeff was resolute, there was little chemistry between the band and their producer. Many involved, not least of all Columbia, were happy to write the venture off as a failed experiment, but to Berkowitz's despair, Jeff obstinately stuck by his choice. As far as he was concerned, for now the future still lay with Verlaine.

'The Verlaine recordings were just a test,' reckoned George Stein. 'No one thought that recording session was necessarily going to be the record... it was just an experiment.'

Berkowitz was not completely disappointed by the sessions, and found himself almost beguiled and enthused by the heavier numbers, but the overall feeling was one of depression. These recordings were not even considered worthy of a Sin-é, pre-album EP-type of release, and any plans for such (which had been speculatively earmarked for the end of the year) were shelved. Jeff himself was increasingly troubled and attempted to lose himself in his city, taking to the temporary and partial life of a barfly while he reconsidered his options. Away from the stage and studio, he revelled in enjoying his city as a common civilian. He attended Sufi meetings. 'It was embarrassing. It felt like a hippy ashram. And I think I would know the difference between that and the real thing. I think Sufi meetings are untraceable; you'll never find them.' Earlier that spring he had enrolled in a poetry class. New York writer and Jeff Buckley fan Scott Cohen was stunned to find himself in class with an idol. After introducing himself to a charmed and charming Jeff, Scott then kept his distance, going so far as to take notes on Jeff even as he sat across from him. 'I avoided him over the next few weeks, choosing instead to observe him furtively,' he confirmed. 'My notes from the second class include: "Greasy hair." "Exquisitely shy. How could this be the guy I saw in concert?" "Feminine, high-pitched voice." "Delicate, almost apologetic laugh." "Trance-like countenance." "Pale." '

The two students became friendly as the classes progressed, and at the end of one class Jeff invited Scott to a Sin-é show the following Monday. 'He never showed up to that gig or in class again,' said Scott. 'And a couple of weeks later, the teacher announced that Jeff had called her to say he'd had to drop the class.'

Yet even as he unwound during this much-deserved downtime, scribbling in his journals through long, smoky, Guinness-coloured afternoons, previous work began to surface in the form of collaborations. In the busy years just passed, Jeff had always been a generous creative force, contributing to and collaborating with handfuls of fellow musician friends and artists whenever the opportunity had arisen. 'Jeff had a habit of sitting in on recording sessions wherever he went, especially if a friend needed a hand,' confirmed Mary Guibert. 'Jeff used to sit in on all kinds of recording sessions, to strike a triangle at the appropriate moment, to add guitar riffs or background vocals.'

That June, as Jeff quietly agonised over his own creative impasse, the summer finally saw the release of Patti Smith's *Gone Again* album, featuring Jeff's contributions to 'Beneath the Southern Cross' and the scrappily haunting 'Fireflies'. Just as intriguing was Jeff's ghostly guitar and vocal presence on old friend and touring partner Brenda Kahn's 'Faith Salons', from her *Destination Anywhere* album, released on the same June day as Patti Smith's LP. Kahn recalled the birth of this particular collaboration as being typical of Jeff's devotion to living in the spur of the moment.

'We played music together and hung out together,' she says. 'The only song we recorded together was "Faith Salons"... I lived in a big loft space in Brooklyn and he was over playing my guitar, and I started reading out of various journals I had lying around. Suddenly he stopped and said, "Four-track." So we put down a basic version of the song. Later we recorded it for real. The clicking sound on the track is Jeff tapping his foot, and he's singing all the background vocals.'

When the time came to record the song proper, Jeff was a mellow, encouraging presence in the studio. 'We had recorded "Faith Salons" at a studio in New York,' recalls Brenda. 'I can't remember the name of the studio. It might have been Quad. I don't know how Jeff was with his own records, but with me he was always very easy-going. We just played the song and it was always perfect the first time through. It's just me and him on the track, and I think maybe the producer put a couple of organ notes on it... but the real beauty, to me, is Jeff's background vocals.'

Outside of the studio, Jeff's problems with his own muse were manifested in strange mood swings and occasionally eccentric behaviour, with some friends reporting enigmatic answerphone messages, seeing him speaking to himself in clubs, and haunting doorways.

Somehow the music went on, with Jeff writing a new song, 'Haven't You Heard', which addressed the paranoia he now courted, or at least felt he should be experiencing: 'Make sure you learn to beware your neighbour / Bolt the doors and then hire your guards.'

Despite the feeling of anti-climax hanging over them in the wake of the initial Verlaine sessions, the group continued to rehearse at studios in Chelsea. Irrespective of their best efforts, however, the summer would prove to be a listless one. Tentative plans had been made to release

Grace's follow up in the spring of 1997, but this clearly wasn't going to happen. Jeff could not focus himself or sufficiently rally his unregimented inner forces.

During this time Jeff occasionally revealed to his closest friends his thoughts and feelings about his father, although this certainly wasn't something one brought up of their own accord. Jeff's performance artist friend, Penny Arcade, recalled that during this time Jeff 'confessed to me that he "wanted to be better than my father", revealing that night the extent to which he had studied Tim, something he hid from the world. He called me up raving drunk,' she concluded. 'And he was freaking out about the new record.'

Lee Underwood, Tim's old musical sideman, continued to track Jeff's progress from afar and had his own very definite views on the causes of Jeff's writer's block. 'Because he could not give proper credit to Tim, he exacerbated the melancholic and self-destructive wars within his own psyche,' diagnoses Underwood, who had been as close to Tim as any musician. He continues: 'The question was not of origins and influences – of course he was influenced genetically and musically. No, the question was of acknowledgment, respect and self-acceptance. The battle was not with Tim, it was with himself. Certainly Jeff's pain was understandable. Jeff suffered from the void his father's almost total absence left... In several interviews, Jeff indicated how angry he was at not being invited to Tim's funeral. He had not been able to say goodbye, and he and his mother had been snubbed. His anger was justified, but he made it sound as if it were Tim's fault, not Judy's. How could he be angry at Tim for not being invited to the funeral? Jeff's rage was preventing him from fulfilling his gifts... [Jeff was] trying to please and defeat the very man he loved and needed most...'

Jeff's angst would only have been engorged by his own gifts and the acclaim and fortune they brought him. Unlike the offspring of many other famous fathers – Frank Sinatra Jr, Hank Williams Jr, for example – Jeff was at least as talented as his father, and the world recognised, embraced and promoted this talent. Being famous in itself can be traumatic, especially for a performer who was at heart a musician. Jeff was definitely not a celebrity wannabe. To add to this enigma within a riddle, Jeff was supremely conscious of all this and more.

'Jeff knew he had a great voice,' Underwood says. 'But he also knew he did not have the strength or range that Tim had. He found it immensely difficult to write songs. At the beginning, it was almost impossible to face a microphone. At the end, it still seemed enormously difficult to write and record. Even when Sony gave him three years and almost unlimited

Jeff onstage with his blue Gibson acoustic guitar
at the Lowlands Festival, Holland, 1994.

moral and financial support, Jeff found it virtually impossible to squeeze out a coherent song.'

To the contrary, Jeff's latest tunes were deeply coherent. While they did not adhere to a typical A-B-A-B structure, they had an authentic flow that was true, concise and emotionally complete. The problem was that there were not enough of them, and in addition, each song stood mostly alone rather than as part of any unifying concept that would have gone towards the birth of a truly great album. Jeff continued, on the surface at least, to be truly unconcerned with outside criticism. 'All I'm trying to do is make beautiful things,' he said simply. 'I don't give a shit about people's cross-references. I have no compassion for their lack of understanding, or their fear of change, their fear of... music. [Although] It can hurt me sometimes, or it can bewilder me.'

While his inner demons wrestled each other, Jeff coped as best he could, and spent the time going through the motions of preparing for 'Grace II'; guzzling Guinness, smoking pot, not washing his hair, and helping friends out with both their own projects and even their sobriety.

One such new friend was Inger Lorre, the underachieving ex-singer of the Nymphs. Inger was a long-term heroin addict in the midst of a battle for her sanity. 'I met Jeff in a club,' she recalls. 'I was trying to quit junk and Jeff came into my life like a fucking... like a fucking angel! He was so keyed-in, so supportive. He would phone me up and leave messages. "Are you *using* Inger? *Don't*! If you get the urge... call me!" He was a beautiful friend, my best friend...'

Jeff would contribute guitar to Inger's debut solo album and go on to cover the feminised grunge rocker 'Yard of Blonde Girls', which Inger had written additional verses for.

'Jeff always loved that song,' says Lorre. 'And he never, ever got to find out that the lyrics I wrote in that song – "It's in your heart / It's in your art / Your beauty" – were actually *about him*! So when he was singing it, he was singing about himself. It's funny that he chose that song of mine to sing, when it was about *him*. And, like I said, he never, ever knew that's what it was about.'

For all his counselling of others, Jeff ultimately needed to help himself.

Once again he figured on taking geographic steps to rid him of the sense of claustrophobia he now felt in New York. Memphis was the likeliest contender, a locale suggested by a musician friend. Jeff had, of course, played there during a tour, and the vibe of the place had stayed with him.

He had found a kind of new Sin-é – the obscure Daydream Café, located on West Fifty-First Street. He'd also, at least, come up with the title of the next record: *My Sweetheart the Drunk*. A slow evolution was falling into place, and new songs followed and flowed; 'Sky Blue Skin', 'Murder Suicide Meteor Slave', and 'Ever Since Then (Opened Once)'.

Although things were looking up, the band was once again falling apart. The initial Verlaine sessions had proved that Eidel was not fitting in, and, as with the departed Johnson, there were tensions between him and his rhythm partner Grondahl making themselves apparent.

Despite this, the pressure from Columbia was a constant factor, and that September the group pulled together for a session at Sony Studios, where they 'auditioned' the new songs for Berkowitz. Signs were encouraging. The ensemble now pumped out two more new tracks – 'Demon John' and 'Gunshot Glitter' – as well as the now-evolved 'Moodswing Whiskey'. ('That started off as a joke,' said Jeff of the latter song, 'a name for a fictitious product that I sort of saw as a euphemism for this life. A thing that takes people away from ordinary strains of life. And which causes a lot of problems.')

The session was the last Eidel would play with the group. Matt Johnson had been aware of the tensions and was once again philosophical. 'I thought that Eric was exactly that – a replacement. He didn't seem to have fully digested the role he'd have to play up to that point,' Johnson commented tactfully. 'And he didn't seem to bring something totally new to it either. The band may have had the idea that because he was an overall very good musician and writer, he would bring a lyricism, and a heightened attention to composition. He did those things exactly, and tastefully. He also seemed to speak only partially through the medium of drumming. His talents were split in different areas. This provided valuable perspective and intelligence. But he seemed never to have totally given himself over to the drums. He hadn't found his voice as a drummer.'

The freezing New York winter was approaching and many of the staff Jeff had been on good terms with at Columbia were leaving, replaced by new employees who knew of him only as a vague name – and one with a difficult reputation.

Such a reputation was not abetted when, on 23 October, Jeff was arrested in the New Jersey farming town of East Amwell for 'public drinking'. In actual fact, Jeff was supping from a single beer while being ferried around by hardcore drunkard (though she was sober at the time) Inger Lorre. On being searched, a tiny amount of pot was discovered on his person. Jeff was taken to a local police station and fined. He was eventually let off with a caution.

To some, such a shabby occurrence as this pathetic arrest highlighted the dichotomy in Jeff. He was, as ever, pragmatic in his defence. Although he was not shy about speaking of 'the divine' in music, neither was Jeff above 'lower' pleasures of the flesh, and the beers and other substances this could involve. 'Flesh is awesome. Lots of people degrade the flesh,' he said. 'Lots of people say flesh is bullshit, that the real party is happening upstairs or downstairs. But I don't agree.'

While Jeff mulled over his recurring drummer problem and considered the mechanics of moving to Memphis, he sent out an internet message to the faithful. Written in Beat-era style rambling prose, his vision of the forthcoming album was not completely discernable from the blog he posted that fall:

...every song will have a quiet part and then a loud part at the shout chorus and the lyrics will totally open up new pathways in the human mind, allowing both sexes to fling themselves into the path of modern boredom and sloth like an oncoming train. It's not just a woman's job anymore. Both must explode as one. There will be no pain or shock at the time of impact. There will only be Coca-Cola and Disney. And hooks, lots and lots of hooks for the kids at summer break. For the employees of the year who suddenly crack under pressure and ascend to the clock towers with their candy bars and automatic rifles, or anyone who has finally come to the answers of life. And lots of songs about chicks, I almost forgot... life. Chicks. Hooks. Life. Chicks. Hooks. Life. Click. Bang. Click click. chicks. click click. hooks. bang. bang. hooks. chicks. hooks .click click. candy bar. bang! bang! bang!

Back in the linear world, on 31 October, a new drummer by the name of Parker Kindred auditioned for Jeff, Mick and Mike at an East Village rehearsal space.

Parker was a jazz-loving, wiry young man with excellent drum chops and, as soon as the group began playing together, the stakes seemed to have been raised. Further sessions were booked, which subsequently proved that the initial meeting had been no fluke.

'Parker is a whole other story,' relates original drummer Johnson. 'He brought sophisticated charisma, understatement, feel, street smarts, and a palpable rebelliousness. Here Jeff and the band had found a good match.'

Still, Jeff did not yet commit. He had a lot on his mind. The Memphis move seemed definite, and he felt like touring again – alone.

That season, things were ending. In November, the Sin-é shut down, marking the end of a minor era. On the seventeenth of that same month,

Jeff and his girlfriend danced around the jukebox in the Daydream Café to celebrate his birthday. It would be his last.

'I'm on the rapids,' Jeff had told an Australian writer earlier that year. 'I see the waterfall ahead. I know I'll fall. I scream. It's never a result of the art form, but there's something about the social life of a musician who lives as a musician and nothing else. It will bring you into the underground.'

10. EXIT MUSIC

'The only way I can rebel against him [Tim Buckley] is to live.'

Jeff Buckley

That December Jeff decided to recalibrate. With as little publicity and hassle as possible, he sought to realign his head, heart and soul by hitting the road again. The journey was also intended to be something of a bond-forging road trip between him and his half-brother Corey. Jeff had asked Corey to drive, but it was ultimately not to happen. The younger Moorhead left his driving licence at home in California and subsequently couldn't hire the requisite car.

Heading out instead with Jack Bookbinder, his manager's assistant, Jeff, packing just his amp, guitar and notebooks, temporarily parachuted out of New York and the musical roadblock he'd found himself stuck in and headed for a nine-date trip starting on the 6 December for his 'Phantom Solo Tour – two guys in a car with a guitar'. It might have seemed to some that Jeff often put his frustrated creativity into tour titles. Ever-playful, rather than go out under his own name, he toured under a number of amusing pseudonyms – A Puppet Show Named Julio, The Crackrobots, Crit-Club, Father Demo, Smackrobiotic, Topless America, Martha and the Nicotines, and Possessed By Elves.

To some at his record label, this was yet another exasperating gesture on behalf of someone who really should have been knuckling down to business. Jeff answered, as ever, primarily to himself.

'There was a time in my life not too long ago when I could show up in a café and do what I do, make music,' he explained. 'In this situation I have that precious and irreplaceable luxury of failure, of risk, of surrender. I worked very hard to get that kind of thing together... I loved it then missed it when it disappeared... All I am doing is reclaiming it.'

All of this put further distance between Jeff and the completion of the album Berkowitz had initially scheduled for release the following

Jeff in his infamous thrift-store fur coat, circa 1994.

January, and further threatened to snuff out the A&R man's stadium-bursting U2 fantasies.

'I'll never play stadiums,' said Jeff cheerfully. 'The conceptual artist in me would see a stadium and would go, "What sort of material would be completely filled with subtlety and nuance in a big fucking stadium and also rock and hold an entire stadium?" I don't like stadium shows... the people take the act for granted. In the middle of a song they don't understand they go away and buy a programme or a hot dog or a beer... that would kill me. I'd be so sad.'

When Jeff drove through and played Westborough, Boston, Buffalo, Cleveland, Manayunk, Baltimore and Washington, the venues and audiences were far removed from stadiums and arenas. Wearing his infamous thrift-shop fake-fur coat, he would turn up at around 11:00pm, unannounced and unconcerned by box-office receipts, and play to as little as twenty people. He continued to throw eclectic cover versions into the sets as and when his mood dictated. This gave the concerts an enduring quality, regardless of the relevance of Jeff's standing in the market place, or if he had a new product to promote. As well as including new originals such as 'Jewel Box' and future sex-mantra classic 'Everybody Here Wants You', he was also currently enamoured of Nina Simone's version of 'Wild Is the Wind', Inger Lorre's re-working of the 360s' 'Yard of Blonde Girls', and indie band Drugstore's 'Alive', as well as the traditional blues of 'Dink's Song'. Whether you knew of Jeff and his work or not, anyone turning up to these shows could be sure of value for money.

Andrew Goodsight, the bassist who had worked with Jeff just after his signing to Columbia, explains why some of Jeff's friends would refer to him as a 'human tape recorder':

'He had what seemed to be an endless well of songs that he knew note for note and word for word,' remembers Goodsight. 'When I say, for instance that during my time with him we jammed on Zeppelin tunes, I mean Jeff knew *every* Zeppelin song from beginning to end. He could sing it better than Plant and play the guitar parts just like Page. The whole of every song from every record. Even that weird middle section – Jeff had it down cold. Do you know how amazing that is? Musicians will claim to know that stuff, but they don't really know it. They know the intro riff to a handful of classics. It wasn't just Zep. He knew the whole Beatles catalogue, Rush – can you imagine? Every Rush song note for note; the words and music at the drop of a hat – Yes, Dylan, Van Morrison, Aerosmith, Black Sabbath, Beach Boys and on and on. And that's just the rock stuff. He had jazz standards down like nobody's business. Folk, show tunes and even some opera. The guy was a prodigy... an encyclopaedia.'

Jeff forbade any DAT recordings to be made during these performances, not wanting to be hampered by the prospect of posterity. Other than this stipulation, he seemed carefree. 'I'll be wandering around in an ugly rented car,' he blogged that winter, replying to the anguished internet cries of frustrated and disappointed fans who had just found out in retrospect that Jeff had actually played their town under some stupid-sounding alias. Jeff's reply was curt: 'Real men maintain their freedom to suck eggs my dear.'

The low-key tour came and went and Christmas glittered in. By Jeff's standards, a relatively uneventful seasonal period passed. Unlike previous years there were no New Year's Eve shows, and the magical Sin-é no longer existed anyway. Yet Jeff knew that this brief resting-up period was merely the calm before the storm. Come the New Year, he threw himself into a dervish whirl of focused activity. Refreshed by his mini-tour, he was now speeding into his future. This, to the mute surprise of some, included working once again with Verlaine, albeit this time in Memphis. He was due to depart for the south's Easley Studios that February. Before then, there would be a handful of shows in which he would bid farewell to the New York that he had now, to some degree, fallen out of love with.

'He lived on a really nice block, but there were prostitutes on the block all the time,' remembered Joan Wasser of his East Village apartment. 'And, you know, he was compelled to look into their eyes. Jeff was giving and compassionate, but it would weaken him.' Such occasions displayed symptoms of how ill at ease Jeff now felt in the city and even in his own image. As far as Jeff was concerned, *Grace* was merely the starting line. He now considered it too polite, too polished, and ultimately indicative of a place he was no longer at or wanted to be. He also saw it as something of a ball and chain. Dambuilders singer Dave Derby remembers Jeff 'self-deprecatingly joking that after you call your first record *Grace*, you can't exactly hand in just anything. I don't think he ever lost his sense of humour about the situation.'

It was now 1997. *Grace* had been recorded almost four years ago. How many albums, how much progression had the Beatles, Bowie, and the Smiths shown in a four-year period? Although there was no physical product to show as such, Jeff had already moved on, even if his label hadn't realised as much. There would be no 'Grace II'. 'That was the last thing that he wanted because that's not what he was any longer,' confirmed Wasser. 'He was planning on losing a lot of fans [with the second record]. He was looking *forward* to losing a lot of fans. So [the second record] wasn't just getting certain feelings of unrequited love out. This was a statement of life, and his life.'

On 2 January he performed at his Sin-é substitute, the Daydream Café, with 'Special Guests' Mike and Mick. It was as close to impromptu as he could get, and the gig was kept secret from his Sony paymasters. He now had a formidable arsenal of as yet unrecorded new songs, and the shows were a bootlegger's delight. Jeff was not passive when he saw punters taping his shows. 'You fuck! Dick! Bootleggin' our show, man!' he admonished one such taper during this period. 'You're going to study it?' It was hard to tell if he was joking.

Offstage, intensive rehearsals began with new drummer Parker Kindred. Jeff's excitement with his new band was palpable and momentum was building. At this time their guitarist had a weird insight. 'When Parker and I rehearsed with Jeff,' Michael Tighe would later recall, 'I had flashes into the future. I saw a premonition that we were playing and Jeff wasn't there.'

Kindred was coming along nicely, finding his way within the established chemistry set of Mick, Mike and Jeff. Increasingly confident, Jeff had Dave Lory make a phone call. To Jeff's management it may sometimes have seemed as if history just kept on repeating itself, but they did as Jeff asked. A hook-up with Verlaine was arranged, once again at Sorcerer, to see how Kindred's swing translated in the recording studio.

Regardless of the newfound band energy, their return to the Canal Street studio was a disappointment. Verlaine once again found fault with Jeff's drummer, and the atmosphere was uncomfortable. Parker, like the ill-fated Eric Eidel, could not seem to adjust to the studio environment.

Still, Verlaine dutifully turned on the tape recorder and the band played through a fistful of Jeff's new tunes. As strong as these songs were, for whatever reason, the group were not happening and everyone present plainly knew it. At the end of the session Verlaine handed Jeff the rough-sounding tape of their latest efforts. Berkowitz and Columbia would once again be disappointed.

Jeff, however, only seemed to be gaining confidence – as if following a secret map of stars that only he had access to. With a few days left in NYC, he played another two shows – the first one was at yet another of his old haunts, the Knitting Factory (where he opened for his old collaborators the Jazz Passengers). Michael Dorf, owner of the small club, had by now been a friend and fan of Jeff's for some time. 'It was very clear that this guy had magic,' he recalled. 'As a person, he was shy but very sweet. When [Jeff's former girlfriend] Rebecca Moore was recording *Admiral Charcoal* for our label in '96, he was involved in every session but wouldn't take a credit. I'll always remember him saying, "Don't screw Rebecca!" Not sexually, but business-wise. He was showing this real care about her – protecting her.'

Although it was arguable that he had by now outgrown such petite clubs, Jeff was always sublimely comfortable playing such locales. 'Columbia recording artist, Jeff Buckley,' read the blurb, 'will be performing a solo electric set at famed NYC avant-music stronghold, the Knitting Factory, at their tenth anniversary celebration on Tuesday, 4 February. Admission will be by invite only, with the invites being issued by the Knitting Factory, not Columbia Records.'

Perhaps seeing himself described as a 'Columbia recording artist' brought home to him the reality of his privileged situation, which wasn't an undesirable one by any means, despite the attendant pressures. Maybe Jeff was about to begin to take his career more seriously, or was at least about to begin to enjoy playing the game a little more. Certainly, when asked where he saw himself in a decade's time, the names he dropped were telling. 'Tom Waits, Lou Reed [who was in the audience at Knitting Factory that night], Ginsberg, De Niro, and Dylan.' Such high-octane expectations, whether placed on himself by himself or by outside forces, did not help Jeff in the short-term, as his friend Dave Derby noticed.

'I sort of sensed that a lot of pressure came from the label, who had tremendous expectations for him, and, I think, his own expectations of what he could have been. I think it would have been hard to be Jeff and have Paul McCartney [who had attended a Fez show the previous year] and Page and Plant turning up at your gigs and still be able to keep things in perspective, especially during that really hard, soul-crushing period of trying to come up with music for a second record. Of course it would be flattering, but I have to imagine that it would also heighten the pressure.'

Despite this, Jeff was mellow and confident throughout the Knitting Factory gig, even inviting the now completely bald Gary Lucas up for a somewhat histrionic rendition of 'Grace'. But although the new material showed promise, to some in the audience this was merely another Jeff solo show, and one within which a follow-up to *Grace* was barely audible. Jeff seemed unworried about whatever perceptions surrounded him and yet another, more informal group get-together happened the following day, with all four musicians once again meeting with Verlaine at an anonymous Chelsea studio. These sessions, whilst no profound improvement upon the last ones, at least evoked a more positive vibe. But the results were, as ever, inconclusive, and Jeff kept this rendezvous a secret from Columbia and his management, a sign of the dividing fault line between them.

Any doubts about Jeff's current band would be exorcised mere days later. The casually assured Knitting Factory show was soon followed by yet another low-key gig, this time to specifically break-in Jeff's new drummer. This appearance, at Arlene's Grocery Store – a new venture of drug-troubled former Sin-é owner Shane Doyle's – proved without a doubt that Jeff and the band had turned a corner. 'Nightmares By the Sea' opened the set; a dark hybrid of Nirvana and Joy Division, with Jeff's vocals limited to a hypnotic mumble. There was little of the melodramatic 'head singing' (a technique wherein the higher registers of the voice are projected from the head rather than the diaphragm) that had worked so well in the past. Kindred's drums were propulsive and keen, showing that his confidence had not been smudged by his encounter with Verlaine days previously. Whatever Verlaine thought of Parker's chops, the young drummer knew he had the support of his band, which Tighe in part put down to 'a tribal link in our blood – Jeff and I both had Irish roots and Parker has Scottish ancestry'.

As a statement of intent, 'Nightmares By the Sea' was a decisive opener. 'Witches' Rave' followed, again a moody mid-tempo song built around Kindred's muscular drumming with a hint of Jeff's perennial favourites the Smiths. The Smiths – more so than Morrissey solo – remained a constant factor throughout Jeff's musical life. The influence was, according to Tighe, 'pretty massive. Jeff went through a phase in his life where he really listened to the Smiths all the time. I remember he would say that, as a lyricist, no one comes close to him [Morrissey]. And he also loved Johnny Marr very much. The sort of scathing, bittersweet quality of Morrissey's lyrics was something that Jeff was fascinated by, and he really admired and respected.'

By default, some of Jeff's 'hits' now sounded oddly bogus. 'So Real', in particular, came across as throwaway, something the band had now outgrown. 'Lover, You Should've Come Over' had aged better, occasionally and spookily evoking Tim Buckley's later output. The new material, the Zeppelin-like 'Haven't You Heard', the sad slow-burn of 'Morning Theft', and the by-now flexing and heaving rock-out of 'The Sky Is a Landfill' all sounded like strong new positive directions. Running through the show like the writing through a stick of seaside rock were Jeff's hilarious monologues. Looking swishy in one of his girlfriend's dresses, he riffed with ace comic timing on everything from Sufi performance artists with genitalia like 'carrots' to his foiled attempts at trying to give up smoking. 'I'm an ex-quitter!' he professed joyously. Near the end of the set he treated all in attendance to a spot-on Tom Waits impression. Yet for all his goofy stream-of-consciousness patter, as a singer Jeff had obviously matured, much less inclined towards the overdramatic dynamic of previous shows. Parker, Mike, Mick and Jeff sounded ready to fly, as if they were performing an album already recorded.

Sadly this wasn't so. (It's intriguing to wonder at the lost possibility of a full-length, full-band live recording as the follow-up to *Grace*.) Jeff had promises to keep and miles to go before he and his band would try to recreate such magic under Verlaine's tutelage.

Jeff was due to fly to Memphis on 11 January. 'He had to get out of New York just to literally find the time to sit down and write some music,' stressed Mary Guibert. Before then, he seemed determined to pack as much as he could into his remaining time in the city.

On the night before his departure he revisited Sorcerer Sound Studios. This time it was a Verlaine-free zone. Jeff was there at the bequest of Hal Willner, whose latest project was a tribute album to Edgar Allan Poe, eventually entitled *Closed on Account of Rabies*. The company that Jeff scruffily ambled in on was high calibre; including Debbie Harry, Marianne Faithfull, Allen Ginsberg and Christopher Walken, and if Jeff wasn't yet as established a legend as any of these artists, then it was generally accepted by all in attendance that he one day would be. What no one at this session would have assumed was that the very album Jeff was contributing to would, on its release, be dedicated to both him and Ginsberg, for reasons both unforeseen and unimaginable.

Jeff's performance, affectionately and expertly coached by elderly Beat poet Ginsberg, was powerful and convincing. Out of those offered to him to read, the piece Jeff chose was 'Ulalume' – Poe's 1846 meditation on the untimely death of a beautiful woman.

The relaxed, champagne-infused recording session must have seemed like a mini-vacation in his own backyard, and showed that Jeff was multi-faceted and in control of his ego – he never had any trouble working with others or their material if he felt comfortable with the basic premise. Returning to his own musical struggle after the brief sojourn of working with Ginsberg may have seemed less than desirable, but at least he had a good support team in his manager, road crew, band and friends. 'He was lucky to have some really great people around him,' confirms Dave Derby. 'They helped to keep him inoculated from some of that pressure, but it still got to him. That said, I know he was pretty happy about where things were going musically... I think the music was really starting to come together and he was really psyched about the band going down south to record.'

Verlaine, Jeff, Parker, Mick and Mike arrived in Memphis the next day, as scheduled, just after one in the afternoon. After reclaiming their luggage and instruments they drove to the city and booked into hotels.

Typically, Jeff hadn't been explicit about their reasons for relocation. Some of the group thought they were there to continue jamming, whereas Kindred assumed they were there to nail the album. Verlaine remained cool regardless – as he saw it, he was there to turn on the tape recorder, whenever the boys were ready. In Jeff's mind, however, he was here specifically to record an album.

Before the real work began, they needed to make base, and home became the run-down Claridge Hotel. They already had friends there – principally their old touring buddies the Grifters – and within those first few balmy Memphis days, bar-hopping and checking out local eateries and listening to street musicians, Jeff soon felt inspired and energised by his new neighbourhood. So much so, in fact, that by their second day in town, Jeff and the band were playing a two-night residency at a local, sleazy club called Barrister's. Before a small gaggle of regulars who weren't sure who or what they were experiencing, Jeff was once again using the forced focus of the live stage to prepare for the high-definition scrutinisation of the studio.

David Shouse, Jeff's close friend from the Grifters, confirmed that it was he who'd put a bug in Jeff's ear about relocating the band to his hometown. 'I put pressure on Jeff to come to Memphis because I realised he wanted a rougher sound than *Grace*. He asked where we made our records and I said, "Oh there's this amazing studio where you can just do anything you want." ' Thus the group had introduced themselves and their equipment to this 'amazing' place – Easley McCain Recording Studios. The drab and down-home-looking facility had begun as local musician Doug Easley's four-track studio, originally situated in the Memphis woods near the Wolf River in the late 1970s. There, Doug had begun his business by recording local blues musicians such as Mose Vinson. By the early 1980s, Doug had re-branded his operation as 'Easley Recording' and relocated closer to home, near the city's university. As an 'alternative', mostly white music scene grew in Memphis throughout the new decade, Easley became *the* studio to record in for low- to mid-level local groups, and its reputation spread, mostly by word-of-mouth. By the time Jeff and the band turned up, its reputation was on the rise, and the studio's clientele had included both the Breeders and Sonic Youth – two groups Jeff admired. Easley had also relocated once more – to a dead-end street on the south-east outskirts of Memphis. Behind the nondescript façade of the outer building, Jeff instantly felt at home in the funky, folk art-decorated lobby, and also in the company of the gentle, easy-going owner, Doug Easley. Doug kept the studio well-stocked with a wide variety of instruments (not always a given) and the vibe was resolutely analogue, something Jeff and Verlaine were keen on.

'Doug Easley and his people were very mellow,' said Shouse, 'very encouraging of musicians who take chances and try weird stuff.' Doug had been in thrall to both music and his hometown all his life, and understood why someone like Jeff would want to come to Memphis, saying, 'I think the mystique of Memphis really goes deeper than anything anyone can put a finger on.' His studio, with its organic ambience, kooky decor and mellow atmosphere, was testament to such mystery. Initially, a two-week session had been booked, with days starting at noon and ending at midnight. The works in progress included the bulk of the recent Arlene's Grocery set, as well as other stragglers, such as the liquidly erotic 'Everybody Here Wants You'. Despite everyone's best efforts within the conducive atmosphere, and with all the will in the world, much to their deep disappointment, the songs still refused to come together on tape.

'It was really stale – lifeless,' said drummer Kindred, speaking of all his Verlaine experiences to date. 'We were learning how to play these songs, translating to tape, and hearing what wasn't working.' Parker was still unaccustomed to playing drums in a studio environment, and Jeff would often yell out, 'Okay, you don't know this one... and one, two, and three...' Each musician would air their own Verlaine-related woes if pushed, although the atmosphere, if tense, was rarely actually fractious. Yet the truth remained obvious: the sessions were just not happening. Even going back as far as the sessions with Eric Eidel, the work with Verlaine had never gelled. This was no slur on Verlaine as a person, musician or technician. For whatever mysterious reasons, there was simply no chemistry. The Grifters returned from a tour that month and David Shouse would later confirm the worst: 'Things had kind of hit the wall. Things weren't really jiving with Tom. The atmosphere was pretty bad and I don't think Jeff was really happy with the songs.'

The playback of the material recorded so far only served as aural confirmation of all Jeff's fears. While he was at least not replicating *Grace*, it was also abundantly clear that he had not yet found whatever it was he was looking for. There was a neutral quality to the recordings that was somehow worse than if they'd been fucked-up. Jeff half-joked that when they next recorded they would first 'burn the current tapes down'. Omnipresent good humour aside, he was deeply wounded by the lack of progress, and his reaction that late February was to retreat into himself within his top-floor hotel room. The last song Jeff, Verlaine and band would play together was 'Everybody Here Wants You'. 'I remember he said that he was happy with it,' said Tighe, 'but that he wanted to really make it more of our own song, with an even more unique voice. Which is interesting because if you hear the song now, it sounds very realised and beautiful and definitive, and it makes you realise that maybe sometimes things are finished even when you don't think they are.'

Steve Berkowitz and Dave Lory flew in from Manhattan early that March to check in on progress and report back to their bosses at Columbia. It seemed like a lifetime ago that Berkowitz had taken a similar trip to the Sag Harbor house, back in the first month of 1996. Back then *Grace* had finally bruised the *Billboard* chart, Matt Johnson had still been the drummer, and although a lot of water had flowed in the time since then, it also seemed as if little tangible progress had been made. It was a dispiriting meeting. Jeff even went so far as to hide one track from Berkowitz and his manager. The sensual strut and swagger of 'Yard of Blonde Girls' was Jeff's guilty secret, simply because he feared it sounded too catchy. So much so that it almost rang out like a novelty song amongst the denser and darker original material. As a result, he feared that Berkowitz and Columbia would want to do something untoward with it – release it as a single for instance. The irony of this situation was not lost on Jeff. He had vowed long ago not to rely on other people's songs for his own records, and now here he was, sweeping one such track under the mat for fear that his label, on hearing it, might find it the prime pick of all he had to offer. Berkowitz, seeing the song noted in the studio log book, rumbled Jeff, and the singer fled the studio in tears. Jeff was not only upset over the 'Yard of Blonde Girls' debacle, but also by the fact that the incident had somehow exploded the indisputable truth. Despite having relocated to a new state, despite getting a new drummer, despite writing a bunch of great new songs, the actual recordings were still, after all this time, simply not happening. Jeff could hide the elephant in the room no longer – Verlaine would have to go.

Jeff didn't announce as much immediately. Instead, when the band

'Right before his death,' said Jeff's guitarist Michael Tighe,
'he was having amazing realisation about the way he wanted to live.'

prepared to return to NYC as scheduled, Jeff opted to stay on in Memphis with Verlaine. He needed yet more time to dive into himself and see what he could come up with. The sessions had by no means been a disaster, but the new plan was that the group return to Memphis in a month's time, although that would ultimately depend on how Jeff was feeling. Berkowitz, having come this far, could only roll with it. Jeff had spent a serious amount of money since *Grace* looking for the next step, and as yet they had nothing to show for the expense, at least not in terms of anything approaching a record release. Yet *Grace* was still selling, particularly abroad, and it would have been seen as churlish for Sony to drop Jeff. Besides which, any number of other labels would have been only too happy to sign him up and indulge him further.

Yet again, Columbia had given their enigmatic investment what he needed without fully understanding what that was, and in the band's immediate absence, Jeff got to work with Verlaine completely alone. This seemed to mark a sudden change in tension, a seismic shift in atmosphere. Jeff played most of the instruments himself. (Curiously, it seems he never considered employing Verlaine's virtuoso guitar skills for any recordings.) Verlaine actually thought that without the band, Jeff was improved.

'They weren't holding him back. But his desire to get stuff right with them was taking time.' Jeff and Verlaine only spent a few days alone together in the studio. Verlaine too was due to return to New York. After a heart-to-heart at a local café, Jeff and his producer discussed the general disappointment with their work together. 'When he was saying that he wasn't satisfied with the Tom Verlaine sessions,' explained Tighe, 'he was mostly referring to the fact that he felt he hadn't really entered into the cores of those sessions; also, sonically it wasn't as extreme and exciting as he had wanted it to be.' Thus Jeff magnanimously shouldered the bulk of the blame himself. The two parted on good terms, although it was undecided if and when Verlaine would return to Memphis, or when Jeff would return to New York.

Meanwhile, Jeff needed a new base. The hotel life had lost its appeal. He had decided he would be there for the duration and transient lodgings were no longer appropriate. He set about looking for a home.

Jeff had already met local writer Robert Gordon. 'Jeff and I had met accidentally. We laughed a lot at that first meeting... I left thinking he was just some new guy in town. He was a blast to be around. His core bubbled with energy.' Through Robert, Jeff was introduced to local landlord Pat O'Brien, a perky lady not much older than himself. They soon came to an arrangement, and Jeff took out a three-month tenancy on a little cottage on North Rembert Street in midtown Memphis, near the golf course and zoo.

Jeff moved in during late March with his guitar, four-track, bursting journal and a few clothes. The set-up was sparse, monastic and meditative. He was as about as far away from a tour bus as it was possible to get. He felt as if he had found, finally, a place to write. As he sat down in the bare unfurnished rooms (he changed bedroom whenever the mood suited him, dragging around a scrappy piece of spongy foam for a mattress), Jeff felt a long way from New York and all its distractions, and a lot closer to himself. Setting up his four-track tape recorder on a milk crate, with the Memphis pre-harvest moon blazing in the curtainless window, he stomped and strummed, sang and screamed, crooned and wailed. The houses were detached and there was no complaint from his neighbour – the local Avon Lady.

The next few weeks were spent within a harmonious balance of solitude and socialising. To some it seemed as if Jeff were auditing himself, and finally processing everything that had happened since *Grace*, digesting it and setting it out in words and chords. He also took it upon himself to start calling people on the phone. Some of whom he hadn't seen in years.

'He literally called everybody,' confirmed Mary Guibert. 'He called old buddies from elementary school just to say hello and to apologise for not returning their phone calls and letters. He called everybody 'cause he knew that the next thing he had to do was lock himself in the studio and record an album that he would then have to come out and promote.'

'Yeah, he did contact certain friends that he hadn't spoken to in a long time,' recalled Tighe. 'In retrospect, it does feel as though he was sensing some type of departure or massive transition that he was going to undertake. He was realising so much about his life at that time... all these old memories and connections opened up in him. He felt it was really important, and had a sense of urgency to contact certain musicians that he had played with, and certain friends that meant a lot that he had fallen out of touch with.'

Although some aspects of Jeff's life had a hermetic quality, he was not a remote figure and he did not communicate with the outside world only by phone. Since 31 March he had been playing every Monday at Barrister's, woodshedding raw material as he had done in the Sin-é days.

Outside of the balmy, rough-and-ready club, he socialised feely, once again getting to know the neighbourhood. In David Shouse and his band the Grifters, he already had an established friend-base, besides which, Jeff had always had a talent for finding buddies. He also began to play with his dress sense, often kitting himself out in lime-green pinstripe suits and fedoras, the outfit topped off with spats. At the local pool halls some wondered who the new pimp in town was. As 'Jeff Buckley' he was recognised by the occasional in-the-know waitress or tourist, but rarely to a level where he felt hassled, and in fact some friends saw this as a welcome insulin boost to his otherwise under-stimulated ego. His mother summed up this period succinctly. 'He lived in a little house and was just this weird guy who wrote songs and went to the zoo for a while.'

By their very nature, the solo shows at the local club sometimes caused him grief, determined as Jeff was to use them as a forge for his brand-new material. But he seemed able to rise above audience expectations now, without alienating them, or himself. This was surely a sign of a musician evolving.

'He was playing new material, which was a little difficult, dense, you know, for people who wanted to hear *Grace*,' remembered Joan Wasser, who made monthly trips to Memphis to see her man. 'After about 30 minutes of songs they couldn't sing along to, it became too much. They began yelling. "Grace! *Grace*! Play Grace!" Jeff looked at these four and said, a little sweetly, a little playful, "You're gonna have to wait." '

Ever-courteous and mindful that the occasional fan had flown in from as far away as London, Jeff usually did a crowd-pleaser or two towards the end of each Monday show, dipping back into what he now considered within his own personal mythology as 'the *Grace* period'. These gigs showed that Jeff was finding a balance between his own musical needs and those of his audience. 'It was gorgeous,' said Wasser, 'because you saw the coming together of two people that really were in a battle previously.'

'I was at the last show he played there,' recalled Gayle Keleman, one-time webmaster of an unofficial Jeff Buckley web page, 'on 26 May 1997. There were probably about 50 or 60 people there. He was wearing a grey dress-suit with a tie. A couple of songs into the set he said, "There's some red wine over at the bar." He'd been pouring wine into little plastic cups for the audience.' Aside from this typically playful and seductive gesture, Gayle reported that, 'It wasn't the usual joking Jeff. It was more intense than that.'

He seemed to have found equilibrium within himself, and a daily self-imposed routine that worked between the twin poles of major label expectation and pressure and his own more mysterious and intangible needs. When he wasn't performing at Barrister's or writing and recording in his bedroom, Jeff walked the town, bought goofy clothes at the local flea market and army salvation warehouses, became a regular at the zoo (the butterfly exhibit was his favourite) and occasionally went for a solitary swim in the nearby Wolf River.

As spring snuck in through the woods and the junkyards, a be-suited Jeff was also regularly attending three-hour ceremonies at the church of soul singer and preacher Al Green. He hadn't 'found God' in the accepted sense, but Jeff definitely took something real and nurturing from the sermons, from the loss of self in the heaving congregation, and from the singing. After all, his first ever public performance, many light years ago, had been in a church. He usually wound down after these Sunday meetings at Ellen's Soul Food Restaurant. Dressed in his thrift-shop T-shirts and old-fashioned suspenders, Jeff supped on iced tea and joked with his friends. When not getting to know his new town by foot, he drove around in a modest rental car, listening to the Dead Kennedys at full volume on the stereo.

Like any true musician in Memphis, he was occasionally hassled by the local cops. After one such pat-down, Jeff was fortuitously picked up by a passing friend, Robert Gordon, who tried to placate him by explaining that he had merely been strolling through an area well-known for drug deals, and no doubt his slightly bohemian, Salvation Army-informed appearance had alerted the on-duty cop. Sadly Jeff's mood did not lift, and he ended up letting himself out of his friend's car, into the downpour of southern rain that had just broken. 'I'll walk,' he pouted. 'It's nice out.'

Besides the occasional inconvenience of a troublesome cop, star-struck waitress or disappointed fan, the intermittent Columbia-endorsed visits from Berkowitz were a more tangible hassle for Jeff, even though the two men got on well personally.

The problem was what the A&R man represented to the musician. It was by now obvious that Jeff was not designed to work within the record/release/tour treadmill that major companies like Columbia liked their artists to adopt. But Berkowitz had a job to do, and as gentle and sympathetic as he was, he was ultimately the company man and thus represented issues that Jeff would have preferred not to have hanging over him. David Shouse recalled that his own conversations with Jeff were 'along the lines of "fuck the label", you know? He was unhappy with that side of things.'

At least Verlaine was no longer a bone of contention. Jeff freely admitted to Stein that he didn't think there was much mileage left in that experiment. At this point, the idea of using Andy Wallace was resurrected. As well as Berkowitz, Jeff had old friends visit – most regularly Joan Wasser, who revealingly remembered his tiny house as being mansion-like, 'Because he filled it up with his giant self.'

Meanwhile Jeff kept busy sanding the wooden floors of his new home and letting the grass out front grow to meadow-like lengths. Inside he continued to whittle away, even finding a way to indulge his mischievous nature within the process of laying down demos. Instead of buying blank cassettes, Jeff preferred to use commercial tapes by other artists and record over them. He usually got these from a dishevelled man in town who often wandered from table to table in the bars with a box full of music cassettes of dubious origin. Jeff was ecstatic to one day stumble across a Michael Bolton tape amongst the clutch of ripped-off Columbia products. Once he'd mixed down his latest musical trophies to these recycled tapes, he'd mail them north to his band. 'Yeah, he was proud of those four-track recordings,' said Tighe, 'because he felt that the hearts of the songs had been realised. He knew that once that was realised, it would quickly take shape from there. He was someone that liked to have a song live in him for a long time. He didn't just write songs off the bat or rely on songwriting craft. He really had to experience a song and have it come from a place of truth. A lot of times he was almost reticent to let a song go because he wasn't sure if maybe three months down the road, he would gain some other wisdom about whatever he was singing about. He was also a perfectionist.'

Jeff called Parker Kindred on 25 May to see what he thought of the latest offering – a clutch of Buckley originals taped over Fiona Apple's album *Tidal*. Mid-conversation, as the drummer put across his thoughts, Jeff cut him off abruptly and said, 'I love you, man!' before hanging up.

The end of May was now approaching, and with it the return of Jeff's band. Around 21 May Jeff had called his guitarist, who recalled that the singer sounded grounded, focused and confident. Jeff was ready. 'He called me and told me that he was very proud of this new music because he had felt that he had contacted the source or the cores of these new songs,' recounted Tighe, 'which was something that was eluding him for a while… He really wanted to express other facets of himself musically that he felt weren't represented on *Grace*, but which were very much a part of his musicality or his musical mind and soul. He told me that he was really proud of this new music; that it felt like it did when we first started making music together. He was referring to a time that had a lot of levity and was very innocent, with a lot of forward motion and a very triumphant feeling. You can hear on his four-track recordings some of the ideas that he was going for. They were very, very extreme at certain points, very gentle and soothing, and at other times, very terrifying... He used to say that he wanted the second record to have "terror music" on it. Music that would be so haunting and seductive that listeners would have no choice but to be somewhat stunned and a little bit repelled, but really attracted to what they were hearing. I think that he had begun to enter the first phase of orchestrating those kinds of songs.'

The next phase toward orchestration involved the arrival of his band. They flew out of JFK airport on the afternoon of Thursday 29 May. Gene Bowen, Jeff's sometime tour manager and assistant to manager Dave Lory, had driven up to arrive a day ahead and help prepare the little house – which Jeff had finally made steps toward buying – for the incoming musicians. Producer Andy Wallace, now definitely booked, was due to arrive later still, on 23 June, but it was assumed he wouldn't be slumming it with the band.

For now Bowen had to set up bedding, sweep the floors, and generally make the place hospitable. As it was, it looked as if a weird monk had been living there. Shortly after 8:00pm, Jeff casually let Bowen know that he and his friend Keith Foti – who had journeyed up with Bowen in a guitar-stacked van – would be checking out Easley Sound Studios in anticipation of their sessions there. Besides which, Jeff fancied a bash on the studio's drum kit. Bowen concerned himself with the state of the house while Jeff and his friend, grabbing a boom-box and guitar, took off for the studio in the beat-up van. Dusk was settling, midges buzzed in small static clouds, and the weather was typically mild for Memphis at that time of year. It was just another southern evening coming in.

Driving along while listening to a mix as eclectic as Jeff's own tastes on the boom-box – the Beatles, Jane's Addiction, the Dead Kennedys – the two friends gradually realised they were lost. They appeared to be driving everywhere and nowhere, through residential districts and industrial estates, past garages and the odd thrift store. Strange as this must have seemed, although Jeff had been to the studio almost every day for over three consecutive weeks, he had usually been driven and hadn't paid much attention to the route. As for Foti, this was his first time there. One place Jeff did know how to get to was Barrister's. Thinking they could pick up directions there, Jeff directed Foti to the club, still singing along with his portable stereo. To their dismay the club was closed, shut up, and no one was answering either the door or the phone.

Stumped and feeling a bit embarrassed, Jeff asked his younger friend if he wanted to get something to eat. Foti declined. There was a beat, and then, with the mild boyish excitement that had never left him, Jeff suggested an idea – they should hang out near the river.

It was nearly 9:00pm now, and at this moment Mick, Michael and Parker would be flying over the city itself, coming in to land. Bowen was on his way to pick them up. They wouldn't reconvene back at Jeff's house for a while yet. There was still time to kill. Foti shrugged. Maybe Jeff would like to hear a song he'd been working on?

Back in the van they were soon passing the markets and driveways, the shops and the storefronts and the inevitable statues of Elvis and B. B. King. Within minutes they had parked and were strolling west of Tennessee and north of the Mississippi, through the cool dusk and onto the banks of the Wolf River.

Jeff's band had arrived at the airport and was passing through its corridors, down its escalators and along its mechanised walkways. Thankfully Bowen, who was waiting for them in the arrivals lounge, had driven all their gear up the day previously. Once the two guitarists and drummer had picked up their personal luggage, they steamed into the Memphis air, pumped up at being back in the birthplace of rock'n'roll, ready to nail the second album and, most of all, happy to be seeing their friend Jeff.

Jeff stood on the riverbank playing with the fistful of keys that hung from his belt, planted solidly on the earth in his heavy work boots. He scanned the water, took in the dusk air and felt the encroaching night. It was still warm, and both the first evening star and Jupiter were visible. The sky was neither blue nor black. Hundreds of years ago this very riverbank had been home to various Native American, Spanish and French communities – a mix as rich as Jeff's own family's racial heritage. In the 1600s a Native Indian guide had gone missing along the riverside while guiding a group of French settlers – one of the river's first reported casualties. The Wolf River itself was estimated to be 12,000 years old, give or take a decade. Jeff would have been 31 the following November.

Beyond the waterfront and less than a hundred feet away was Mud Island, a large sandbar a century old and formidable enough to house the local museum perched atop it. Beyond that was more dark, calm water, and beyond that the other side of the river. With Foti sat behind the singer, strumming along beside the parked boom-box, Jeff decided to go for a swim.

By now, Jeff's band, driven by Bowen, were well on their way to his house. Spirits were high. Since they'd left Jeff alone in Memphis, it seemed like he'd finally found a focus. In the previous weeks each band member had been delighted to receive a package from Jeff – his signature scrawl evident on each envelope – containing Fiona Apple and Michael Bolton cassettes that Jeff had gleefully recycled, taping over them with rough mixes of his latest songs. The powerful, hymn-like quality of compositions such as 'I Know We Could Be So Happy Baby (If We Wanted to Be)' and the poignant, hypnotic 'River of Dope' came close to turning Jeff's bandmates into fans. There was a confidence, a totality in these solo recordings that had been missing from the Verlaine sessions. The group had been plagued by a season of stops and starts for the previous two years. In addition to the obvious quality of the latest material, the fact that Jeff was calling his band back *now* could only mean that he had slayed whatever demons of doubt had been stifling him. A perfectionist to the point of neurosis, he would nevertheless not be regrouping the band unless he felt totally ready. His approach to this 'difficult' second album could be deemed many things, but casual was not one of them. The very fact that Mick, Mike and Parker were now heading toward their singer could only mean that something special was on the horizon. The time was now. There were only good vibes aboard the van as it left the freeway and sped into the lamp-lit Memphis night.

He waded into the brown water fully-dressed. The Memphis government had long since banned swimming in the Wolf River, which was still said to claim at least one victim a year. But there were no warning signs in place to make this explicit, and Jeff probably would have taken little heed of them even if there had been. Previously he had told friends that he'd swum there before. He found it 'refreshing'. No one knew if he was joking or not.

As Foti watched, Jeff's lower body began to disappear, his signature belt of keys ceasing their jangle as the water enveloped them. He had on his army pants and a Rolling Stones 'Altamont' T-shirt. Perhaps wary of the spiky shingle strewn across the muddy shore, Jeff hadn't bothered to take off his boots.

'You can't swim in that water,' Foti cautioned. 'What are you doing, man?'

Soon he was doing the backstroke while chatting to the guitar-strumming Foti on the pluses and minuses of being a rock star. Referring to both *Grace* and the as yet unborn follow-up album, he told Foti: 'You know, the first one's fun, man, it's the second one...' Foti, himself an aspiring rock star who would eventually surrender his dream to become a full-time celebrity hairdresser, continued to fidget with the guitar's fretboard. He had hoped to play Jeff a song of his own, but by now it was he who was the audience as Jeff, still swimming on his back, began singing a familiar song. 'I'm gonna give you my love,' he wailed, no doubt aping Robert Plant's screech perfectly. Foti must have been almost impressed – there was Jeff, fully-clothed, out in the middle of the river, singing Led Zeppelin's 'Whole Lotta Love', and he hadn't even had a drink or smoked a joint. The singer's reputation as a somewhat naturally eccentric star was being more than justified.

It was almost 9:15pm, and it looked like a calm, peaceful evening was settling. One could sense the shift of the air's density in the mornings and evenings – the way the dogs barking in the distant dusk sounded different now that the air was warming.

Meanwhile Jeff was going for it – he was now swimming in a forward stroke, apparently trying to make Mud Island, feeling happy and strong and audacious and maybe showing off just a little – to himself, Foti, and the dead father he had outlived.

Suddenly Jeff had competition. From the direction of Beale Street – home of the blues – came a tugboat. Jeff deftly avoided its path and its wake, manoeuvring his slight body out of its range. He'd been swimming for almost twenty minutes now, and for the first time in a long time. No one who knew Jeff would ever have described him as a 'water baby'. He was far more aesthete than athlete and always had been. The only recent enthusiasm for water sports that anyone could recall was when he and Joan Wasser had – ignoring warnings about the tides – gone for a midnight swim off Queensland's Gold Coast, and another time when he'd jumped into a pool while on tour. Even then he'd been fully-clothed. Out there in the dark water, heavy in his waterlogged boots and clothes, dodging the river's traffic, he must have been getting tired.

Then came the barge. Carrying grain from a local wholesaler up the river, it was a hundred-feet long and churned-up a deep but slow-moving wake in its path.

Jeff once again swam out of its way and was soon bobbing in the heavy waves it created. It was almost dark now, and the deepening blackness of the sky was beginning to render the light from even the weakest stars visible. Jeff would have known that the light from many of those stars came from a source that was long extinguished.

Foti, having abandoned his guitar, turned from Jeff – whose silent head was still visible above the lapping dark water – and moved his stereo clear of the rising swell.

When he looked out again, Jeff was gone.

AFTERGLOW

'People freaked out about how sad it is that Jeff didn't lead a full life. I just feel so certain about the fullness of his life. It's really hard to understand, because we haven't lived out our full lives, but I'm certain he did. I guess I just want that feeling to overwhelm this whole... the whole tragedy element. Because I just don't feel that. That his death was a tragedy. You know?'

Joan Wasser, 1998

Within five minutes of the band's arrival at Jeff's house there was an edgy, breathless phone call from Keith Foti. Jeff was missing. They needed to come down to the river *now*. His tone of voice, the subtext in what he was telling them, was disturbing.

The band had walked into the house of a living, breathing young man. Food containers with fresh leftovers were strewn about the place, there was unopened mail on the floor, the four-track recorder was set-up and ready to roll. There were even locks of freshly cut hair on the hardwood floor. (Jeff had given himself a trim earlier that day.) The answerphone machine was blinking manically.

Before they'd been able to check the messages – mostly a distraught Foti's – he'd called again. Putting down the receiver, Bowen barely had time to collect his thoughts before it rang yet again. This time it was the police.

The local cops and river police were all over the scene by the time the group arrived at Wolf River. Foti was being questioned in a state of shock. There were helicopters overhead and police in the water itself. The group stood around on the riverbank utterly disorientated, bewildered and unable to comprehend the reality offered them. Jeff was *gone?*

The authorities advised them to return home for the night. There was little the stunned musicians could do except get in the way, and, inexplicably, insultingly, there seemed little sense of hope. Everything was

Jeff Buckley: 1966 – 1997.

black – the sky, the water, and the prospects. Back at what had been Jeff's home, the dull shock of the unacceptable began to saturate the group's collective consciousness. Tighe remembered the gradual numbing acceptance. 'I think everyone there, before the night was through, felt that he had gone somewhere else.'

The place was strewn with fragments of Jeff, quite literally in the clumps of hair that Parker Kindred would eventually dazedly stuff into his pockets. Midnight came and went, and the first day on earth without Jeff began. His green Gretsch guitar lay like a defunct prosthetic limb. Tighe noted the butterfly stickers on its back. Going through Jeff's room looking for clues earlier – was there a suicide note? – he had seen that in one of the journals in Jeff's bedroom, the singer had recently written about rebirth, reincarnation and becoming 'molecules and rain'.

By 12:30am Jeff had not been found. So, lifting up a telephone receiver that felt as heavy as granite, Bowen began to make the dreaded phone call. At the top of the list was obviously Jeff's mother, followed by his management and friends. The initial reaction across America's vast time zones was muted. This was Jeff, after all. He was always going AWOL. Yet for some the situation tasted different this time. Jeff's manager, Dave Lowry, began the process of collecting his possessions and currency – the master tapes, the notebooks, the demos – salvaging them before the vultures came picking. Evidently for a few, Jeff was not returning any time soon.

Michael, Parker, Mick, Mary Guibert and a growing ensemble of colleagues were holed up in Jeff's house for the six days that Jeff was missing. Six days that, in the words of the drummer, were spent 'crying, and listening to all his CDs. His mom came down, and we had people come over and cry with us. We'd go down to the river, look at some records, make sure we got nice and drunk. Days and nights just fell into one another... Nobody could leave. It was just basically all of us trying to make sense out of something that was just completely taken away instantaneously.'

Out in the wider world and especially within the media, articles and notices were already appearing – reporting and speculating on the disappearance. Such notices already read like made-to-order rock myth. As with most random acts of tragedy, many tried to apply logic to seemingly illogical happenstance – there were rumours of drugs, Jeff was drunk, it was a hoax, it was a macabre ritualised suicide tribute to his father.

The hardest fact of all to accept in this case was that it was an accident – that Jeff was utterly sober and in a distinctly non-suicidal frame of mind.

'People were always trying to paint Jeff as this dark, self-destructive artist,' said Tighe of the public reaction, 'but… right before his death, he was having amazing realisation about the way he wanted to live.'

Obviously, with Jeff having disappeared in such an indiscriminate way, no one wanted to hear words like Tighe's. Could the universe be that perverse, that cruel, or that indifferent?

Yet Jeff had to take some of the responsibility, even if he were acting as a pawn in the game of his own destiny. 'I think he was impulsive,' reckoned Eric Eidel. 'That sort of explains why he went into the river and why he was a great musician. He went with his impulses, which were many and varied. He could be really weird, and funny, and kind of shamanistic sometimes too. I think he went with impulses, and he had an intense impulse to go into the water and he went with it.'

What was planned as a musical rebirth, as a new chapter in a great adventure, had turned into a wake, an intense season of mourning. By 3 June the Memphis summer was in full slow-burn. Jeff was still gone, and for his ex-band members it felt as if there was nothing to be gained here. The band had to move on. They returned to New York, leaving Bowen to guard the house and wait for news that might never come.

The reappearance of Jeff's physical form the very next day categorically defined his ultimate absence. The singer's body was spotted by a tourist from the deck of the American Queen riverboat at 4:40pm. Six days after he had strolled into the Wolf River Jeff's body had come to rest amongst an eddy of water-flooded branches at the very foot of Beale Street.

Bowen identified the body, citing the belly button ring and clothes as the most obvious proof that this was his old friend and boss. An autopsy was duly carried out at the city's university, where the toxicology report deemed Jeff drug-free. There was the slightest, merest negligible trace of alcohol in the blood; 0.04 milligrams. This was the equivalent of one beer or a small glass of wine. Jeff had at least cheated one more rock'n'roll cliché. The official explanation of his death was simply, horrifically, 'due to drowning by misadventure'. (The medical definition of drowning is not as peaceful as its name evokes. 'Drowning is death as caused by suffocation when a liquid causes interruption of the body's absorption of oxygen from the air leading to asphyxia. The primary cause of death is hypoxia and acidosis leading to cardiac arrest.') No foul play was in evidence, and the case of the death of Jeff Buckley was – at least as far as the authorities were concerned – closed.

The inevitable low-key fan vigils were held the world over, and Michael Stipe and Bono both dedicated songs to Jeff during their current tours. But he was no John Lennon, Kurt Cobain nor Bob Marley in terms of his fame, and even these small public displays of mourning were touchingly private affairs.

Jeff's body was ultimately cremated in a private ceremony. For all in attendance the whole course of events must have seemed like a macabre waking nightmare, yet one they would have to realign their lives to as reality.

As the shockwaves of Jeff's sudden loss ebbed into the grain and rhythm of the lives of those he'd left devastated, Columbia got on with the job of marketing the future mythic icon. (Although at far from the same level, on hearing of Elvis's death, Colonel Tom Parker had allegedly barked, 'This changes nothing,' in Jeff's case his tragedy could potentially increase his sales and critical reputation.)

Over it all hovered the pungent sense of unfinished business, both in his life and work. 'At the moment that Jeff walked into the water, he was ready to finally go in and make the second album,' confirmed his mother. 'He knew exactly what he wanted. He and I had a long conversation just previous to that. We talked about everything about his life. We even covered some stuff that we needed to clean house on as a mother and a son.'

The record company appeared to move a bit too eagerly for some. 'We had been in Memphis, and Jeff's A&R guy Steve Berkowitz came down, and the lawyer came down, and there were tears from people in the company,' remembered Parker Kindred. 'I was like, "Okay maybe their hearts aren't gristle." But then when we got back to New York, these same people were saying, "Okay, we have to get in there and listen to everything we can possibly listen to right now. The time is now. We have to put something out." '

Ultimately, as sole executor of her son's estate (Jeff had not made a will), Mary Guibert would oversee the project. 'I knew I wanted to be the one to sort of monitor what was going to happen to his music, though I had no way of envisioning how difficult it would be,' she said. 'There were tapes from the different sessions... the early ones with Tom Verlaine producing, which Jeff was not happy with, and the four-track demos...'

'The stuff that he did on his four-track – that is the shit,' said Joan Wasser. 'That's what he was going for. I'm very thankful that any of that got on this record. If it hadn't, it would be beyond misrepresentative.'

And so, in Jeff's eternal absence, the planned *My Sweetheart the Drunk* became *Sketches for My Sweetheart the Drunk*. The assorted DAT and reel-to-reel tapes were collated from the various sources, and so began the journey through Jeff's massive amount of unfinished work. Bearing in mind that disc one of what would become *Sketches* is essentially a group of recordings that he allegedly didn't want heard, the collection would sound profoundly flawed to some of the musicians involved. Although as Tighe has pointed out, works like 'Everybody Here Wants You', that seemed unfinished at the time of recording, ultimately sounded complete with the objectivity of time and space.

This release would be the first of many, fulfilling the needs of a growing worldwide fanbase who were ultimately drawn to the music, and not merely the stoked myth.

The later posthumous albums – eight to date – collate live tracks, demos and outtakes, and include the inevitable remastered and expanded version of *Grace*. While never coming across totally as mere mop-up operations, these releases seem to have lost the splinters of hard and bright quality that *Sketches* imbued, which is only to be expected. 'It's a given that nothing we have, in its state, would ever have got out if Jeff had lived,' said Mary. 'Would any of these songs have been included on an album if Jeff was still alive? Why was he disappointed or dissatisfied with the Verlaine sessions? I don't have the answers to those questions.'

Jeff seemed to live a life as wide and deep as it was brief, and this has allowed for a prolific stream of unheard material. But the source is obviously more finite than most. It's tempting to ruminate on the career that never was. With time, Jeff becomes more of an anomaly among his peers, and it's intriguing to wonder about what, where and who he would have been today. There would have been, perhaps, the inevitable return to a totally acoustic work, the orchestral record, the countless guest appearances on tracks ranging from disco to jazz freak-outs. Jeff would have taken a foray into production, perhaps – the inspiration his work has provided for other groups could have made such a scenario inevitable. A new full-on project with Gary Lucas may have happened, as certainly the best of their material stands as classic amongst the glittering, patchy Buckley canon. Then there was cinema. Aside from the inevitable soundtrack commissions, many would have argued for Jeff's presence in front of the camera. Although after early nineties forays into avant-garde theatre Jeff had decided that 'acting was not for me', it's easy to imagine him playing variants of himself, *à la* Bob Dylan. (Dylan had once told Jeff: 'You're handsome enough to be in movies.')

Yet, in the end, Jeff's first and last love was music, and it's doubtful that he would have strayed from this in any meaningful way other than to have forsaken the material world completely, wandered into the woods and became a holy man – which, in one sense, is what he ultimately did.

Yet again and again, scrutiny of his life up to that point gives no sense of Jeff other than that he was to continue making music. 'He was becoming a man. He was a seasoned performer, he'd travelled around the world several times, he'd written – in addition to a phenomenal first album – 35 incredible songs, and he was ready to take charge,' confirmed his mother.

Despite the arguments against the ultimate meaninglessness of Jeff's death by those closest to him, in most ways his passing seems like the very embodiment of human tragedy. Perhaps in the grand scheme of things it was right that he left when he did, but it's hard to see how.

If life is by default defined by death, then this was certainly an element that Jeff was aware of – and verbally so – throughout his life and work. 'You mean lyrics like "I've had so many loves and I've drowned them all"?' asked his mother. 'Or, from "So Real", "The nightmare that pulled me in and sucked me under." Or, "I lost myself on a cool damp night" from "Lilac Wine". Yeah. Well, if the boy knew he was going to die by drowning, he couldn't have given folks more stuff to chat about, could he? He was very into metaphysical symbols, and I'm as much to blame for that as anybody. A focus on the soul and spirit really shaped his lyrics.'

One of Jeff's favourite writers, William Burroughs, has said that, 'When death finally comes to us it comes in the form of the most appropriate and the least expected.' While this could be said to be true of Jeff's own demise, it was not something he had consciously instigated. In the shadow of his father's tragedy, Jeff had grown up fostering a deeper awareness of the state of things than most, and thought he'd had a defence against this. He seemed to think that, given his father's choice, it was enough simply to want to live and to reject death in all its forms. 'Really, I wish to grow old,' he said a mere year-and-a-half before wading into his fate. 'That is a definite difference between the way I live my life and the way Tim lived his. He was convinced he wasn't going to live past 30. That was the second-hand information I was given and all the things pointed to it... [But] I think he would have made a really fabulous old man.'

ACKNOWLEDGEMENTS

Author Interviewees
Matt Johnson, Daniel Harnett, Mark Brend, Gary Lucas, Nicholas Hill,
Brenda Kahn, Jan Hellriegel, Andrew Goodsight, Iain McDonald, Lorna Goldie,
Jared Nickerson, Lee Underwood, Cressida Johnson, Tom Clark, Tony Lewis, Tom Shaner,
Reggie Griffith, Inger Lorre, Dave Derby, Mary Timony, Tripp Lamkins, Andrew Strong,
Joe Giuseppe, Leah Reid, Clif Norrell.

Secondary Sources
The following publications, websites, documentaries, radio stations and books were
extremely helpful in the writing of this book: The *New York Times*, *Rolling Stone*, *Rolling
Stone Australia*, *Interview*, *Q*, *NME*, *Melody Maker*, *Guitar Player*, *Juice*, *Mojo*, *Uncut*, *Hot
Press*, *Scam*, *Rock and Folk*, *OOR*, *Puncture*, *Sky International*, *Oxford American*, *DoubleTake*,
B-Side, *Rip It Up*, *Puncture*, *Black Book*, *Musician*, *Now*, *Commercial Appeal*, *Les
Inrockuptibles*, *Dallas Morning News*, *New Jersey Beat*, *Raygun*, *Buzz*, *Tim Buckley Fanzine*,
the *Times*, the *Guardian*, the *Independent*, jeffbuckley.com, jeffbuckley.com/rfuller/buckley/
(Kingdom for a Kiss), jeffbuckleycommunity.com, jeffbuckley-fr.net, jeffbuckley.tk,
mojopin.org, salon.com, *120 Minutes*, *The Making of Grace*, *Fall in Light*, *Amazing Grace*,
Spotlight, BBC Radio One, XFM, BBC Manchester, RRR Radio Australia, KROQ FM,
KCRW FM, *Blue Melody: Tim Buckley Remembered* by Lee Underwood and *Dream Brother:
The Lives and Music of Jeff and Tim Buckley* by David Browne.

Picture Acknowledgements
We would like to thank the following for supplying photographs: Cover phoptograph
Retna/ Niels Van Iperen; Corbis/ Nicola Dill; Retna/ David Tonge; Front Row Photos/
Jack Vartoogian; Front Row Photos/ Jack Vartoogian; Front Row Photos/ Jack Vartoogian;
Retna/ Benjamin Oliver; Corbis/ Jeffrey Thurnher; Getty/ Bob Berg; Retna; Retna/ Kelly
Dervish; Getty/ Sony; Retna/ Martyn Goodacre; Redferns/ Getty; Redferns/ Getty;
Getty/ Paul Natkin; Redferns/ Getty; Corbis Sygma; Corbis/ Nicola Dill; Front Row
Photos/ Jack Vartoogian; Redferns/ Getty/ Michel Linssen; Corbis/ Nicola Dill;
Corbis/ Stephen Stickler and Retna/ Rob Watkins.

Thankyou
The Publisher would like to make a special thankyou to Tom Branton for his
dedication and patience in the editing of this manuscript.
The author's thanks go to Charlotte and John, Juan-Luis and Olga,
Leonard D'Onofrio, Christopher Brooke, Lloyd and Sion, Bernard
and Margaret, and The Vulcan public house, Cardiff.

In memory of Sean Body, Ian Brown, Cassie and all of those gone too soon.